ONLY ONE PLACE OF REDRESS

CONSTITUTIONAL CONFLICTS

A Series with the Institute of Bill of Rights

Law at the College of William and Mary

Neal Devins, series editor

ONLY ONE PLACE OF REDRESS

African Americans, Labor Regulations, and the Courts from Reconstruction to the New Deal

David E. Bernstein

DUKE UNIVERSITY PRESS

Durham & London

2001

FOR MY PARENTS,

Stanley & Lillian Bernstein

Contents

✳

Preface

�֎

THIS BOOK EXAMINES how several different types of labor regulations enacted between Reconstruction and the New Deal era — laws restricting interstate labor recruitment, occupational licensing laws, railroad labor laws, public works labor legislation, and New Deal minimum wage and collective bargaining laws — harmed African Americans. Labor regulations were vulnerable to constitutional challenges until 1937. Court decisions invalidating labor laws on constitutional grounds have traditionally been seen as irredeemably reactionary. The judiciary is said to have been blind to economic realities that required government to intervene to ensure that labor markets functioned properly, and to redress inequalities of bargaining power.

The traditional sanguine view of the intent and effects of labor legislation neglects a very simple but powerful insight provided by modern political and economic theory — regulatory legislation tends to benefit those with political power, at the expense of those without such power. Many labor laws were blatant special-interest legislation that, at best, helped certain workers at the expense of others, while reducing market efficiency. Even laws that were initially motivated by legitimate public health, safety, and welfare concerns were frequently drafted and/or enforced to benefit the politically powerful at the expense of the politically vulnerable.

Acknowledgments

✳

MY INTEREST IN the effects of facially neutral economic regulations on African Americans was first stirred by a lecture by economist Jennifer Roback Morse at the Cato Institute during the summer of 1998. Her article, "Southern Labor Law in the Jim Crow Era: Exploitative or Competitive?" 51 *U. Chi. L. Rev.* 1161 (1984), directly inspired my research on emigrant agent laws, which eventually became chapter 1 of this book.

A cryptic note in my first-semester law school constitutional law casebook, Paul Brest and Sanford Levinson, *Processes of Constitutional Decisionmaking* (Little, Brown 1988), asking how to reconcile the holding of *Plessy v. Ferguson* with the holding of *Lochner v. New York,* encouraged me to explore how constitutional law decisions on economic regulation affected African Americans.

During the second semester of my first year at Yale Law School, Professor Geoffrey C. Hazard Jr. agreed to supervise an independent study project on economic regulation and African Americans. He strongly suggested that I investigate whether prounion legislation negatively affected African Americans. Geoff certainly put me on the right track, as evidenced by chapters 2–5 of this book.

I continued my research throughout law school on how labor regulations affected African Americans. My *Yale Law Journal* note, published as "The Supreme Court and 'Civil Rights,' 1886–1908," can be considered something of a prologue to my later work on race and legal history. Special thanks are due Alex Azar for his role in facilitating publication of that note. An "intensive semester" spent at the Landmark Legal Foundation Center for Civil Rights in Washington, D.C., supervised by Professor Paul Gewirtz, gave me the opportunity to investigate the history of the Davis-Bacon Act, the subject of chapter 4 of this book.

During my last semester of law school, I had the good fortune to take a seminar in constitutional history with Professor Michael Les Benedict, who was visiting Yale from Ohio State's history department. As he told me later, Les was initially very skeptical of my thesis that African Americans benefited from Lochnerian jurisprudence. After I wrote a seminar paper that was in effect a skeletal outline of this book, however, he changed his mind and encouraged me to write a book on the subject. I greatly appreciate Les's encouragement, as well as the training he gave me in the methodology of legal historians.

Much of the research that went into this book was initially published in law review articles in the *American University Law Review,* the *San Diego Law Review,* the *National Black Law Journal,* and the *Texas Law Review.* The editors of these journals provided helpful editorial assistance. Many colleagues, mentors, and friends commented on one or more of these articles, including Ian Ayres, Randy Barnett, Les Benedict, Lloyd Cohen, John Donohue, Hal Edgar, Dan Ernst, Jim Ely, Richard Epstein, Paul Finkelman, Lawrence Friedman, Richard Friedman, Geoffrey Hazard, Bruce Johnsen, Michael Klarman, Michael Krauss, David Mayer, John McGinnis, David Nelson, Rick Pildes, Eric Rasmussen, Mark Tushnet, and William Van Alstyne. Heartfelt apologies to anyone inadvertently left off this list.

Susan Rose-Ackerman, Randy Barnett, and Guido Calabresi offered me consistent encouragement as I searched for and ultimately received an academic appointment.

Most of the initial work on the aforementioned law review articles was conducted when I was a law student and young lawyer. Converting these articles into a book required substantial additional time and resources. Time was provided by the John M. Olin Foundation, which awarded me a research fellowship for the 1998–99 academic year, relieving me of teaching and administrative duties for twelve months. The fellowship was of invaluable assistance to me in completing this book, which involved, among other things, rereading every source I had cited in the articles, along with hundreds of new sources. Resources were provided by the George Mason University School of Law library staff, which managed to track down even the most obscure interlibrary loan requests.

As a professor since 1995 at George Mason, I have been blessed with engaging and extremely productive colleagues. The Institute for Humane Studies at George Mason University has been of invaluable assistance to me in many ways, not least in introducing me to an international scholarly community dedicated to exploring the foundations of free societies.

Finally, I owe great thanks to Neal Devins of William & Mary School of Law for soliciting a book proposal from me in the summer of 1998, and for shepherding the proposal and manuscript through the review process of Duke University Press.

Introduction

✳

BETWEEN RECONSTRUCTION AND the New Deal, American courts struggled with the issue of how much protection the Fourteenth Amendment of the United States Constitution, adopted in 1868, accorded economic activity. The amendment was primarily intended to secure the rights of the freedmen against hostile state and local governments, but its supporters also sought to extend federal constitutional protection of liberty against state action more broadly. Unfortunately, the scope of the protections provided was left extremely vague. The amendment does not explain what is meant by "privileges or immunities of citizens of the United States," and "equal protection of the laws," which the amendment purports to protect from hostile state action. Nor does the amendment spell out what it means when it prohibits states from depriving persons of "life, liberty, or property, without due process of law."

Because contemporary American ideology placed high value on the right to make and enforce contracts, particularly labor contracts, litigants quickly challenged economic regulations as violations of the vague terms of the Fourteenth Amendment. In the *Slaughter-House Cases,*[1] decided in 1873, a one-vote majority of the Supreme Court embraced a narrow reading of the amendment. The majority stated that the Court may not interfere with state and local economic regulations that did not explicitly discriminate against African Americans. The dissenters, however, vigorously argued that the amendment gave courts latitude to invalidate legislation that interfered with prevalent notions of economic freedom, particularly the right to pursue a lawful occupation without unreasonable government interference.

Several state courts implicitly or explicitly rejected the *Slaughter-House* majority opinion in favor of the dissent and invalidated economic regulations, especially labor regulations, as violations of the Fourteenth Amendment and analogous state constitutional provisions. Lower federal courts, led by courts in the West that overturned facially neutral labor regulations intended to harm Chinese immigrants, meanwhile developed case law holding that the Fourteenth Amendment protected occupational liberty.[2]

In 1905 the United States Supreme Court adopted in *Lochner v. New York* the *Slaughter-House* dissenters' view that the Fourteenth Amendment barred certain types of state economic regulation.[3] In *Lochner* the Court invalidated a provision of a law regulating bakeries that prohibited business owners from employing bakers for more than sixty hours per week. From 1905 to 1937, during the so-called *Lochner* era, the Supreme Court was relatively sympathetic to plaintiffs who challenged government regulations, especially occupational regulations, as violations of the implicit constitutional right to "liberty of contract."

Lochnerism was never consistently practiced.* Even at the height of the *Lochner* era, from 1923 to 1934, federal and state courts upheld the vast majority of challenged regulations. Nevertheless, *Lochner* did inhibit government regulation to some extent and was therefore always extremely unpopular with the statist Progressives and Legal Realists who dominated the legal academy. Once New Deal constitutionalism triumphed and *Lochner* was explicitly overruled, Lochnerian jurisprudence was widely discredited.

Nevertheless, the ghost of *Lochner* continues to haunt American constitutional law. Supreme Court justices consistently use *Lochner* as an

---

*Throughout this book, the phrases "Lochnerism" or "Lochnerian jurisprudence" are used to refer to the liberty-of-contract jurisprudence associated with the *Lochner* era, instead of the more common "substantive due process" or "laissez-faire jurisprudence." The phrase "substantive due process" was never used by Lochnerian judges or, for that matter, by their opponents. The phrase has no known use before the early 1930s, and caught on only years later as a pejorative oxymoron used by opponents of Lochnerism and, later, opponents of the Warren Court. The phrase "laissez-faire jurisprudence," meanwhile, is a misnomer. Although *Lochner*-era courts sometimes invalidated economic regulations, they never attempted to institute a regime remotely approaching the sort of Nozickian night watchman state normally associated with the phrase "laissez-faire." See James W. Ely Jr., *The Guardian of Every Other Right: A Constitutional History of Property Rights* 103–4 (2d ed. 1998); James W. Ely Jr., "Reflections on *Buchanan v. Warley*, Property Rights and Race," 51 *Vand. L. Rev.* 953, 956 (1998); Gary D. Rowe, "The Legacy of *Lochner: Lochner* Revisionism Revisited," 24 *Law & Soc. Inquiry* 221, 244 (1999).

epithet to hurl at their colleagues when they disapprove of a decision declaring a law unconstitutional. Conservative justices accuse their colleagues of Lochnerizing when abortion restrictions are curtailed, while liberal justices return fire when property regulations are declared unconstitutional under the Takings Clause, and when the Court uses the Commerce Clause to invalidate congressional edicts.[4]

Lochner was discredited primarily on two grounds. First, since the Progressive era, critics have argued that *Lochner* and related decisions had no basis in the text or history of the Constitution, but were instead based on the personal political predilections of the justices.[5] Worse yet, scholars have frequently contended that these predilections were based on pernicious Social Darwinism.[6] Meanwhile, Cass Sunstein's assertion in his 1987 article "*Lochner*'s Legacy" that Lochnerian judges believed that "market ordering under the common law was part of nature rather than a legal construct," and formed a baseline from which to measure the constitutionality of state action, has been very influential among legal scholars.[7]

The accusation that Lochnerian jurists were Social Darwinists is based on a misreading of Justice Olive Wendell Holmes's dissent in *Lochner,* and little else.[8] The historical basis of Sunstein's argument, meanwhile, is extremely thin. Besides *Lochner* itself, Sunstein cites only five of the hundreds of state and federal cases decided between *Slaughter-House* and the New Deal relevant to his thesis, and even then misreads these cases from both a legal and an economic perspective.[9]

More generally, the view that constitutional protection of liberty of contract was essentially made up by willfully political or formalistic judges has been persuasively rebutted by revisionist scholars. These scholars — including political scientists, historians, and law professors — argue that Lochnerian jurists genuinely tried to enforce what they saw as the mandates of the Fourteenth Amendment. Lochnerian judges relied primarily on two long-standing American intellectual traditions that heavily influenced American conceptions of liberty and the proper role of government in the postbellum era when the Fourteenth Amendment was framed: the abolitionist natural rights and "free labor" tradition, and opposition to "class legislation" — legislation that aided politically powerful interest groups at the expense of the public at large.[10]

As a result of the convergence of the free labor and anti-class-legislation traditions, *Lochner*-era courts were especially skeptical of laws regulating

Introduction

3

the employment relationship—at least when such laws appeared to be special-interest legislation, rather than legislation aimed at protecting the health or safety of either the general public or workers themselves.[11] Legitimate health and safety laws were not constitutionally vulnerable because they came within the states' inherent "police powers."

In *Lochner* the defendant bakery owner submitted a brief showing that mortality rates for bakers were only slightly above average, and lower than the mortality rates for many unregulated occupations. Moreover, other unchallenged provisions of the law regulated bakery sanitation, while the hours provision was widely known to be special interest legislation benefiting unionized German bakers at the expense of unorganized recent Jewish and Italian immigrants. The Supreme Court therefore concluded that the hours provision of the law was not a constitutional measure protecting bakers' health, but was class legislation "passed for other motives."[12] Because the law was not within the police power, and interfered with the constitutional right not to be deprived of liberty without due process, it was unconstitutional.

Largely because of the courts' hostility to labor legislation, especially legislation aiding labor unions, the second major criticism of Lochnerian jurisprudence has been that judicial invalidation of economic regulations benefited the wealthy and powerful at the expense of the poor and helpless. Concomitantly, scholars argue that the Supreme Court was out of touch with the need of a modern economy for a strong regulatory state.[13] Implicitly influenced by Marxist interest-group theory that attributes nearly all societal conflict to economic "class" conflict, and by Progressive myths contrasting "The People" with "The Interests," scholars have assumed that political conflicts over labor regulations during the *Lochner* era involved oppressed "workers" with a common interest on one side, and powerful "employers" or "capitalists" on the other.[14]

More modern and sophisticated economic analysis appreciates that not all workers have a common interest in supporting labor regulations, nor do all employers gain from opposing such regulation. Unionized workers, for example, benefit from legislation favoring labor unions, whereas such legislation harms workers excluded from unions. Employers who already have high-wage union shops or who are on the cutting edge of mechanization, meanwhile, also gain from prounion legislation, because such legislation forces a disproportionate rise in their competitors' labor costs.

Skilled high-wage workers gain from legislation that prices less-skilled lower-wage competitors out of the market. High-wage employers also benefit from such legislation. During and after the New Deal era representatives of northern industry consistently supported high-minimum-wage laws to reduce competition from the lower-wage South.[15]

More generally, as noted in the Preface, economic regulations tend to benefit those with political power at the expense of those without such power. There was much merit to Lochnerian jurists' instincts that labor legislation that was purportedly ameliorative and humanitarian could in fact be used as a subterfuge to give certain politically powerful workers special privileges at the expense of those, including other workers, who had less influence.

African Americans, for example, were largely disenfranchised during the *Lochner* era. They were also typically excluded from the most politically powerful labor interest groups of the *Lochner* era, such as craft unions and professional associations. One would therefore expect that much labor legislation challenged in the courts during the *Lochner* era advanced the interests of the dominant native white majority at the expense of African Americans and other politically weak groups.

This book presents several case studies of how facially neutral occupational regulations passed between the 1870s and the 1930s harmed African American workers. Sometimes racism motivated the laws, either directly (as when the sponsors of the legislation were themselves racists) or indirectly (when legislative sponsors responded to racism among their constituents). Some laws had the primary goal of restricting African American access to the labor force, whereas in other instances this was a secondary goal related to the broader goal of limiting competition faced by entrenched workers. In yet other situations, racism did not motivate the laws, but the adverse effects on African Americans were foreseen, and critics pointed out the likely adverse effects when the legislation was under consideration. And, finally, whether intended or not, whether actually foreseen or not, the adverse effects of some legislation were foreseeable in light of the way labor markets operate.

Much of the early post-Reconstruction legislation that harmed African Americans originated at the state and local level. Between the 1870s and the 1920s, states and localities that faced the out-migration of African American workers passed laws restricting labor recruitment (chap. 1).

Introduction

5

The goal and effect were to restrict the mobility — and, therefore, the market power — of African American workers.

Labor unions and professional associations used occupational licensing laws (chap. 2) to reduce competition from unorganized, politically weak rival workers by preventing them from obtaining needed licenses. The organizations that controlled licensing processes generally barred African Americans. Not surprisingly, the exclusionary effects of licensing disproportionately affected African Americans.

By the 1920s federal labor legislation was an emerging threat to African American workers. The Railway Labor Act (chap. 3), passed in 1926 and amended in 1934, marked the culmination of railroad unions' attempts to monopolize the railroad labor market. Several whites-only unions used the monopoly power the act gave them to force employers to oust their African American employees and to cease hiring new African American workers.

The Davis-Bacon Act (chap. 4), a 1931 statute requiring that the federal government's construction contractors pay the prevailing wage, similarly marked the realization of construction unions' goal of using their political power to dominate the public construction labor market. Racist legislators sponsored the act, and its supporters had the specific (though not exclusive) goal of preventing African American workers from competing with white labor union members. The act successfully restricted African American participation in the construction industry for decades.

Broad-based New Deal labor legislation (chap. 5), meanwhile, typically did not have discriminatory intent but had harsh, foreseeable, discriminatory effects. Many unions used the power they received under the National Industrial Recovery Act "to organize a union for all the workers, and to either agree with the employers to push Negroes out of the industry or, having effected an agreement with the employer, to proceed to make the union lily-white."[16] The effects of the Wagner Act were more complex, but ultimately African Americans suffered from the power that law granted to unions, too.

The federal minimum-wage laws passed during the 1930s, meanwhile, were applied selectively so that African American workers who generally did not compete with whites, such as domestics, were not covered at all. The minimum-wage laws did cover African American industrial workers, but at rates dictated by wages affordable in the unionized and indus-

trialized north, not in the impoverished South, where the vast majority
of African Americans still resided. The result was to create more jobs
for white union workers in the North, and to protect northern industry
from southern competition, while reducing employment opportunities for
southern African American industrial workers.

Some courts relied on *Lochner* and related doctrines to resist emigrant
agent laws, licensing laws, laws granting monopoly power to the railroad
and construction unions, and the cartelization of the labor market
brought about by New Deal labor legislation. African Americans benefited greatly from such decisions preserving free labor markets. In each
instance, however, the courts, led by the United States Supreme Court,
ultimately acceded to these regulations, much to the detriment of African
American workers. The triumph of proregulation constitutional arguments was complete by the late 1930s, when the Supreme Court rejected
Lochner and declared that it considered liberty of contract a nonfunda-
mental right worthy of no more than a bare minimum of constitutional
protection.

Few have noticed that Lochnerian jurisprudence, when applied, protected African Americans from facially neutral legislation that restricted
their access to, and mobility in, the labor market. Indeed, legal scholars
and historians have traditionally seen Lochnerism as at best irrelevant to
the welfare of African Americans, and at worst a menace.[17]

As this book shows, however, in the context of a racist American polity
between Reconstruction and the New Deal, the problem with Lochnerism
from African American workers' perspective was that it was much too
timid and ineffectual; courts gave far too much leeway to the regulatory
powers of government, allowing powerful interest groups to profit from
labor regulations at the expense of African Americans. To the extent that
Lochnerian jurisprudence did restrain government, it lasted far too short
a time to provide much protection to African American workers from
harmful labor regulations.

ONE ✶ Emigrant Agent Laws

ABOLITION OF SLAVERY was an economic disaster for white plantation owners in the South. Not only did emancipation destroy much of their capital wealth,[1] but mobile, free African American laborers replaced a docile supply of African American slave labor. In response to African Americans' new market power, planters lobbied their state and local governments to regulate the labor market to African Americans' detriment. This chapter focuses on one type of law used to restrict African American workers — "emigrant agent" laws that inhibited the interstate recruitment of workers.

THE SOUTHERN LABOR MARKET AFTER THE CIVIL WAR

Consistent labor shortages in the post–Civil War South led to fierce competition among planters for African American workers, who generally were not inclined to remain on their former masters' plantations.[2] Just after the Civil War, various southern states passed explicitly discriminatory "Black Codes" to control African American workers. The more severe laws practically recreated slavery for African American agricultural workers by prescribing their labor terms in detail.[3]

The federal 1866 Civil Rights Act invalidated these laws. The act granted African Americans the same rights to make and enforce contracts "as is enjoyed by white citizens," as well as equal protection of the laws.[4] Passage of the Fourteenth Amendment ensured the constitutionality of the act.

Reconstruction governments repealed or ceased enforcing all explicitly discriminatory laws within a few years of passage of the Civil Rights Act. African Americans' wages rose from the implicit subsistence wage of slavery to a wage closer to the value of their marginal labor product.[5]

Although the vast majority of African Americans remained dependent agricultural workers, they were willing to move when an opportunity to improve their situation or the prospects for their children presented itself. Many of those who did not take direct advantage of their mobility nevertheless used it to their advantage by demanding better employment terms. As one scholar notes, "during the period from 1865 to 1880 the action of supply and demand enforced more freedom for the Negro than any of the post-bellum amendments to the Constitution of the United States."[6]

Of course, as generally unskilled, often illiterate workers living in an impoverished, war-ravaged region, most African American workers were extremely poor, and many remained so for decades.[7] African American workers' prospects were further dimmed by official and informal white violence and lawlessness, and the refusal of southern governments to give them the same basic public services routinely provided whites. Nevertheless, African Americans' ability to migrate ensured that employers could not easily pay them below-market wages, and African Americans' living standards gradually improved as the southern economy recovered.[8]

Employers responded to rising African American wages after the Civil War by attempting to create voluntary cartels to assure a noncompetitive labor market. Despite appeals to class interest and white solidarity, the employers' attempt to form cartels did not survive the strain of the marketplace. Individual planters offered continuously higher wages and better working conditions to entice African American workers to their plantations.[9]

When landowners found themselves unable to create viable voluntary cartels to control labor costs, they turned to violence and government compulsion to restrict the free market in labor, particularly after Reconstruction governments fell to the "Redeemers."[10] Because the Fourteenth Amendment outlawed overt legislative discrimination, the planters lobbied for facially neutral legislation that would subdue labor market forces. Planters were particularly keen to promote legislation restricting African American workers' mobility.[11]

Certain facially neutral provisions of the Black Codes designed to restrict African American labor mobility and guarantee a labor supply for planters survived Reconstruction. For example, Republican governments had not repealed laws providing for the hiring out of prisoners convicted of minor offenses. These laws were often used to procure labor for planters, to force African Americans to fulfill the terms of their labor contracts — even if their employers were cheating them — and to keep "troublemakers" in "their place."[12]

Moreover, by the end of Reconstruction, Alabama, Georgia, North Carolina, and Florida still had "enticement" laws that made it a crime, rather than simply a tort, to hire a worker who was under contract with another employer.[13] Vagrancy statutes promulgated in 1866 in Georgia, North Carolina, Texas, and Virginia, also survived. These laws — which essentially criminalized unemployment, even temporary unemployment — had almost never been enforced during Republican rule.[14]

INTERSTATE MIGRATION BY AFRICAN AMERICANS
AND THE RISE OF EMIGRANT AGENT LAWS

In contrast to vagrancy and enticement laws, emigrant agent laws were largely a post-Reconstruction innovation. Between the Civil War and World War I, African Americans migrated in substantial numbers within the South. Over the years, agents representing planters in the higher-wage states of Mississippi, Arkansas, Louisiana, and Texas recruited tens of thousands of African Americans from the lower-wage states of Alabama, Georgia, North Carolina, and South Carolina.[15]

With or without emigrant agents, determined individual men almost always found a way to migrate. Emigrant agents were nevertheless helpful to such migrants because the agents lowered the information costs of migration by using their resources to advertise distant opportunities. Agents also often subsidize the economic costs of migration by either paying for or advancing the money for migrants' train tickets. The agents sometimes even retired debts their recruits owed to plantation owners. Migrants also preferred to affiliate with agents because the agents provided guaranteed employment, ensuring that migrants could leave their old jobs without fear of arrest for vagrancy.[16]

While emigrant agents were of some help to individual migrants, they played a crucial role in group migration, which involved daunting information and economic costs. Some groups of African Americans overcame these costs by forming migration societies. More often they relied on agents; even large families had great difficulty moving without the help of

Only One Place of Redress

an agent. As historian William Cohen concludes, "In the main, . . . large-scale long-distance movement in the era before World War I required the agents' participation."[17]

Many historians treat intrasouth long distance migration by African American farmworkers as at best largely inconsequential, and at worst a product of African American self-deception or false promises by emigrant agents. In fact, group migrations within the South were crucial to African American welfare for several reasons. First, such migrations were a potent form of political protest, and one of the few forms of protest available to African Americans after Reconstruction and subsequent disenfranchisement. African Americans frequently deserted regions in response to lynchings and other forms of white lawlessness, or in response to unfavorable legislation.[18] African Americans moved to places where they could expect relatively good treatment or had relatively good economic prospects. "Mobility," one historian notes, "became the most pervasive form of resistance."[19]

Second, in the era before the welfare state, emigrant agents helped groups of destitute African Americans flee areas devastated by flood, drought, or boll weevils and other pests.[20] Finally, and perhaps most important, mass migration, and even the threat of such migration, was critical to improving the treatment of African Americans by white southerners. In response to large-scale migrations, many plantation owners and other employers raised wages, improved the living and working conditions of African Americans, and, with the cooperation of local and state government, granted African Americans greater educational opportunities and greater protection in their property and person.[21] Because African Americans could migrate when faced with economic hardship, African American living standards rose even during the worst period of post–Civil War American political racism, from 1895 to 1915.[22]

Planters in states or regions hit with widespread out-migration were disturbed by the agents' threat to their labor supply. They therefore lobbied for laws that would curtail the agents' activities. Unlike antienticement laws, emigrant agent laws did not target employers who recruited workers already under contract to another employer. In fact, emigrant agents frequently recruited workers after the fall harvest and before the spring planting season, when African American workers were not under contract.[23]

Opposition to emigrant agents and African American migration, therefore, was not a question of enforcing contracts or ensuring that planters could recoup the value of the materials they often advanced their employees. Rather, planters sought to discourage or effectively ban emigrant agents to inhibit a free market in labor. As William Cohen argues, "To the extent that the North had imposed a free labor system on the South, the agents represented that system in operation."[24] Therefore, one cannot understand the operation and attempted suppression of the labor market in the postbellum South without understanding emigrant agent laws.

EARLY EMIGRANT AGENT LAWS

Virginia imposed the first known statute restricting emigrant agents in 1870. The law required labor agents to pay an annual license fee of twenty-five dollars.[25] Over the next two decades, much more onerous emigrant agent laws were promulgated in the states most affected by African American out-migration: Alabama, Georgia, North Carolina, and South Carolina. Agents challenged the laws in the first three of these states. The Georgia Supreme Court upheld its state's emigrant agent law, but the Alabama and North Carolina supreme courts declared their states' emigrant agent laws to be unconstitutional. In 1900 the United States Supreme Court upheld Georgia's emigrant agent law in *Williams v. Fears.* After *Williams,* emigrant agent laws spread throughout the South.

Georgia's Emigrant Agent Law

In 1873 approximately twenty thousand African American residents of Georgia migrated to other southern states. In response to this threat to Georgia's labor supply, a Georgia lawmaker proposed to require each county in the state to impose a license tax on "immigrant brokers," but the bill was rejected.[26]

In 1875 thousands of African American agricultural workers left Georgia for Arkansas, Mississippi, and Louisiana. This time the Georgia legislature passed a law that required labor agents recruiting for out-of-state concerns to pay a fee of one hundred dollars per county.[27]

Two emigrant agents paid the hundred-dollar fee, then filed a petition with the Sumter Superior Court asking that the law be declared void and that their money be returned.[28] The court denied the writ. The plaintiffs then appealed to the Georgia Supreme Court.

The plaintiffs argued that the emigrant agent statute was unconstitutional because "the subject matter of the Act as well as its obvious object [is] that of preventing colored laborers from being induced to leave this state to be employed in another state." The plaintiffs also argued that the law was illicit class legislation because it applied only to those who chose to recruit laborers for out-of-state employment, but not to those who chose to recruit labor for in-state employment.[29]

The Georgia Supreme Court upheld the law in *Shepperd v. County Commissioners*.[30] The court contended that it was an inherently legitimate function of the state to disfavor people who tried to recruit state residents to migrate to other states. The legislature soon raised the amount of the emigrant agent tax to five hundred dollars.[31]

The Kansas Exodus and Alabama's Emigrant Agent Law

From 1873 to 1875 labor agents helped thousands of African Americans abandon Alabama for Mississippi and other southern states.[32] In December 1876 the Alabama legislature considered a proposal to impose an annual license fee of five hundred dollars on emigrant agents in each county where they worked. Due to opposition in strong Republican areas where many African Americans resided (and still voted), the legislation was defeated. In January 1877 the legislature passed a watered-down law that set the fee at one hundred dollars per county and restricted its scope to fourteen specified Black Belt counties.[33]

In reaction to the withdrawal of federal troops from the South in 1876, between 1877 and 1880 tens of thousands of African Americans fled north, mostly to Kansas. Many white plantation owners feared they would lose their labor supply. Some responded with violence against African American migrants and their leaders. Others lobbied their legislatures to restrict the activities of emigrant agents.[34] In January 1879 the Alabama legislature revised the state's emigrant agent law to cover an additional seventeen counties. The following year the legislature raised the license fee to $250 per county.[35]

An agent was arrested for violating the statute, and he challenged the constitutionality of the law. In argument to the Alabama Supreme Court, the agent's attorney, appealing to free labor ideology, argued that the statute violated the "natural right to labor for subsistence" protected by the Alabama and United States constitutions. The agent emphasized that the act impaired the laborer's right to emigrate because it "prevents advances to enable him to leave, on the faith of his promise to labor in his new home."[36]

In response, the state admitted that it passed the law to stem the Kansas exodus, and to otherwise prevent African-American agricultural workers from pursuing opportunities out of state. The state argued the statute was necessary because recruitment of African American workers was "endangering the farming interests."[37]

In one of the earliest Lochnerian decisions, the Alabama Supreme Court held that the law was unconstitutional. The court concluded that the $250 license tax amounted to far more than the value of a laborer's work. The tax was therefore prohibitory, and "its natural effect, pursuant to its obvious purpose, [was] to seriously clog and impair the laborer's right of free emigration." The court pronounced the law "void as an indirect tax upon the citizen's right of free egress from the State, operating to hinder the exercise of his personal liberty, and seriously impair his freedom of emigration."[38]

Peg-Leg Williams and the North Carolina Emigrant Agent Law

In 1881 the North Carolina Senate, apparently responding to a relatively large-scale migration of North Carolina African Americans to Indiana between 1879 and 1880, voted in favor of proposed restrictions on emigrant agents similar to those enacted in Georgia and Alabama. The state House of Representatives did not pass similar legislation, however, so the proposal never went into effect.[39]

About a decade later a resurgence in African American migration from North Carolina, apparently prompted by passage of a discriminatory election law, led to calls for restrictions on emigrant agents.[40] Robert A. "Peg-Leg" Williams, known in the South as the "king of labor agents," actively promoted the migration. A Civil War veteran and native of Mississippi, Williams lost a leg while serving in Forrest's Cavalry during the war. One newspaper described him as "the Moses of the Carolina exodus, the Brer Fox of his profession, the luckiest, pluckiest, spryest labor agent south."[41]

By 1890 Williams claimed to be able to document having moved more than eighty thousand people over the previous seven years. He also claimed responsibility for moving more than twenty thousand people over the five-month period beginning in October 1889, of whom sixteen thousand were from North Carolina.[42]

North Carolina planters grew impatient with Williams's recruitment of their workers. A North Carolina landlord told the legislature: "We are bothered by people from other states persuading away our laborers, which ought to be a criminal offense." The *Tarboro Southerner* approvingly reported that in several cases mobs obstructed the activities of emigrant agents. A law enforcement official in Charlotte attempted to stymie Williams by arresting him on bogus charges. Initially, a judge refused bail. A sympathetic railroad ticket agent wrote a poem in Williams's honor:

> Peg Leg Williams,
> Charlotte jail;
> Peg Leg Williams,
> Can't give bail.

A few days later Williams gave bond and was released. When he arrived in his home in Atlanta, he embellished the story for the benefit of *Atlanta Constitution* readers: "I broke jail. Rescued by the niggers. Never had such a time. Kidnapped the sheriff. Brought him out a piece and dropped him. Come mighty near lynching me."[43]

To stop Williams from continuing to recruit North Carolina African Americans, the state passed a law that required emigrant agents to pay a huge tax of a thousand dollars per county before they could recruit laborers from certain counties. The law applied only to counties with a high percentage of African Americans.[44]

An agent, apparently an employee of Williams's, was arrested and tried before a jury.[45] The jury issued a special verdict finding that the defendant acted as an emigrant agent without a license. The judge apparently believed the law was unconstitutional and instructed the jury to acquit the defendant.[46] The jury did so, and the state appealed to the North Carolina Supreme Court.

In *State v. Moore,* the North Carolina Supreme Court upheld the lower court's ruling in another Lochnerian decision. Quoting Christopher Tiedeman's laissez-faire-oriented treatise on the Constitution, the court held the law unconstitutional because it applied only to certain counties and therefore lacked uniformity, and also because it illicitly restricted people from pursuing the occupation of emigrant agent without persuasive police power justification.[47]

THE GEORGIA EXODUS

Well before mass African American migration to the North began, a visionary Peg-Leg Williams contemplated promoting such migration from Georgia. He considered advertising his services in the *New York World* to provide northern employers with African American workers. He told the *Atlanta Constitution:* "I never heard of the thing being tried before, but I'm going to give it a fair trial."[48]

Williams could not proceed with his plans, however, because Georgia continued to enforce its emigrant agent statute. He announced to the media that he was going to test the Georgia emigrant agent law in court. Williams declared that "[a] man in this country has the right to go where he pleases." The emigrant agent law, he argued, "amounts to saying that a man can't leave the state if he chooses — at least, he shan't be given information or help."[49]

Williams proclaimed that he would prove the law to be unconstitutional and then stimulate a Georgia exodus similar to the North Carolina exodus. Large-scale African American migration had not previously affected Georgia because the emigrant agent tax amounted to a prohibition — no agent could afford the five hundred dollar per county tax. In 1893 authorities in Macon County, Georgia, arrested Williams for working without an emigrant agent license, but they dropped the charges before he could challenge the law.[50]

In 1894 Williams became involved in a failed plan to colonize thousands of southern African Americans in Mexico. Little is known about Williams's whereabouts and activities in the few years after the Mexico venture collapsed.[51]

Apparently, however, he had not given up his dream of tapping the Georgia labor market. A report in the *Birmingham News* in February 1899 stated that Williams was transporting a "car load of Negroes" from Columbus, Georgia, to Arkansas. At this time Williams worked with Mary E. La Vitte, his cousin. Authorities apparently arrested La Vitte in

Columbus for operating as an emigrant agent, but she somehow managed to avoid conviction.[52]

In September 1899 La Vitte entered Morgan County, Georgia, and began recruiting African American workers for landowners in Mississippi. Morgan County, in the heart of Georgia's cotton-producing Black Belt, had suffered a major drought in the summer of 1899, leaving many African American tenant farmers and farm laborers destitute.[53]

At this time the Delta area of Mississippi "exercised a strong hold on the imagination of many blacks."[54] The Delta suffered from an acute labor shortage. As late as 1900 wilderness occupied two-thirds of the Delta's four million acres. Planters were in constant need of labor as new plantations were established, particularly after cotton prices began to rise sharply in 1899. Because of this labor shortage, work in the Delta paid relatively well, and, for a time at least, Delta African Americans were well treated: they participated in government, held supervisory positions on cotton plantations, and even owned more land in the region than did whites.[55] Not surprisingly, then, African American workers responded eagerly to La Vitte's entreaties.

Morgan County farmers soon became concerned about "the outlook for laborers and farm hands" for the following year. In response to complaints by farmers, the mayor of the city of Madison ordered La Vitte's arrest, fined her fifty dollars for operating without a license, and put her under a five hundred dollar bond. La Vitte nevertheless continued her activities. A few weeks later she unsuccessfully appealed the mayor's action to the city council, arguing that the emigrant agent law was unconstitutional.[56]

Shortly after that, the county tax collector attempted to force her to pay the state's annual emigrant agent tax of five hundred dollars. La Vitte refused to pay the fee, and she was arrested again. She posted bond and, for a time, continued to recruit African American workers at secret nighttime meetings. Apparently concerned for her safety, she soon left the county.[57]

Within weeks after La Vitte was forced out of Morgan County, Williams began operating as an emigrant agent in neighboring Greene County, Georgia. Like Morgan County, Greene County had suffered a drought. Williams recruited African American laborers to work in the Mississippi Delta in Bolivar County, Mississippi. Plantation owners paid Williams ten

Emigrant Agent Laws

to fifteen dollars per head for able-bodied workers. At first he made an agreement with local leaders to recruit only one thousand destitute African Americans, to refrain from recruiting workers under contract, and to desist when requested to do so.[58]

Several important planters believed that allowing Williams to work at all was dangerous. They feared that his recruitment of African American workers would eventually cause a labor shortage. However, Greene County's prosecutor, Colonel James Davison, was one of the local leaders who approved of Williams's activities, and he resisted appeals to prosecute Williams. The planters next complained to the state comptroller general, who instructed Greene County's tax collector to demand the five hundred dollar tax from Williams. Williams refused to pay and argued that the tax was unconstitutional. Luther Boswell, one of the county's most prominent planters, swore out a warrant, and Williams was arrested on December 16, 1899. Williams posted an appearance bond and went back to working as an emigrant agent.[59]

Word of Williams's arrest quickly spread through the African American community, helping to publicize Williams's recruitment efforts. More planters panicked; African Americans were reluctant to make contracts for the coming year, and among them "[d]iscontent, dissatisfaction, unrest and uneasiness" prevailed.[60]

In early January 1900 some local leaders who had originally promised not to molest Williams requested that he cease recruiting workers. Williams stated that he was going to make two more trips to recoup losses stemming from his arrest. He learned, however, that discontented planters had arranged to have him arrested when he arrived in Greenesboro, the county seat, for not paying the five hundred dollar license fee for 1900. Acting on the advice of his attorney, Williams paid the fee under protest.[61]

After these events Williams no longer considered himself bound by the agreement to limit his recruiting. After establishing a permanent office in Greenesboro, he escalated his activities in Greene and Morgan counties and sent assistants into neighboring counties to distribute circulars and urge African Americans to move west.[62]

The entire population of Greene County in 1900 was 16,542, of whom approximately 11,000 were African Americans. The exodus of approximately 2,500 African-Americans from Greene County (and 1,500 or more from neighboring Morgan County) created a severe labor shortage. Those who remained successfully demanded higher wages and lower rents from their landlords, creating a "revolution in the labor circles of the county."[63]

Alarmed planters became determined to stop the exodus. Some whites promised Williams that if he stopped recruiting, they would use their influence to have the charges pending against him dropped. Other whites threatened Williams with violence. Nevertheless, he continued to recruit workers.[64]

Williams asked laborers who wanted to leave to gather in the Morgan County town of Madison on Wednesday and Saturday nights at the railroad station. He would meet them there and give them tickets to their next destination. On January 12, 1900, a crowd of local whites gathered at the train depot in Madison. They intended to prevent Williams from providing the train tickets, by force if necessary. Violence was preempted when Sheriff Oliver Fears arrested Williams and one of Williams's assistants for operating in Morgan County without a license.[65]

Some African Americans had boarded the train at an earlier stop. They intended to meet Williams in Madison, where he was to give them tickets for the rest of their journey. The railroad discharged them from the train at Madison, and railroad workers scattered their luggage along a mile of track. A group of masked Klansmen, who had been lying in wait to attack Williams on Sunday morning, had to content themselves with terrorizing the discharged African American passengers instead. The migrants were stranded in Madison and had to walk home to distant counties. The rest of the potential migrants were not allowed to board, and they too returned home.[66]

Williams's ordeal did not end with his arrest. A mob of angry whites prepared to storm the jail. The governor, meanwhile, activated the local militia to protect Williams and the jail. Despite this show of force, whites plotted to capture Williams, flog him, and tar and feather him.[67]

Acting on the advice of his attorney, and attempting to mollify the crowd, Williams released a signed statement declaring his intention to cease recruiting African Americans from the area. The statement, addressed to "All Colored Farm Hands," stated that "unless the farmers with whom you are living will agree for you to leave, I cannot move you. . . . My advice to all of you is to go to work here to make the crop for this year. . . . [Y]ou should settle down and go to work and stop the agitation that now prevails."[68] Meanwhile, Williams vowed to challenge the constitutionality of the emigrant agent law. He told the *Augusta Chronicle:* "I have whipped this law in Alabama and North Carolina, and I will whip it in Georgia."[69]

Williams also attempted to defend himself in the court of public opinion. In response to critical comments in the *Atlanta Constitution* by an African American, Smith W. Easley, Williams wrote:

> I am the man moving the people. . . . I am a democrat and always have been. . . . If [Easley] will take a trip down the Georgia road . . . and see the condition of his colored brethren he would not need an explanation of why the negroes are leaving Georgia.
>
> The reason is a bread and meat problem — in the first place, very little work, if any; two to three years' failure in crops and the starvation prices paid them for farm labor — 15 to 25 cents a day and they board themselves — as they tell me. Unfortunately it is not only the negroes suffering condition, eight out of ten of the white farmers would be broke if they paid their debts; they are not able to furnish the negroes two to three months' rations during the winter months while there is no work for them on the farms. Hence the negroes have to go west where there is work the year round at $12 to $15 per month and board, and cotton to pick at 50 cents per hundred and day work at 75 cents. . . .
>
> I would like to invite the public's attention to the condition [of the emigrants] as they pass through Atlanta. These people are half clad and starving. I have to feed them from the time they start until they arrive at their destination.[70]

On January 16 Williams was transported to Union Point in Greene County for a habeas corpus trial before Judge John Collier Hart. Williams's attorney, Greenesboro prosecutor Colonel James Davison, argued that the emigrant agent law was an unconstitutional regulation of interstate migration. He added a plea on behalf of African American workers: "These negroes have a right to go to Mississippi in quest of honest employment, whereby their conditions could be benefitted."[71]

Judge Hart ultimately upheld the statute. Hart stated that "when a man comes into a community and takes all — from the grandfather to the babe — then he comes in under the head of an emigrant agent" and can be restricted by law. He ordered Williams to pay a five hundred dollar bond for an appearance in Morgan County Superior Court in March.[72]

After Judge Hart denied Williams's habeas corpus petition, Davison filed a new habeas corpus petition in federal court. When that petition was denied, Williams established a new headquarters in Atlanta. He vowed to take his case to the Supreme Court of the United States, if necessary.[73]

After Williams's arrest African Americans continued to leave the area where he had worked, but much more slowly; without a labor agent to help them, learning of employment opportunities was harder for African Americans. And without an agent to pay their train fare, many impoverished sharecroppers could not leave no matter how good an occupational opportunity awaited them elsewhere. Soon the exodus shifted to other counties in central Georgia, but in at least one county the emigrant agent, an employee of Williams, was arrested and convicted, stemming the migration.[74]

A group of African Americans from Clarke County, Georgia, met with Williams in Atlanta to discuss emigration possibilities. Williams then arranged for the Seaboard Airline Railroad to transport African Americans from Athens, the biggest city in Clarke County, to Atlanta, where another railroad would take them west. Williams also paid African American assistants to work quietly in Clarke and neighboring Oglethorpe counties to encourage people to emigrate.[75]

Meanwhile, African Americans organized meetings on their own initiative to discuss whether they should move. The number who decided to leave steadily increased. In early March a group of white planters petitioned the Clarke County commissioners to help stem the exodus. The commissioners replied that they were actively seeking to arrest emigrant agents but had been unable to learn their identities.[76]

On March 11 five hundred African Americans, many of whom had sold all their possessions, gathered at the Athens train station, expecting to be transported to Atlanta. The railroad, however, refused to honor an agreement with Williams and would not board anyone who did not have a paid ticket. This refusal may have been in response to boycott threats from local whites, or may have been a reaction to news that Williams had been arrested in Atlanta and was to be extradited to Clarke County to stand trial. (For unknown reasons, he was released from jail in Atlanta before he could be extradited, much to the annoyance of whites in Clarke County.)[77]

White planters arrived and, with the help of the police, took into custody any African American who was allegedly under contract for the year. One policeman was badly wounded when the crowd resisted these efforts. Most members of the crowd refused to disperse until the police threatened to arrest them as vagrants.[78]

Exactly how much better off African American migrants were in Mississippi is not clear. Georgia newspapers occasionally reported that some unhappy migrants sought assistance from whites to return home. On the other hand, African Americans had access to the U.S. mail, and the exodus would likely not have lasted for months and spread to neighboring counties if most of the initial migrants regretted their move.[79] Also, the Delta area, unlike the rest of Mississippi, was still an attractive destination for African Americans at this time.[80]

The political situation for African Americans in Bolivar County, Mississippi, where Williams sent his Georgia recruits, was deteriorating rapidly, but the demand for labor in the Delta region was sufficiently high that African Americans retained a great deal of economic leverage. African American speculators in Bolivar County had land for sale at reasonable prices, and the number of African American landowners increased sharply between 1900 and 1910.[81] In fact, while the Delta was hardly a nirvana for African Americans, conditions there remained sufficiently favorable that it was one of the few areas of the South that did not become a net loser of African Americans through migration until World War II.[82]

THE DOOMED SUPREME COURT APPEAL

Meanwhile, Williams was convicted in Morgan County in absentia of violating the emigrant agent law. He appealed to the Georgia Supreme Court, but the court, relying on its earlier opinion in *Shepperd,* upheld his conviction.[83]

Williams next appealed to the Supreme Court of the United States. While the appeal was pending, Williams continued to operate as an emigrant agent from his office in Atlanta, but refused to pay the five hundred dollar tax for operating in Fulton County. He also refused to pay the tax in other counties where he recruited workers.[84]

Only One Place of Redress

During the summer of 1900 Williams told Memphis newspapers he planned to recruit thousands of good workers for Delta cotton growers. He told a Georgia newspaper that he already had requests for five thousand workers for the coming winter, but could probably place twice that many.[85]

As it turned out, Williams's recruiting days in Georgia were numbered. In late 1900 Williams's case was argued before the U.S. Supreme Court. In his Supreme Court brief, Davison, still acting as Williams's attorney, did not directly argue that the law discriminated against African Americans.[86] Instead, he relied on the two mainstays of Lochnerian jurisprudence in his appeal to the U.S. Supreme Court — the free labor tradition and opposition to legislation benefiting special interests. He argued that the tax "impairs the natural right of the laborer to labor" and was an example of "class legislation." He cited the two favorable state supreme court decisions from North Carolina and Alabama on his client's behalf.[87]

Neither of these arguments was likely to be successful. Although state courts in the late nineteenth century invalidated economic legislation on "free labor" and "class legislation" grounds, the Supreme Court — having yet to decide the *Lochner* case — remained extremely reluctant to rely on amorphous constitutional theories to overturn state legislation on Fourteenth Amendment grounds.[88]

Davison also made the more promising argument that the emigrant agent statute violated the dormant commerce clause.[89] The Fuller Court, despite its tendency to defer to state authority, was relatively sympathetic to commerce clause challenges, and there seemed to be favorable precedent on point.[90] Davison also argued, among other things, that the statute violated the right to interstate travel.

The Supreme Court upheld the statute in an opinion by Chief Justice Melville Fuller. Fuller acknowledged that both the right to travel and liberty of contract were protected by the Fourteenth Amendment. However, he argued that even if the law "can be said to affect the freedom of egress from the State, or the freedom of contract, it is only incidentally and remotely. The individual laborer is left free to come and go at pleasure, and to make such contracts as he chooses, while those whose business it is to induce persons to enter into labor contracts and to change their location, though left free to contract, are subjected to taxation in respect of their business as other citizens are."[91]

Emigrant Agent Laws

Fuller also argued that the law might be necessary to protect citizens from fraudulent practices by emigrant agents. Fuller claimed that if the emigrant agent business was "not subject to regulation, the citizen may be exposed to misfortunes from which he might otherwise be legitimately protected."[92] Yet the law did not regulate emigrant agents — it simply taxed them out of existence.[93]

Fuller next rejected Davison's contention that the emigrant agent law violated the equal protection clause of the Fourteenth Amendment because it applied only to out-of-state labor recruiters. Fuller ignored the North Carolina and Alabama Supreme Court opinions cited favorably by Davison, even though the Alabama opinion was reprinted in an appendix to Williams's brief. Instead, Fuller adopted the Georgia Supreme Court's 1877 argument in *Shepperd v. County Commissioners* that the state could properly discriminate in its police and fiscal legislation between occupations that tended to induce the laboring population to leave the state, and those that tended to induce that population to remain.[94] This argument seems to contradict Fuller's earlier claim that the emigrant agent law did not substantially affect the right to travel.

Having disposed of Davison's Fourteenth Amendment arguments, Fuller next rejected the argument that the emigrant agent law amounted to an unconstitutional regulation of interstate commerce. Fuller conceded that laborers recruited by emigrant agents must eventually be transported beyond the limits of the state, "but it does not follow that the emigrant agent was engaged in transportation or that the tax on his occupation was levied on transportation." Fuller asserted that Williams was in "the business of hiring laborers," which was not closely enough connected with the interstate transportation of those workers to constitute interstate commerce.[95] In fact, however, Williams did not hire laborers himself but was solely engaged in the business of recruitment of laborers for out-of-state employers, and the interstate transportation of those workers.

Justice John Marshall Harlan, the Great Dissenter in *Plessy v. Ferguson,* dissented in *Williams* without opinion.[96] One is tempted to conclude that Harlan dissented because he thought the Court's opinion represented an injustice to African Americans. Harlan, however, was far from consistent in his jurisprudence,[97] and because he chose not to write an opinion, the rationale for his vote in *Williams* must remain something of a mystery.

Defeated in court, Williams paid Fulton County's license fee and then notified the tax collector that he was filing suit to recover it. Ultimately, however, the Supreme Court's decision marked the end of Williams's activity in Georgia.[98] Other agents who attempted to operate in Georgia, but did not have Williams's connections or money, suffered heavy fines and imprisonment. For example, in April 1907 an emigrant agent was convicted of violating Georgia's licensing statute, and was fined one thousand dollars and sentenced to six months' imprisonment.[99]

THE IMPACT OF *WILLIAMS V. FEARS*

Williams led to widespread legal harassment of emigrant agents in the South. In 1903, just three years after *Williams,* Alabama, Florida, North Carolina, and Virginia enacted emigrant agent laws, while the laws of Georgia and South Carolina remained in effect.[100] The other southern states enacted emigrant agent laws when out-migration of African Americans rose dramatically during World War I.

Labor agents continued to challenge emigrant agent laws in court without success. Lower courts relied on the Supreme Court's decision in *Williams* and uniformly rejected such challenges. The North Carolina Supreme Court distinguished away its previous decision holding emigrant agent laws to be unconstitutional. South Carolina's supreme court added insult to injury by claiming that laws restricting emigrant agents were actually "for the protection of the laborers themselves."[101] Peg-Leg Williams was apparently forced to quit the emigrant agent business due to the enforcement of emigrant agent laws.[102]

Despite emigrant agent statutes, hundreds of thousands of African Americans managed to migrate both within and from the South after *Williams.* But the emigrant agent law placed "a major obstacle in the path of agents who tried to lure laborers away."[103] Economic theory suggests that emigrant agent laws had particularly harsh effects on rural African Americans. The laws substantially raised the economic and information costs of interstate migration, which would logically have had particularly harsh consequences for poor, isolated African American farmworkers who often worked in a cashless economy.

Empirical support for this theory is difficult to come by. Little research has been done on pre–World War I migration within the South, even though by the 1890s every southern state except Mississippi, Alabama, and Florida had rates of African American out-migration almost as high during the 1890s and 1900s as during the much more famous "Great Migration" to the North of the 1910s.[104] Meanwhile, quantitative data on the effects of emigrant agent laws are nearly impossible to gather, given that enforcement of the laws was often sporadic and inconsistent, and that an almost infinite range of factors could account for divergences in migration rates.

Nevertheless, data for World War I migration suggest that emigrant agent laws had the disproportionately harsh effects on rural African Americans that economic theory predicts. The data show that, although urban African Americans had better economic opportunities and suffered less from white violence than did rural African Americans, urban African Americans were substantially overrepresented in the Great Migration to the North during and after World War I.[105] Despite popular mythology to the contrary, most African American migrants to the North during World War I were urban dwellers, not rural farmworkers.[106]

Among urban African Americans, information regarding opportunities in the North and how to pursue them circulated rapidly. African Americans already in the North wrote letters to relatives or friends in the South. The letters were passed around the community, or their contents were passed on by word of mouth among illiterates. Such transmission of information was far more difficult in isolated rural areas.[107]

Urban African Americans also learned of distant opportunities from African American newspapers. The *Chicago Defender,* for example, not only promoted migration to the North in its editorials, but also published advertisements from potential employers.[108] Southern white authorities tried to ensure that as few copies as possible of the *Defender* circulated. In dozens of communities, the police confiscated the *Defender* from dealers. The governor of Arkansas asked the Postmaster General to exclude the paper from the mails, and some southern African Americans believed that letters to the *Defender* were confiscated.[109] Isolated rural African Americans were obviously at greater risk from such tactics than urban African Americans.

Even when African American farmworkers became aware of distant opportunities, many could not take advantage of them because they could not afford the necessary train ticket without the assistance of an emigrant agent. For example, it cost $22.52 per adult to go from New Orleans to Chicago in 1918.[110] Thus, the *Williams* decision had its harshest effects on some of the poorest, most desperate Americans.

Southern plantation owners recognized that emigrant agent laws retarded African American migration. In the 1910s and 1920s they persuaded state legislatures to place ever harsher restrictions on emigrant agents. Certain local laws banned emigrant agents entirely.[111]

Emigrant agent laws were hardly the worst example of southern oppression of African Americans. Still, they were an important strand of the web of laws, violence, and custom that restricted the economic prospects of African Americans in the South. The history of emigrant agent laws also provides an excellent example of how Lochnerian jurisprudence, when applied, aided African Americans, while judicial deference to government regulation harmed them.

TWO ✳ Licensing Laws

OCCUPATIONAL LICENSING LAWS provide a potent historical example of how labor regulations often served discriminatory purposes. Licensing laws prevented African Americans from competing with established white workers in a variety of occupations nationwide. Because of strong employer opposition, and potential constitutional problems with regulating "ordinary trades," industrial labor unions rarely used licensing laws to achieve a closed shop. Licensing was instead imposed on occupations where workers were primarily skilled and self-employed.

Licensing laws inherently had disproportionate exclusionary effects on African Americans. Skilled African American workers often could not satisfy rigid, formal licensing requirements even if they had practical expertise — unions did not admit African Americans into their apprenticeship training programs, and southern public schools gave African Americans very little vocational training compared to whites.[1] Moreover, most African Americans had little formal education, making the typical licensing exam with written sections a tremendous hurdle to many African Americans. Thus, even a purely public-spirited licensing law, if there was such a thing, would necessarily have harmed African Americans.

In fact, despite public-spirited rhetoric, states and municipalities frequently passed licensing laws at the behest of organized members of the licensed profession to grant them a state-sponsored monopoly at the expense of those who would not be able to meet licensing requirements. Even in cases of "hostile" licensing, when the licensing process was originated to regulate an industry in the public interest, the licensed group generally quickly gained control of the licensing process. The group used the process to benefit its members by limiting the number of new entrants, thus assuring higher incomes to those already in the field.[2]

Organized groups of workers controlled the licensing process through their unions or professional societies. These groups usually excluded African Americans. They therefore used the licensing statutes to prevent African Americans from gaining licenses in professions in which African Americans were once numerous — particularly, though far from exclusively, in the South — and to prevent African Americans from getting a toehold in other fields.[3]

Occasionally, states or municipalities passed laws explicitly barring African Americans from a profession. A Maryland statute, for example, restricted admission to the bar to white males.[4] Far more often, however, facially neutral laws that had a plausible public health or welfare justification kept African Americans and other minorities out of a field.

For example, *Yick Wo v. Hopkins*,[5] one of the first Fourteenth Amendment equal protection and due process cases to reach the Supreme Court, involved a San Francisco ordinance that made it unlawful to run a laundry business in a wooden building without having first obtained a license from the city's Board of Supervisors. The city asserted that the ordinance was a prophylactic measure against a potentially disastrous fire. The law, however, was clearly designed to eliminate Chinese hand laundries, which were almost always housed in wooden buildings. Competing white-owned steam laundries, meanwhile, were typically housed in brick or stone buildings. The law was also administered unevenly, so that whites who owned wooden laundries managed to get the necessary operating licenses, while the government prosecuted Chinese laundry owners.

The Court held that the ordinance was unconstitutional on proto-Lochnerian grounds. First, the Court suggested that the law was facially unconstitutional, because it left laundrymen at the mercy of the "purely personal and arbitrary power" of the supervisors to grant or deny a license.[6] Free labor ideology influenced this section of the opinion. Having one's livelihood at the mercy of the "mere will of another," the Court stated, "seems to be intolerable in any country where freedom prevails, as being the essence of slavery itself."[7]

Second, the Court found that, as applied, the law illicitly discriminated against the Chinese as a class. The Court wrote that "the facts shown establish an administration directed so exclusively against a particular class of persons . . . , with a mind so unequal and oppressive as to amount to a practical denial by the state of that equal protection of the laws which is secured to the petitioners . . . by the broad and benign provisions of the fourteenth amendment to the constitution of the United States."[8] Justice Stanley Matthews, for the Court, then proclaimed a lasting principle in American constitutional law: "Though the law itself be fair on its face, and impartial in appearance, yet, if it is applied and administered by public authority with an evil eye and an unequal hand, so as practically to make unjust and illegal discriminations between persons in similar circumstances, material to their rights, the denial of equal justice is still within the prohibition of the constitution."[9]

Despite *Yick Wo*'s potential power to restrain licensing officials from arbitrary and/or discriminatory action, courts rarely relied on it in licensing cases. One problem was that unlike the situation in *Yick Wo*, licensing decisions were rarely wholly arbitrary, as licensing boards usually had some formal standards. Moreover, the equal protection element of *Yick Wo* arguably applied only to laws enforced *solely* against a discrete group. The typical licensing law disproportionately excluded African Americans, but also excluded others who could not pass the relevant examination.

Because of *Yick Wo*'s limitations, an 1888 case, *Dent v. West Virginia*,[10] in which the Supreme Court upheld the licensing of physicians on public health grounds, became the most important licensing precedent. The Court had subsequent opportunities to rule on the question of physician licensing laws and invariably sustained them. On the strength of those cases, lower courts universally accepted the general proposition that licensing statutes were constitutional and gave only minimal scrutiny to licensing laws that appeared to protect public safety.[11]

It was not inevitable that *Dent* would establish the rule in licensing cases. The Supreme Court explicitly articulated the right of a person "to earn his living by any lawful calling" in *Allgeyer v. Louisiana* in 1897.[12] *Lochner v. New York* also gave hope to antilicensing forces. Not only did the decision hold, in rather strong terms, that liberty of contract is a constitutional right, but the Court, in dicta, also specifically discussed the dangers occupational licensing posed to that right. Justice Rufus Peckham, for the Court, warned that "interference on the part of the legislatures of the several states with the ordinary trades and occupations seems to be on the increase." Peckham cited with approval state court decisions invalidating licensing regulations on the trade of shoeing horses.[13]

Yet *Lochner*, like *Yick Wo* and *Allgeyer* before it, ultimately had little effect on most state court licensing decisions. As Lawrence Friedman observes, the Supreme Court apparently believed that professions, but not ordinary trades, could be regulated through licensing. A profession was "an occupational group whose activities touched subjects of public interest legitimately included in the scope of the police power."[14] State courts adopted this notion and were generally inclined to believe licensing authorities when they claimed they were licensing a profession. If the government cited a plausible public health purpose for a licensing statute, the statute was almost always upheld.

Any hope that the Supreme Court would require more stringent review of occupational licensing laws was dashed in 1921 by *Douglas v. Noble*. The issue before the Court was whether it was constitutional for the Washington legislature to delegate to the Washington Board of Dental Examiners the power to decide who was fit to practice dentistry in that state. The case presented the Court with the opportunity to put some limitations on the practices of licensing boards. Instead, the Court gave carte blanche to state legislatures to delegate to licensing boards the authority to "determine the subjects of which one must have knowledge[;] the extent of knowledge in each subject; the degree of skill requisite[;] and the procedure to be followed in conducting the examination."[15] So long as licensing boards treated all people alike, and the decisions by the boards were not wholly arbitrary, the criteria established by the boards were not subject to constitutional review.[16]

Judicial deference to licensing laws allowed racist white unions and professional organizations to monopolize certain professions. The rest of this chapter will explore three examples of occupations from which African Americans were restricted through the application of facially neutral licensing laws: plumbing, barbering, and medicine.

PLUMBERS' LICENSING LAWS

States and municipalities had potentially justifiable police power reasons to regulate plumbers, as incompetent plumbers could threaten public health. For example, defective and improperly installed plumbing fixtures were responsible for dysentery epidemics in Chicago in 1933 and in Kansas in 1942.[17] But even licensing statutes initially proposed for public health reasons are susceptible to being used primarily as barriers to entry. If an organized group of workers can influence the legislative process, it can ensure that the statute is written to benefit itself at the expense of current competitors and potential future competitors. Alternatively, the group can capture the licensing board after the statute has passed and public attention has waned. The group can then use control of the board to achieve its anticompetitive ends.[18] Nevertheless, for the most part courts refused to give more than cursory scrutiny to the motives behind plumbers' licensing statutes or to the statutes' implementation.

Licensing statutes for plumbers generally delegated the power to license individuals as plumbers to a licensing board composed of members appointed by the mayor and/or city council. Not surprisingly, local plumbers' unions, representing the politically best-organized plumbers, exerted a great deal of influence over who was chosen to serve on boards of examiners. The Plumbers' and Steamfitters' Union, affiliated with the American Federation of Labor (AFL), excluded African Americans nationally throughout the *Lochner* era. Through their influence on boards of examiners, the unions were often able to deny licenses to African Americans.[19]

Despite liberty of contract and free labor arguments made by unlicensed plumbers, state courts almost uniformly upheld the power of the state to license plumbers on public health grounds, and rarely looked closely at how licensing was being administered. Judges of the day, often infused with nascent Progressive optimism about the benevolence of government and the value of institutionalized expertise, seem to have had little awareness of the misuses to which licensing laws could so easily be put. In 1898, for example, the Wisconsin Supreme Court upheld a plumbers' licensing law, noting that it did not "anticipate that any examining board would go further than the act requires, and insist upon more than this practical knowledge acquired in the school of experience."[20] The Wisconsin court apparently believed that the licensing authorities' only interest would be to protect the public health from incompetent plumbers.

Yet by the time the Wisconsin Supreme Court decided *Winkler*, complaints about discriminatory treatment by licensing boards were already showing up in reported judicial decisions. In an 1895 New York State case, *People ex rel. Nechamcus v. Warden*, Peter Nechamcus, a master plumber, alleged that he was unable to get a plumber's license because of "his religion and his Russian nationality."[21] The brief he submitted to the New York Court of Appeals, the state's highest court, gave examples of other applicants who could not get certificates because of their "race and religion" and because they did not belong "to an association of master plumbers." In other words, Nechamcus argued that the licensing board discriminated against Jews, immigrants, and those who did not belong to a union. He argued that the law was unconstitutional because it created a monopoly and was applied in a discriminatory fashion.

In a 4–3 decision, the court rejected Nechamcus's argument that the law created a monopoly, and added that it would not invalidate licensing laws even if they were applied in a discriminatory manner: "Nor is the constitutionality of an act to be determined by the manner in which its provisions may be carried out by those upon whom devolves the duty of acting as examiners. If they act unfairly or oppressively, as alleged by the relator in his petition, that is conduct which may call for a remedy against the persons who compose the board; but it does not furnish ground for assailing the validity of the statute."[22]

Rufus Peckham, who later authored *Lochner* as a U.S. Supreme Court justice, wrote a sharp dissent. His dissent was joined by the same New York judges who would later dissent from the Court of Appeals' decision upholding the New York maximum-hours law for bakers eventually invalidated by the Supreme Court in *Lochner*.

Peckham asserted that the licensing law was "vicious in its purpose" because it "tends directly to the creation and fostering of a monopoly." He accused the majority of shutting its "eyes to the evident purpose of the statute and . . . imput[ing] a purpose to the legislature which it plainly did not have." Peckham added that the law "detracts from the liberty of the citizen acting as a tradesman in his efforts to support himself and his family by the honest practice of a useful trade." "Taking the act as a whole," Peckham concluded, "it would seem quite apparent that its purpose is to enable the employing plumbers to create a sort of guild or body among themselves, into which none is to be permitted to enter excepting as he may pass an examination, the requisites of which are not stated, and where his success or failure is to be determined by a board of which some of their own number are members. In order to be at liberty to exercise his trade as a master plumber he must pass this examination and become a member of this favored body."[23]

Despite occasional protests like Peckham's, throughout the late 1890s and early 1900s state courts continued to uphold the licensing of plumbers on public health grounds. In one of the most important and widely cited licensing cases, the Ohio Supreme Court upheld the general authority of the state to license plumbers. The court rejected a challenge based on *Yick Wo*, and cited *Dent* and *Nechamcus* as precedents.[24]

None of the previous cases discussed above involved African American plumbers directly, but the results nevertheless were devastating for them. Once unions gained control of the licensing process, they promptly used this power to exclude African Americans. After the *Nechamcus* decision, unions used the licensing process to exclude African Americans from plumbing in New York City. By 1902 African American plumbers in Memphis were unable to pass the licensing exam. The plumbers' union used the power it gained under Ohio's licensing law to exclude African American plumbers. As a result, by 1910 Cleveland had only five African American plumbers, even though African Americans had once been prominent in the skilled trades there.[25]

White plumbers in other states brazenly lobbied for licensing laws to exclude African American competitors. A Virginia plumber, for example, wrote in the *Plumber's Journal* that a pending licensing bill would, if enacted, "entirely eliminate" African Americans from the plumbing field. He added other locals could accomplish the same result "if they would devote a little time and money."[26] Despite its discriminatory intent, the bill did not mention race at all. Rather, the bill provided, among other things, that members of local plumbers' unions would serve on the board of examiners that would judge the competency of applicants.[27]

As the years passed, the courts continued to ignore the abuse of plumbers' licensing laws. African Americans made significant inroads into the plumbing trade in Philadelphia and Chicago until licensing laws were used to exclude them. Courts proceeded to uphold the laws.[28]

A few state courts recognized the danger of allowing licensing authorities unmitigated discretion to control entry into the plumbing profession. For example, in *Replogle v. Little Rock,* the Arkansas Supreme Court, citing Peckham's dissent in *Nechamcus,* emphasized the importance of an individual's right to pursue a lawful occupation. The court noted the plaintiffs' allegations that the licensing exam tested obsolete knowledge not relevant to modern plumbing. The justices concluded that nothing in the relevant statute prevented the licensing board from relying on such a test. This "illustrate[d] the arbitrary and oppressive power that the board of examiners might exercise to deprive one who is thoroughly qualified to do the practical work of plumbing of his constitutional right to pursue his avocation, and perhaps his only livelihood, because, forsooth, he was unable to answer some technical or theoretical question, not in any sense germane to the real and practical trade of a plumber, and not having even the remotest connection with the actual conversation of the public health." Citing *Lochner,* the court concluded that the measure vested illicit arbitrary authority in the licensing board and was not truly a public health measure but was " 'passed from other motives.' "[29]

The Georgia Supreme Court, meanwhile, ruled in favor of a plumber who argued "that although he is a competent plumber he could not stand a written examination, due to his lack of education." The plumber also argued that "the ordinance is not for the protection of the public, but is for the purpose of reducing competition in the plumbing trade" and "that it is the inalienable right of every man to work at his trade and earn a living." The court held that the licensing statute was unconstitutional because it granted arbitrary authority to the mayor and city council to grant a license to a plumber who had failed the licensing exam.[30]

In 1950 the Illinois Supreme Court invalidated a plumbers' licensing law that required an apprenticeship before one could become a master plumber. The court noted that the master plumbers could deny such an apprenticeship for any reason, including the applicant's race, creed, or color. The apprenticeship requirement, the court concluded, was an "arbitrary denial to a citizen of his inherent and inalienable right to engage in a legitimate activity by his own free will and choice."[31]

These sporadic decisions did not stem the overall tide of state court decisions upholding plumbers' licensing laws. The results of judicial acquiescence to the licensing system, combined with other factors benefiting the plumbers' union — particularly inspection laws (with inspectors recruited from the plumbers' union), discriminatory government funding of vocational training, and local government's inability or unwillingness to curb union violence against African American competitors — were disastrous for African Americans who sought to work as plumbers.[32]

The magnitude of the effect of licensing laws on African American plumbers is difficult to quantify because most studies underestimate the effect of licensing by relying on self-reported census occupational data. Such data are skewed because many African Americans reported their

occupation as plumber but were forced to work in the underground economy without licenses, or to pay whites to do "officially" the plumbing
work actually done by African Americans. More generally, white plumbers usually did not interfere with unlicensed African American plumbers
who worked only in African American neighborhoods, or who worked
on unpleasant jobs union plumbers disdained.[33] Thus African Americans
retained a foothold in plumbing, but a tenuous one that restricted their
income and occupational status.

The efforts of the plumbers' unions to keep African Americans from
getting licenses were extraordinarily successful. In some states, examining
boards required a union apprenticeship before a potential licensee could
even qualify to take the licensing examination. Because unions banned
African Americans from apprenticeship programs, they could not even
qualify to take the test.[34] Other tactics favored by unions to prevent African Americans from getting licenses were requiring a high school diploma
and/or requiring a highly subjective personal interview before one could
take the exam. If those tactics did not work, examining boards were not
above doctoring test scores.[35]

Because of union control of the licensing process, a 1953 investigation
discovered that out of thirty-two hundred licensed plumbers in Maryland,
only two were African American. The first African American passed a
plumbers' licensing exam in Colorado in 1950 only after pressure from
civil rights authorities. There was only one licensed African American
plumber in Charlotte in 1968. As late as 1972, Montgomery County,
Alabama, had only one licensed African American plumber, and he was
able to get his license only after a ferocious struggle with the local plumbers' union. By the early 1970s there were still very few licensed African
American plumbers in the United States.[36]

BARBER'S LICENSING LAWS

In the late nineteenth century, southern African Americans had a near
monopoly on the profession of barber. Many northern African Americans
worked as barbers as well. Overall, 20.5 percent of the barbers and hair-
dressers in the United States were African American in 1890.[37] Because of
an increase in immigrant barbers and a rise in racism, many whites started
to patronize white barbers.[38] By 1910 only about 11 percent of American

barbers, beauticians, and manicurists were African American. Encouraged by this decline, white barbers, typically operating through the Journeyman Barbers' Union, aspired to use the licensing laws to limit African American barbers to African American customers, whom white barbers did not wish to serve.

The official policy of the Journeymen Barbers' Union was to admit African Americans. Some locals, particularly in the North, apparently followed this policy, though most did not. In any event, the union never acquired many African American members. In 1903 there were only 1,000 African American members of the Journeymen Barbers' Union, and by 1928 this number had declined to 239.[39]

White barbers were sometimes unsubtle in their attempts to use regulation to monopolize white customers. In 1926 the Atlanta City Council passed an ordinance requiring barbers to serve members of their own race exclusively. Unlike many facially neutral laws that served intentionally or unintentionally to advantage white workers at the expense of African Americans, this law caused an uproar among both African Americans and sympathetic whites. The city modified the ordinance to prohibit African American barbers from serving white women — who were just beginning to patronize barbershops — or children under fourteen years old. A group of independent African American barbers and white barbers who employed African Americans challenged the law in state court. The Atlanta Chamber of Commerce, which feared bad publicity for the city and further restrictions on African American workers to the detriment of its members, financed the challenge.[40]

In 1927 the Georgia Supreme Court held that the law was an unconstitutional violation of state and federal constitutional guarantees of equal protection, the "right to labor," and due process. The court rejected Atlanta's argument that the city could place special restrictions on African American barbers because African Americans in general had a higher rate of infectious diseases than did whites.[41]

Unlike the Atlanta statute, laws that served to restrict African American barbers were usually facially neutral. One such bill was introduced every legislative session in Virginia from 1928 to 1940 at the behest of the barbers' union, which sought to stop African American barbers from serving white patrons. When the bill was introduced in 1929, the *Norfolk (Va.) Journal and Guide*, an African American weekly, complained that the bill had as certainly been designed "to effectively limit the opportunity of colored persons to follow the trades [as] if it had been openly drafted to accomplish that purpose." The bill mandated that licenses in Virginia be issued only to those who had served as registered apprentices for eighteen months and had passed an examination given by the board of examiners. One could become a registered apprentice only if one graduated from a school of barbering approved by the board. Schools of barbering, meanwhile, would be prohibited from accepting applicants having less than an eighth grade, or equivalent, education.[42]

These facially neutral regulations were in fact discriminatory, the paper editorialized. First, the newspaper noted that no currently existing barbers' school in Virginia would admit African Americans. The editors predicted that the board would simply refuse to approve any new school that did. Moreover, the editorial continued, "prejudice or politics involved with organized labor's voting strength might easily operate through the board to destroy the usefulness of Negro barbering schools and, of course, cut off the source of apprentices." Also, according to the editors, many African Americans in the state could not meet the eighth grade educational requirement. Even those who met that requirement could not afford to spend six months at a barbering college. "The proposed barbers' licensing law is a real menace to the economic opportunity of colored people," the *Journal and Guide* warned. "The social consciousness and responsibility of the State must be aroused against this pernicious measure, masquerading as a public health effort, but obviously an organized labor union project drawn in the special interest of white organized labor."[43]

The proposed Virginia law was supported by the Virginia Federation of Labor and the barbers' union. The Virginia Commission on Interracial Cooperation and the Barbers' Protective Association, an organization of African American barbers, both vigorously opposed the bill. Opponents of the bill argued that the proposed board of three white barbers could sooner or later eliminate all licensed African American barbers on one pretext or other. As one commentator noted, if under the proposed licensing regime a certain African American barbershop was to take too much business from its white rivals, "a question or two [from a board of white barbers] to the operator concerning sebaceous glands and the problem is quickly solved." Ben Taylor, an African American barber, testified before the state legislature that his colleagues would "whiten the mountains with their bones" and "dye old Virginia with their blood" before submitting to the authority of a state board of barber examiners.[44]

Although the Virginia bill was proposed every year and consistently defeated, by 1941 every state except Virginia and New York licensed barbers, and in those two states local governments had their own laws.[45] The laws often had many elements objected to by the *Journal and Guide*. Indeed, although the Virginia bill intentionally sought to restrict African American barbers, it was typical of license laws lobbied for by unions and passed by many states, including those with few if any African American barbers.[46] Established barbers, after all, were interested in restricting all potential competitors, not just African Americans.

Regardless of intent, licensing laws disproportionately prevented the licensure of the poorest and least-educated barbers and potential barbers,[47] a greatly disproportionate percentage of whom nationwide were African American. Moreover, union-dominated licensing boards applied facially neutral licensing standards in a discriminatory fashion, as predicted by the *Journal and Guide*.

African Americans were not mute in the face of this threat to their livelihood. In some states where they had political power, African Americans mitigated the effect of licensing on African American barbers. In Ohio, African American barbers and nonunion white barbers successfully opposed licensing bills in 1902, 1904, 1910, and 1913. A licensing law finally passed in 1915 after some issues of contention were compromised. African American barbers in West Virginia, meanwhile, managed to convince the state legislature to protect their interests through a statutory requirement that one member of the four-man licensing examination board be African American.[48]

In Florida, meanwhile, an African American barber named Andrew Fulton launched a successful court challenge to the refusal of the State Board of Barbers Examiners to renew his license. The refusal was based on Fulton's failure to comply with the board's decree — based on its statutory authority to fix prices for barbering services — of certain minimum fees for haircuts, shampoos, and other services.[49]

A concurring justice noted that the price "fixed for the entire county of Duval may have been entirely reasonable as minimum prices to be charged in the expensively equipped and gleaming white barber shops located in the central business district of Jacksonville." Fulton's shop, by contrast, "was located in a section of the city inhabited almost entirely by people of small means, most of whom were poor and not able to pay the minimum price." The board's price fixing, therefore, threatened to put Fulton and similarly situated barbers out of business.[50]

Although African American barbers and other licensing opponents had some success in blocking or mitigating the effects of licensing, they often failed. Opponents of licensing then turned to the courts but rarely managed to persuade judges that licensing laws violated their right to occupational liberty. Beginning in about 1900, cases almost uniformly upheld licensing of barbers.[51] Even the Washington State Supreme Court, which had invalidated the licensing of plumbers, upheld it for barbers. A dissenting justice demonstrated how little the provisions of the law related to public health. He demanded to know why the court should "declare blindly that the public health is involved when all the rest of mankind know[s] full well that the control of the barber business by the board and its licensees is the sole end in view."[52]

As with plumbers, the major effect of the licensing of barbers was not necessarily to exclude African Americans from the field completely, but to restrict their numbers and keep them unlicensed to limit their ability to compete for white customers. Ironically, the unionized barbers' racism protected African Americans to some extent from the effects of licensing laws. If union members discovered an unlicensed African American barber who continued to serve white customers, the union would complain to the authorities. But white union barbers had no interest in serving African American customers. Legal authorities, therefore, did not harass unlicensed African American barbers who restricted their trade to African American customers. In the 1970s a researcher could locate only six licensed African American barbers in Alabama, Georgia, Louisiana, North Carolina, South Carolina, Tennessee, and Virginia, though clearly far more African American barbers practiced their trade.[53]

Barbers' licensing laws continued to harm African Americans for decades. As late as the early 1980s, researchers reported that unlicensed African American barbers and beauticians commonly practiced their trade in the inner city because of difficulty in getting licensed, sacrificing not their careers but their level of income. Interestingly, the reasons African Americans had trouble getting barbers' licenses in the 1980s were remarkably similar to some of the problems the *Journal and Guide* foresaw with the Virginia law proposed over fifty years earlier; African Americans who aspired to be barbers often could not afford trade school tuition (where students are taught how to pass the exams) and had generally inferior educational backgrounds.[54]

One relatively recent study of cosmetology licensing found that although the failure rates of African Americans and whites on the practical part of the examination were about even, African Americans failed the written portion of the examination at a much higher rate than did whites. Qualified African American beauticians were unable to get licenses because they could not answer questions only tangentially related to their jobs.[55] Besides those who failed the test, many others were discouraged from taking it because they did not believe they could pass. The situation surely was far worse in the days when the tests were often intentionally used to exclude African Americans.

PHYSICIANS' LICENSING LAWS

Physicians' licensing laws are an example of laws initially passed for a public purpose that wound up hurting African Americans unintentionally. The effects of the growth of licensing laws on the number of African American physicians were not that severe at first. For example, despite the spread of licensing laws, between 1900 and 1910 the percentage of physicians in the United States who were African American rose more than 50 percent, from 1.3 to 2 percent.[56]

In 1910 Abraham Flexner published the *Flexner Report,* his famous and extremely influential study of medical education in the United States. Flexner's study argued that many American medical schools provided severely inadequate education, and that many doctors were therefore incompetent to practice medicine.

The *Flexner Report* was written at the height of Progressive faith in social planning and distrust of market competition. Flexner believed that society would be far better served with fewer, but better trained, physicians, who would be educated at universities instead of at for-profit medical schools. Flexner believed in technocracy and was something of an elitist. He contended that physicians should not only have a strong background in the sciences, but should also be more generally well educated.[57] Flexner argued that premedical and medical education should take at least six years after high school, and preferably eight, compared to the four years that the typical for-profit medical school allocated.

To Flexner no middle ground existed: either a physician was trained properly, according to modern standards, or he was worse than useless, even if the physician was to serve a poor community that otherwise would do without medical help altogether. He failed to consider directly an obvious, more moderate alternative: legislatures could have created a category of medical professionals akin to today's nurse practitioners, permitted to see patients and provide basic medical care though lacking the full panoply of training and skills possessed by physicians. Recommendation of this alternative would have been contrary to the elitist spirit of the *Flexner Report* and would have faced vociferous opposition from the American Medical Association (AMA), which has historically opposed any challenge to physicians' legal monopoly on the direct provision of medical services.

The African American community was in dire need of more African American doctors. Physicians were rare in the rural southern Black Belt, and white physicians who were available often charged fees beyond most African Americans' means. Many African Americans relied on local "healers" who had no formal medical education. Nevertheless, Flexner explicitly rejected the notion that the African American community would be better off with less costly and more readily available medical personnel whose training did not meet his standards than with a great shortage of medical personnel.

Flexner's views on African American medical education were condescending, paternalistic, and not at all grounded in the reality of African American life. He wrote:

> The negro is perhaps more easily "taken in" than the white; and as his means of extricating himself from a blunder are limited, it is all the more cruel to abuse his ignorance through any sort of pretense. A well-taught negro sanitarian will be immensely useful; an essentially untrained negro wearing an M.D. degree is dangerous. . . .
>
> The negro needs good schools rather than many schools, — schools to which the more promising of the race can be sent to receive a substantial education in which hygiene rather than surgery, for example, is strongly accentuated. . . .

Of the seven medical schools for negroes in the United States, five are at this moment in no position to make any contribution of value.[58]

Flexner did not explain how two medical schools could possibly meet the demand for African American physicians, nor did he suggest prodding other medical schools to accept African American students.

In response to the *Flexner Report,* some states put medical licensing directly in the hands of the American Medical Association. Other states required that potential doctors be graduates of a medical school rated "A" or "B" by the AMA, which based its standards on Flexner's report. The AMA had for decades been agitating for legislation that would reduce the number of physicians in the United States.[59]

Once the AMA took control of licensing procedures, state physician-licensing laws began to have marked effects on the number of African American doctors. Most important, states followed Flexner's advice and forced five of the seven existing African American medical schools, which educated most African American doctors, to close. These schools received "C" or lower ratings from the AMA despite desperate attempts by their administrators to raise their standards. On Flexner's recommendation, the charitable foundations that supported African American medical schools cut off funds to these schools and instead directed their philanthropy to the two African American medical schools that survived, Howard and Meharry. Even those two schools were in danger for a time of losing their accreditation.[60]

If licensing officials had taken the interests of the African American community to heart, they could have temporarily bent standards to allow the other African American schools to catch up. Despite Flexner's dismissal of these schools as worthless, approximately half their graduates passed their states' licensing examinations, and several of their graduates became prominent physicians.[61]

Alternatively, licensing authorities could have pressured the other medical schools to admit African American students, or at least to create parallel programs for African Americans. But the AMA, which controlled the licensing process, was concerned mainly with the interests of its members, who were, by strict rule, all white. Most AMA members were indifferent to the shortage of African American physicians, and some southern white doctors resented even the minimal competition they received from African Americans: poor whites sometimes sought out African American physicians because their fees were generally much lower than those of white doctors, and wealthier whites concerned about confidentiality sometimes went to African American doctors instead of to local white physicians with whom they shared a social network.[62]

Moreover, there was opposition in the South to allowing African Americans to serve as medical personnel at all. Mississippi authorities were reputed to fail African American physician and dentist candidates routinely, especially if they were not from the South. Most southern states either forbade African American nurses from taking registration examinations, or only permitted them to take separate tests.[63]

Meanwhile, ever-increasing premedical educational requirements made it difficult for students from impoverished backgrounds to achieve the financial means to attend medical school. Flexner argued that his recommendations for additional premedical education would not discourage poor students, because nonprofit medical schools, subsidized by foundations and alumni, could offer six years of education for the price that for-profit schools charged for four years of education. Apparently, Flexner not only had excessive faith in the efficiency of nonprofit institutions, but also was not familiar with the concept of opportunity cost; the prospect of an extra two years of lost wages could easily divert a promising but impecunious student from medical education to a more immediately remunerative endeavor.

Not surprisingly, after 1910 the percentage of African American doctors, which had been rising dramatically, leveled off. Because of the medical establishment's attitude toward African Americans, which ranged from indifference to hostility, as late as the 1940s over 80 percent of African American medical students received their education at Howard and Meharry.[64] The discriminatory effects of facially neutral physicians' licensing statutes helped create a shortage of medical personnel to serve the African American community that continues to this day.

CONCLUSION

This chapter has focused on how occupational licensing laws reduced opportunities for African Americans to work as plumbers, barbers, and

Only One Place of Redress

physicians. Licensing laws served a similar exclusionary purpose in other occupations, ranging from well-known examples (African Americans had great difficulty acquiring electricians' licenses) to the obscure (West Virginia mining supervisors needed a license, and for decades the state provided only whites with classes needed to prepare to take the licensing examination).[65] Had the courts been more willing to scrutinize closely the purpose and effect of these laws to ensure that they did not unreasonably interfere with the right to pursue a lawful occupation, African American workers would have greatly benefited.

THREE ✳ Railroad Labor Regulations

FROM THE LATE nineteenth century through the New Deal era, tens of thousands of African Americans found relatively remunerative work on American railroads. Most of these workers were unskilled laborers, but African Americans were also well represented in semiskilled positions, such as firemen and trainman, particularly in the South. These jobs were highly sought after among African Americans. Finding employment as a fireman or trainman "made a man a notable in the Negro community, gave him a house with a shaded yard and sent his children to high school and beyond."[1]

The opportunities semiskilled African American workers found on the railroad were perpetually endangered by the racist policies of railroad unions. Unions representing workers in train and engine service, the so-called operating unions, launched collective bargaining in the 1880s and developed into some of the strongest unions in the United States.[2] The shop crafts and other nonoperating unions developed more slowly but gradually gained power, particularly when they received government assistance. Railroad unions consistently tried to use their power to exclude African Americans from skilled and semiskilled positions in the industry.[3] With a great deal of help from federal laws granting the unions monopoly power, they eventually largely succeeded.

ORIGINS OF THE CONFLICTS BETWEEN AFRICAN AMERICANS AND RAILROAD UNIONS

From their inception, the most powerful railroad unions, which were known as "brotherhoods," were modeled after fraternal organizations. Fraternalist ideology not only created solidarity among the initiated, but also served as a justification for excluding others not deemed worthy of membership, including African Americans.[4] Almost all of the major railroad unions — including the Brotherhood of Locomotive Engineers, the Brotherhood of Railway Conductors, the Brotherhood of Locomotive Firemen and Enginemen, the Brotherhood of Railway Clerks, and the Brotherhood of Maintenance-of-Way Employees — banned African Americans from membership by constitutional provision. African Americans were also banned from other unions that had large memberships among railroad workers, including the Boilermakers, the International Association of Machinists, and the Blacksmiths.[5]

Admitting African Americans into the brotherhoods would have meant implicitly acknowledging that African Americans were the "social equals" of whites, something few white workers were willing to do. Moreover, if the brotherhoods had admitted African Americans, African Americans would naturally have sought the same access to the most desirable railroad positions that their white co-unionists enjoyed. Yielding to this expectation would have required whites either to lower their self-image or to raise their view of the competency of African American workers, neither of which they were inclined to do.[6]

White workers understood that excluding African Americans undermined labor solidarity and made it much more difficult for their unions to negotiate successfully with railroad management. They accepted this vulnerability because the alternative of sharing their organization with African Americans seemed even worse. One Texas fireman declared, "[W]e would rather be absolute slaves of capital, than to take the negro into our lodges as a [sic] equal and brother."[7]

The brotherhoods were initially successful in excluding African Americans from any jobs where few African Americans were entrenched; railroad management did not want to risk racially motivated strikes if there was not a ready reserve of African American workers to replace striking whites. For example, because African Americans had never acquired many jobs as conductors or engineers, it was not difficult to exclude them from those jobs. Government restrictions on entry, such as licensing laws, doubtless made the task of exclusion even easier in a few states. In 1910 only about 3 percent of southern engineers and southern conductors were African American.[8]

In the North and West, firemen and brakemen were initially overwhelmingly white. The entrenched white workers insisted on a stringent color line, and railroad managers usually capitulated, although some African Americans found jobs as brakemen.[9] The trainmen's and firemen's brotherhoods had far more difficulty excluding African Americans from their crafts in the South, because many African Americans had entered those occupations at a time when the jobs were hot and dirty and therefore considered "Negro work." As technological improvements made these jobs easier, they became attractive stepping stones to conductors' and engineers' positions and therefore increasingly appealed to white workers. Meanwhile, white firemen and trainmen sought recognition as skilled, respectable craft workers. The presence of many African American workers in their occupations, combined with the racism of other white workers, made this respectability difficult to achieve.[10]

Despite union pressure, railroads had incentives to hire African American workers. African American firemen and trainmen earned about 10–20 percent less than whites (though railroad representatives insisted that this was due to productivity differences). Moreover, white engineers preferred to work with African American firemen; African American firemen were more willing than whites to serve as the engineers' valets, and the engineers wanted new engineering jobs to be reserved for unemployed engineers, not for white firemen seeking promotion.[11]

Beginning in the 1890s, the Firemen, along with the Brotherhood of Railway Trainmen, launched public, organized efforts to exclude African Americans from their occupations nationwide. In 1898 the Grand Master of the Brotherhood of Locomotive Firemen declared that he looked forward to the day "when every locomotive in the country would be fired by a white man" and promised "a campaign in advocacy of white supremacy in the railway service."[12] In 1899 the national convention of the trainmen's union voted to support the exclusion of African Americans from the railroads.[13]

One way the unions attempted to achieve their exclusionary goal was by engaging in strikes for a whites-only hiring policy. Such strikes often involved violence against African American railroad workers. In 1911, for example, a strike against the Cincinnati, New Orleans and Texas Pacific Railroad protesting the employment of African Americans led to the murder of ten African American firemen. The strikers and the railroad eventually agreed that African Americans would not be employed on the company's line north of Oakdale and Chattanooga, Tennessee, and that the overall percentage of African American firemen would not rise. Workers soon reached a similar agreement with the Southern Railroad.[14]

In general, however, similar "race strikes" failed. In 1909, for example, white firemen in Georgia went on strike to demand that the Georgia Railroad dismiss its African American workers. The railroad had started hiring African American firemen in 1902, and 42 percent of the railroad's firemen were African American by 1909. African Americans and whites had equal seniority rights on Georgia railroads, but only whites were eligible for promotion to engineer. Therefore, as senior whites received promotions, African Americans dominated the ranks of senior firemen and claimed a large percentage of the best runs. Whites were often left with less desirable runs, which offended their white-supremacist sensibilities. The white workers' simmering resentments boiled over into a strike when ten white assistant hostlers — firemen who had engineering duties in the railroad yards — were dismissed in favor of African Americans. The strikers demanded that the railroad dismiss its African American firemen, as well as its other African American workers.[15]

The firemen's union called on the white population of Georgia to support them against the railroad's alleged preference for African Americans. Whites responded by attacking trains as they went through various towns. State and local officials resisted appeals to enforce order. After two weeks the railroad, which adamantly rejected the workers' demands but was helpless against the violence, suspended operations.[16]

The railroad and the union ultimately agreed to federally sponsored arbitration. The railroad agreed because it was desperate; the union agreed probably because it faced the threat of a federal court injunction of its strike. The arbitrators voted 2–1 to allow the railroad to continue to employ African American workers if they paid African Americans and whites equal wages. Some white workers claimed victory because they assumed that the railroad would no longer hire African Americans if it had to pay equal wages. They were wrong; the Georgia Railroad continued hiring African American workers until 1928, two years after passage of the Railway Labor Act, which gave the railroad unions new power.[17]

When the unions found they could not exclude African Americans through the collective bargaining process, they began to consider ways the government could aid them. For a time, several unions contemplated using licensing laws to monopolize the railroad labor force. In 1902 the Brotherhood of Locomotive Firemen considered lobbying Congress for a bill that would require firemen to pass a literacy test. The union's leaders believed that such a bill would eliminate two-thirds of African American firemen. In 1906 the firemen's union suggested that southern lodges lobby their state legislature for laws "whereby the standard of the men in railroad service will be raised to what it should be in every state."[18]

During the Georgia race strike, the firemen submitted a licensing bill to the Georgia legislature. The union's journal contended that "[t]he justice which has been denied the white firemen of the Georgia Railroad may be secured, not only for them, but for every white fireman in the South, through legislation such as that now pending in the lawmaking body of the State of Georgia." The union expected that the bill's enactment would "have the effect of reducing to a minimum the number of Negro firemen eligible to fill that position on locomtives [sic] in the state of Georgia."[19]

The licensing bill failed, but the union did not give up. Just after the strike concluded, the state legislature considered, but failed to pass, a bill to require all passenger trains to carry one white fireman. Another licensing bill, requiring that all railway firemen be able to read train orders, was introduced in 1912 but also failed to pass.[20]

Far more common than licensing laws were "full crews" laws, which slowly spread across the United States. These laws provided that a train crew must consist of an engineer, a fireman, a conductor, a brakeman, and a flagman. Full-crew laws were ostensibly passed for safety reasons, but enjoyed much of their popularity because they served the interests of the railroad unions. Not only did full-crew laws force railroads to hire unnecessary workers, but railroad unions sought to ensure that the laws encouraged the railroads to hire union members.[21]

For example, full-crew laws led to discrimination against African Americans in both the North and the South who had gradually acquired positions as brakemen while remaining officially classified as porters. At the behest of the trainmen's union, state railroad officials — and federal officials who controlled the railroads during World War I — decided that the many African American porters who did brakemen's work were not brakemen for the purposes of the statutes. The porters therefore had to be replaced by white brakemen — generally union members — in order to comply with the law. When Ohio passed a full-crew law, railroads fired approximately thirty veteran African American porters who had performed brakemen's duties. Railroad management objected to an Oklahoma full crew because it would prevent the railroad from using African American porters as brakemen. In 1911 and 1916 the U.S. Supreme Court held that full-crew laws were constitutional.[22]

Despite these and other efforts by railroad unions to exclude African Americans, approximately 104,000 African Americans worked in the railroad industry in 1910. Although most worked as unskilled laborers or porters, African Americans also held approximately one-third of southern railroad fireman and brakeman jobs. Approximately five thousand African Americans were employed as firemen, and about the same number worked as brakemen.[23] Moreover, a substantial number of African Americans worked as switchmen. These railroad jobs were among the highest-paid positions available to African Americans in the South. The relatively favorable position of African Americans on the railroads did not change until World War I brought massive federal intervention in the railroad labor market.

WORLD WAR I AND FEDERAL INTERVENTION IN THE RAILROAD LABOR MARKET

During World War I, labor shortages induced skilled African Americans to leave the southern railroads for more lucrative employment in the North. The traditional pay differential between whites and African Americans, which normally allowed African Americans to compete successfully with exclusionary white unions for employment, instead encouraged African Americans to seek greener pastures. In response the federal government, which had taken over the railroads during the war, ordered that African American workers be paid the same wages as whites for the jobs of fireman, switchman, and trainman.[24]

Immediately after the war, railroad unions renewed their efforts to force African Americans out of the industry. Government control of the industry had greatly increased both unionization and union power, which aided unions in their efforts, as did the equal pay order, which in the postwar period reduced the railroads' incentive to employ African Americans.[25]

The federal government also intervened directly in the labor market to the detriment of African American workers at the behest of unions. For example, labor unions threatened a walkout and strike when a northern line hired African American workers for the first time. In response, the Director of Operations for the Federal Railroad Administration issued a directive instructing regional managers that African American "firemen, hostlers, switchmen, brakemen, etc." should not be employed "beyond the practice heretofore existing," nor should they be employed on "any line or in any service upon any line or in any service where they have not heretofore been employed, or to take the places of white men." The directive was rescinded after protests from the NAACP and National Urban League, but the Railroad Administration remained hostile to African Americans.[26]

Basking in their newfound power, the Brotherhood of Railway Trainmen took matters into its own hands and engaged in a series of racially motivated strikes. When those strikes failed, the white trainmen turned to terrorism, killing several African American trainmen, while kidnapping, beating, and threatening others. Finally, to pacify the trainmen's union, which threatened to disrupt all of the southern lines, the Federal Railroad Administration agreed in 1919 to new regulations benefiting white trainmen at the expense of African Americans. One rule required all new applicants for positions of brakeman, flagman, and switchman to pass uniform written examinations. Another rule provided that "Negroes are not to be used as conductors, flagmen, baggagemen, or yard conductors."[27]

On many lines African Americans had customarily served as brakemen, and whites as flagmen. Now the position of brakeman was to be filled by seniority, a change that would allow white trainmen to displace junior African American brakemen, while African Americans were still banned from becoming flagmen.[28] Other provisions were designed to force African Americans out of the occupation of train porter and to prevent African American porters from serving as brakemen.[29] A federal railroad official acknowledged that union blackmail had worked. He told a delegation of African American protestors that sacrificing the interests of African American workers was necessary because "it was better to inconvenience a few men than tie up the entire South for an indefinite length of time."[30]

Over the opposition of railroad unions, government domination of the railroads, including federally imposed labor rules, ended soon after the war. Although this control had solidified the power of operating craft unions, African Americans managed to hold their own in railroad employment. Approximately 136,000 African Americans still worked in the railroad industry in 1924, many of them in relatively high-paying positions. African Americans still could not get jobs as conductors and engineers, but as of 1920 they constituted approximately 27 percent of the firemen, 27 percent of the brakemen, and 12 percent of the switchmen in the southern states. African American workers formed their own unions, such as the Association of Colored Railway Trainmen, which spent much of their energy trying to defend their members from the machinations of whites-only unions.[31]

THE LABOR INJUNCTION: ANATHEMA TO UNIONS,
A BLESSING FOR AFRICAN AMERICANS

Several hundred thousand railroad jobs were eliminated as the railroads mechanized in the early 1920s, increasing competition for the remaining jobs. The unions responded by intensifying their campaign against African American workers, with limited success. Unskilled African American workers suffered disproportionately from mechanization, but their employment situation stabilized by 1922.[32]

For the next several years, railroad unions, particularly the nonoperating unions, weakened dramatically, in part due to the loss of the federal support they received in the late 1910s, in part because of the general decline of organized labor during the 1920s, and in part due to the increasingly aggressive use of injunctions issued by federal judges against strikes, especially railroad strikes.[33] African Americans took advantage of the weakening of the unions and began to enter many nonoperating or shop craft skilled and semiskilled occupations — such as blacksmith, electrician, carman, and machinist — during the 1920s, after serving as strikebreakers.[34] By the end of the decade, African Americans had doubled their

Railroad Labor Regulations

share of jobs in the railroad shops, with particularly large gains in skilled positions.[35]

Labor injunctions had worked to the benefit of African American railroad workers long before the 1920s. One of the first great labor cases to reach the Supreme Court, *In re Debs*,[36] illustrates how labor injunctions served the interests of African American railroad workers. Eugene V. Debs formed the American Railway Union in June 1893. Debs's goal was to unite all railroad workers rather than organize them by craft. Against Debs's wishes, the national convention of the union voted to exclude African Americans. The delegates to the convention agreed to organize Negro affiliates, but few African Americans were interested in joining Jim Crow unions.[37]

Debs led his union into a nationwide strike in 1894. African American railroad workers, fearing for their livelihoods, mobilized to defeat the strike. Some African American workers even formed an "Anti-Strikers' Railroad Union" to help break the strike.[38] Ultimately, the Supreme Court upheld an injunction against the strike in *In re Debs*,[39] leading to the end of the strike and of the union. Had the strike been successful, African American railroad workers would have found themselves in the precarious position of being excluded from an extremely powerful labor union with influence in most railroad occupations. Ironically, Professor Derrick Bell, oblivious to the interest of African Americans in the *Debs* case, points to it as an example of a case in which the Supreme Court "denied rights to labor" just as it was denying rights to African Americans.[40]

In the years after *Debs,* courts often issued injunctions to enforce "yellow dog" contracts, in which employees agreed not to join a union. Because the workers had agreed not to join a union, courts could enjoin their participation in strikes as a violation of their contracts. Courts also enjoined labor unions from attempting to organize workers covered by yellow dog contracts, because such activity amounted to unlawful inducement of breach of contract.

In 1898, in one of the first major examples of federal legislative interference in labor relations, Congress, at the behest of the railroad unions and partly in response to the *Debs* decision,[41] enacted a statute that banned federal courts from enforcing yellow dog contracts signed by employees of interstate railroads. In 1908, in *Adair v. United States,* the

U.S. Supreme Court, relying heavily on *Lochner*, held that the act was unconstitutional because it violated freedom of contract.[42]

To Progressive critics, the *Adair* decision was "diametrically opposed to the spirit of the freedom supposed to be guaranteed by the first ten amendments, and the supporting argument [was] based on an ancient theory of individual rights rather than upon any consideration of actual conditions."[43] For African Americans, however, the main effect of the decision was to prevent the federal government from implicitly continuing to aid the railroad unions' quest to monopolize the railroad labor market at the expense of African American workers.

Several years after *Adair*, the Supreme Court invalidated a state ban on yellow dog contracts on intrastate railroads. In 1917 the Court held that federal courts may issue injunctions against labor unions seeking to organize workers bound by yellow dog contracts.[44] (The National War Labor Board, however, claimed wartime exigency and refused to comply with Supreme Court precedent with regard to railroad labor during World War I.)[45]

The yellow dog/labor injunction combination, anathema to organized labor and its sympathizers, played a key role in helping to maintain African American employment on the railroads. The labor injunction not only helped African Americans indirectly by limiting union power, but sometimes aided African Americans directly. For example, the Georgia race strike of 1909 was brought to an end by arbitration forced upon the union by the looming threat of a federal injunction.[46]

The labor injunction also helped African Americans in other contexts, as when an Ohio court enjoined a union from using misleading tactics in a boycott to try to force a roadhouse owner in a Cleveland suburb to fire his African American employees.[47] The union's pickets claimed that the owner was unfair to organized labor, even though the employer agreed to pay his workers union wages and abide by union rules if the union would allow his workers to form a chapter, a privilege denied to them because of their race. The court, relying on its equity jurisdiction, ruled that the union's picketing was misleading and dishonest, because the owner could not be considered unfair to labor unions in refusing to fire his African American workers on demand. "In its last analysis," the judge stated, this was "a case of white men opposing colored men. . . . [T]he only information these defendants could properly and truthfully give the public about plaintiff is that he employs colored people, and I do not believe these defendants care to advertise that fact as such."[48]

No wonder, then, that two prominent African American leaders from Ohio, where an anti-yellow-dog bill had recently been defeated, testified against the Shipstead anti-injunction bill before the Senate Judiciary Committee in 1928.[49] Charles Chesnutt, an attorney, stated, "The Federal courts, in those part [sic] of the country where the rights of negroes are most limited, have been almost their only bulwark against oppression and other kinds of discrimination, and the power of injunction has been one of the strongest weapons which those courts have employed. . . . The power of injunction has undoubtedly been abused in some cases, but it has been exercised beneficently in a great many others." Chesnutt added that if the power of injunction was taken from courts with regard to labor disputes, a skilled African American worker could "not be protected from unlawful molestation in the exercise of his art."[50]

Chesnutt argued that the bill was "class legislation" intended to aid labor unions. Perhaps, added Chesnutt, if African American workers were admitted into unions, they would support the legislation out of self-interest. However, under the circumstances, a law banning injunctions "can do them no good," and "might be invoked at times to their very serious injury." Unions, after all, "say to the negro, 'You can not become a member of our union; you can not work unless you are a union man,' which in effect is to say, 'you shall not work at all.' " Chesnutt concluded that African Americans "do not desire to see what little protection they have or may have through the courts against union discrimination and tyranny taken away from them by this bill."[51]

"It logically follows," added Harry E. Davis, the leading African American Republican politician in Ohio, and a representative of the Cleveland NAACP, "that a colored worker who is denied the protection and the benefits of organized labor because they will not take him in, has only one place of redress in case his right of employment is assailed, and that is in our courts." Davis noted that the bill would prohibit injunctions unless physical or tangible property was at issue. African Americans, however, did not have "very much physical or tangible property and their biggest asset is their right to a job, recognized as a contract, but an intangible right, and I maintain that if this bill becomes a law it would affect very materially their right to the biggest thing which they have, the right to earn a living." Davis concluded that "it seems to me absolutely unjust for Congress to even think of passing a law which would deny [African Americans] their only appeal, an appeal to the courts for their redress."[52]

Professor William Forbath sees "rich irony" in the fact that the strongest precedents in favor of federal court civil rights injunctions against local and state officials "would spring from uses that the federal courts had made of the . . . fourteenth amendment a half-century earlier against the labor movement and its allies."[53] Surely, this purported irony would have been lost on Messrs. Chesnutt and Davis.

THE RAILWAY LABOR ACT AND THE DOWNFALL OF AFRICAN AMERICAN RAILROAD WORKERS

Despite the relatively hostile climate of the early 1920s, several major discriminatory railroad unions, particularly the operating unions, retained some of the monopoly power granted them by federal control over the railroads during and after World War I. The great blow to African American railroad labor, however, was the Railway Labor Act of 1926, and, even more significant, the amendments to that act passed in 1934.[54]

The Railway Labor Act of 1926
Two of Felix Frankfurter's protégés drafted the Railway Labor Act in close cooperation with the railroad unions.[55] The act guaranteed the right of workers to choose their bargaining representatives, which in effect means that it granted power to the government to force employers to negotiate with certified union representatives. The Supreme Court not only upheld this legislation in 1930, but interpreted it favorably for the unions, holding that a railroad must deal only with the representative chosen by a majority of employees.[56] The Court distinguished its earlier holdings in yellow dog contract cases supporting a free labor market in the railroad industry by arguing that the act did not interfere with the right of the carrier to select its employees or to discharge them, but merely prevented employers from interfering with their employees' right to organize.

White unionists understood that the act would help them tremendously in their quest to exclude African American workers from the railroads. As Richard Epstein notes, the act "did not transform racial attitudes, but it did change the balance of power" by giving whites "control over the choices of both African-American workers and the railroads."[57] In 1926 the president of the Brotherhood of Locomotive Firemen and Enginemen expressed his hope that at the next union convention he could report that no African Americans still worked as firemen. In 1932 a representative of the firemen's union declared at the union's annual meeting that "[a]ll of these delegates and general chairmen share the opinion mutually with this committee, that the Negro is an undesirable in our particular vocation, therefore, should be supplanted by a white man in all instances."[58]

Although nothing so dramatic occurred, the act gave unions the power to negotiate agreements with several railroads that substantially limited the number of jobs available to African Americans. For example, in 1928 the St. Louis and San Francisco system issued regulations based on an agreement with the railroad unions that would necessarily lead to the eventual elimination of all African Americans from train, shop, and rail service.[59] T. Arnold Hill of the National Urban League concluded in 1934, "During recent years considerable new Federal legislation has been enacted to improve the railroads and to promote the welfare of employees working on them. Concurrently with this legislation, the condition of Negroes engaged in train and yard service has grown steadily worse."[60]

Violent attacks by southern white railroad workers on African American workers made matters worse. For example, white trainmen launched terrorist campaigns against African American trainmen in 1931, and at least ten African American firemen and trainmen were killed and twenty-one wounded in the lower Mississippi Valley between 1931 and 1934. The railroad unions failed to condemn the violence and in some cases were implicated in it. The railroads, by contrast, offered rewards and investigative assistance that helped catch the perpetrators.[61]

One railroad executive vowed that the "reign of terror will have no effect whatever on our policy of giving Negroes their employment rights."[62] Indeed, although some African Americans quit their jobs due to labor union terrorism, it was not organized violence that eventually led to the steep decline of African Americans relative to white workers in the railroad industry, but the monopoly power granted unions by the Railway Labor Act.

Only One Place of Redress

The 1934 Amendments to the Railway Labor Act

The act's negative effects on African American workers were exacerbated in 1934, when Congress amended the act to provide: "The majority of any craft or class of employees shall have the right to determine who shall be the representative of the class or craft."[63] In other words, the union chosen by the majority of workers in a particular category defined by government regulations would now have the exclusive right to negotiate for all workers in that category.

Moreover, despite the *Adair* precedent holding that yellow dog contracts were constitutionally protected, the 1934 amendments outlawed such contracts. The amendments also banned the formation of company-financed unions, which, at least as compared to railroad unions organized by white workers, had treated African American workers well.[64] The Supreme Court unanimously upheld the act as amended against a challenge that it violated the Due Process Clause of the Fifth Amendment in *Virginia Ry. Co. v. System Federation No. 40* in 1937.[65]

The 1934 amendments—along with the Norris-La Guardia Act of 1932, which banned most federal court injunctions in labor disputes, and with state "little Norris-La Guardias," which banned state court injunctions—gave tremendous power to exclusionary railroad unions. The unions immediately tried to take advantage of the amendments "to gain a favored position for white workers."[66] The National Mediation Board (NMB) and the National Railroad Adjustment Board (NRAB), both established by the 1934 amendments, abetted the unions' discriminatory actions.[67]

The NRAB had jurisdiction over disputes arising out of the interpretation of collective bargaining agreements in the railway industry. The NRAB was composed of thirty-six members, half chosen by the unions and half by the railroads. National unions were eligible to participate in selecting the union representatives, but African American unions were not permitted to participate.[68]

Dominance of the NRAB by the railroad brotherhoods led the board to promulgate rules that benefited white workers at the expense of African Americans. For example, in 1942 the First Division of the NRAB ruled that railroads could not use porter-brakemen as brakemen.[69] In practice this decision required the railroads to replace African American porters who served as porter-brakemen with white brakemen.

Railroad Labor Regulations

Meanwhile, the NMB determined, based on a poll of workers, which union would act as sole bargaining agent of any class or craft.[70] NMB policy made collective bargaining "a mockery for the black minority on the roads." The election process almost always led to the designation of the discriminatory white firemen's and trainmen's unions as the sole bargaining agent for African Americans in those jobs. Even on the rare occasions when most of the voters in a railroad union election were African American, white unions managed to win the elections through fraud; African American workers protested to the NMB to no avail. The lack of redress logically resulted from the fact that many members of the NMB believed that the certification process should be limited to whites. For example, in 1936 one member of the NMB sent a letter to the engineers' and firemen's unions stating that African American workers' bargaining power represented a "menace to the present setup of railway labor organizations."[71]

African Americans responded to railroad union discrimination by attempting to form their own unions. The NMB frustrated such attempts by ruling that these alternative unions could not represent African American employees because the official unions already represented them. The NMB thus bestowed de facto monopoly representation powers upon white labor unions that refused to extend equal membership rights to African Americans.[72]

The legality of the NMB's policies reached the courts in *Brotherhood of Railway & Steamship Clerks v. United Transport Service Employees*.[73] The case involved forty-five African American station porters ("red caps") from St. Paul, Minnesota. The red caps were covered by a previously executed agreement with the Brotherhood of Railway and Steamship Clerks, Freight Handlers, Express and Station Employees, but were ineligible for membership in that union because of their race. They unanimously voted for the United Transport Service Employees of America (UTSEA), a nationwide union of red caps, to be their bargaining agent. The UTSEA applied to represent the African American red caps.

The NMB dismissed the application, as it typically did when African Americans sought to establish their own union in opposition to a whites-only union. The NMB ruled that the red caps were not entitled to their own union because station porters "are part of the craft or class of clerical, office, station, and storehouse employees" and did not form a separate class of employees for purposes of the Railway Labor Act.[74]

Only One Place of Redress

On appeal the United States Court of Appeals for the D.C. Circuit declared the dismissal order void. The court pointed out that the dismissal forced African American employees to accept representation by an organization in which they had neither the right to membership nor the right to speak or be heard. The Supreme Court, however, reversed the decision on the grounds that the NMB's certification decisions were not subject to judicial review.[75] This decision paved the way for many future certification proceedings that granted discriminatory labor unions exclusive bargaining representation.[76]

African Americans often were not able to get copies of the contracts in force on their roads, though the contracts were routinely distributed to white workers. The NMB, which was supposed to keep a copy of all union contracts, was not eager to help African Americans who believed that a contract was being violated to their detriment. The firemen's brotherhood refused to handle grievances filed by African Americans if the complaint conflicted with the perceived interests of white firemen. This is not surprising, given that in 1937 the union reaffirmed its intent to eliminate African American firemen from the profession.[77]

The firemen's union negotiated a series of discriminatory agreements with the railroads that severely reduced the employment of African American firemen in the late 1930s and early 1940s. By 1940 the number of African American firemen and brakemen had declined by almost two-thirds from the 1920 level. No African American firemen or trainmen were left in Virginia in 1940.[78] This "progress" did not satisfy the brotherhoods; their goal remained the *elimination* of African American competition nationwide. For example, in 1940 the firemen's brotherhood demanded that all future firemen hired by the southeastern carriers be "promotable," meaning white.[79]

When some carriers resisted, the brotherhood called in the NMB. With the NMB's encouragement, the firemen's union in 1941 signed a contract with the southeastern carriers that contained a clause stipulating that the carriers would hire only "promotables" and reduce the presence of nonpromotables on each line to 50 percent. The agreement was eventually amended to state that "nonpromotable" meant "colored."[80] Similar agreements were devised by the brakemen's union.[81]

Unions sometimes forced employers to go beyond the letter of the contracts and engage in wholesale displacement of African American railroad workers already employed. Secret agreements designed to undermine African Americans also marked this period. In one case the firemen's union agreed with the Gulf, Mobile and Ohio Railroad to forgo higher wages for its members in return for more jobs on new stokerized engines at the expense of senior African American firemen.[82]

Not all railroads' managements capitulated to the unions. Faced with the demand that his railroad eliminate African American firemen, one railroad executive protested that African American "people are citizens of the country; it is necessary that they make a living; colored people are patrons of the railroads, and, in our opinion, we should not by agreement entirely exclude them from employment in positions which they have occupied and filled over the years."[83]

Often, however, the railroads acquiesced because union policies put them in a very difficult position. For example, although African American firemen were not promotable, they did get seniority, and because they never received promotions, on many lines African Americans had the most seniority. This allowed them to claim runs, and prevented white firemen from working the minimum number of days necessary for promotion to engineer. The railroads, meanwhile, were left with a shortage of engineers, and the path of least resistance was to eliminate African American firemen. Several railroads covered by the Southeastern Agreement signed contracts reducing the percentage of runs for African American firemen below what the master agreement envisioned.[84]

The National Mediation Board approved the discriminatory agreements made by the unions and railroads. As Malcolm Ross, a director of the Fair Employment Practice Committee during World War II, noted, in doing so the NMB "was no more legally responsible for the antiracial act than an Elkton Maryland marrying parson is for joining in holy wedlock an overstimulated Princeton sophomore and a blonde he has just picked up."[85] The NMB's job was to accept any agreement the designated union negotiated with the railroads.

THE LONG-TERM EFFECTS OF THE RLA: CASTE IN *STEELE*

In 1944, in *Steele v. Louisville & Nashville Railroad*,[86] the Supreme Court unanimously held that railroad unions, having been granted monopolies by the Railway Labor Act, must represent all workers fairly, including

African Americans. The defendant railroad had hired Steele, an African American fireman, in 1910. At that point 98 percent of the firemen in his district were African American; 80 percent were still African American by 1941. After railroads in the southeastern United States agreed to a discriminatory contract with the firemen's union, three-quarters of the African American firemen working for the defendant railroad lost their jobs. Steele, fearing for his own job, and having already been demoted, sued in Alabama state court.[87]

The Alabama Supreme Court upheld the agreement, concluding that it was "a lawful contract entered into in a lawful manner."[88] Prospects at the United States Supreme Court looked bleak. Just a few months before *Steele* was decided, the Supreme Court explicitly ruled that whatever the potential advantages to individual workers from negotiating their own contracts, under the Railway Labor Act "the majority rules." This opinion seemed "to make the union the sole and final arbiter of conflicts of interest among members of the bargaining unit."[89]

The Supreme Court, however, while very much in favor of coerced collective bargaining, also was becoming increasingly sympathetic to civil rights claims. The Court found for Steele, creatively (and perhaps disingenuously) arguing that because there was no evidence that Congress intended to authorize race discrimination under the act, the Court could prohibit union representatives from engaging in it.[90] Of course, Congress knew that the unions to which it was granting tremendous power in 1926 and 1934 were exclusionary, and it obviously had no strong objection to the unions' policies. The Court, however, could not countenance a situation in which the railroad unions used their government-granted monopoly power to drive African Americans from the labor force.

The Court's legal gymnastics were not quite over. It still had to contend with the concern raised by Messrs. Chesnutt and Davis at the hearings on the Shipstead anti-injunction bill: how were the federal courts to enforce a nondiscrimination policy when the Norris-La Guardia Act seemingly banned courts from issuing injunctions against labor unions? The Court answered that when Norris-La Guardia banned injunctions in "labor" disputes, Congress meant disputes between employers and employees. Conflict among employees, the Court stated, did not constitute a labor dispute within the meaning of the act, and courts therefore could enjoin labor unions from discriminating.

Railroad Labor Regulations

One contemporary authority celebrated the *Steele* decision as *"Dred Scott* in reverse."[91] In fact, however, the ruling (and its extension in *Howard v. St. Louis-S.F. Ry.,* 343 U.S. 774 [1953], to prohibit unions from attempting to dislodge African American workers in a different bargaining class) did not effectively reduce discrimination in railroad employment. *Steele* did not require unions to admit African American members and did nothing to reduce monopoly powers the Railway Labor Act conferred on unions. Most railroad unions, meanwhile, remained recalcitrantly racist. Although *Steele* held that the railroad unions had a duty of fair representation, "many opportunities remain[ed] for ostensibly neutral rules to impose disproportionate losses on black workers" so that the possibility of redress through the courts was remote.[92]

Moreover, the promise *Steele* held for African Americans was not realized, because the relevant government agencies did not enforce it vigorously, and because private parties lacked the resources to litigate. Indeed, the discriminatory agreement that led to the *Steele* case remained in force until 1951.[93] By the time *Steele* began to give African American railroad workers some leverage against discrimination in the 1950s, the bulk of African Americans' jobs on the railroads had been lost. For example, the presence of African American firemen in the South declined to only 7 percent in 1960. By the time railroad unions revoked their color bars in the 1960s, overall railroad employment had declined dramatically, and few railroads were doing much new hiring.[94]

To be sure, not all African American railroad workers were harmed by the Railway Labor Act. Some deft political maneuvering in 1934 by A. Philip Randolph of the Brotherhood of Sleeping Car Porters assured that despite the indifference or hostility of the other railway unions, the almost entirely African American porters' union was recognized as the "duly authorized representative of the sleeping car porters." This recognition rescued the brotherhood from near extinction and guaranteed that its members received the advantages union members gained from the act.[95] (The porters, however, soon faced discriminatory legislation in several southern states forbidding the Pullman Company from operating sleeping cars in their states without conductors; a bill that would have required the displacement of sleeping car porters by conductors nationwide died in Congress.) Randolph, meanwhile, became an important African American leader in the labor movement, and in the nation at large.[96]

Only One Place of Redress

Overall, though, labor economist Herbert Northrup concluded in 1944 that "[i]n no other industry has collective bargaining had such disastrous results for Negroes."[97] In a 1971 introduction to a reprint of his earlier work, Northrup added that if equal opportunity was finally to come to railroad employment, it would arrive at least thirty years too late.[98]

Ubiquitous collective bargaining on the railroads did not happen spontaneously. The federal government encouraged, and in fact commanded, it. In no other industry did the abandonment of Lochnerian jurisprudence by the courts and the establishment of government intervention in the labor market have such disastrous results for African Americans.

FOUR ✳ Prevailing-Wage Laws

THE DAVIS-BACON ACT[1] harmed African American construction workers for decades. Initially enacted in 1931, the act requires contractors with federal building contracts in excess of two thousand dollars to pay their workers the "prevailing wage" as determined by the secretary of labor. Davis-Bacon was passed in part to limit the employment of African Americans on federal construction projects, and it accomplished that purpose. Indeed, Davis-Bacon represented the culmination of a decades-long effort by construction unions to exclude outsiders from public works projects.

EARLY PUBLIC WORKS LABOR LEGISLATION

In the immediate post–Civil War period, building-trade unions had several major goals, including an eight-hour workday and a reduction in competition from members of minority groups, aliens, and others whom the unions generally excluded. Indeed, these goals were often intertwined.[2] Given the prevailing anti-interventionist "free labor" ideology of the time, labor leaders expected to achieve these goals through legislation only in the realm of government public works. Union leaders argued that because the government itself was acting as the contractor for such projects, the government could determine who was to be employed on such projects, and on what terms.

Relying on this theory, construction unions had some success in promoting eight-hour-day laws for public works projects. A few states passed such laws,[3] and the federal government's eight-hour law for federal employees also covered workers on federal public works projects.

Unions also occasionally succeeded in promoting statutes that excluded competitors from public works projects. A Louisiana statute limited employment on public works to those who had paid their poll tax. Early Oregon and California statutes banned the use of Chinese laborers on public works projects, and an 1894 New York statute banned the use of aliens generally. Even after the New York law went into effect, the state government continued to receive complaints from labor unions that contractors were employing (nonunion) aliens, especially Italians, on public works projects.[4]

These statutes met with a chilly reception when challenged in the courts. Courts invalidated each law as a violation of liberty of contract and/or equal protection guarantees.[5]

By the early twentieth century, the construction craft unions had affiliated with the burgeoning American Federation of Labor and were among the strongest unions in the United States. They were especially powerful in the North and Midwest. The unions used their political muscle to seek laws regulating employment on public works for the benefit of their members. Illinois, for example, joined New York in banning aliens from working on public works projects.[6]

Other public works laws did not explicitly discriminate based on race or alienage, but had discriminatory effects. The most restrictive statutes required that public works contractors use only union labor. More common were statutes requiring contractors to pay workers the "prevailing wage," which generally meant the union wage. Other statutes were more modest, simply requiring public contractors to adhere to an eight-hour workday.

A challenge to Kansas's eight-hour law reached the United States Supreme Court in 1903. The defendant, a contractor charged with violating the law, argued that the law unconstitutionally limited freedom of contract. The Court rejected this argument, as well as contrary New York and Ohio precedents, and held that the law did not violate the Constitution.[7]

Dicta in the Court's opinion implied that it would reject any challenge by a contractor to a public works labor statute. The Court adopted the unions' argument that the state was like any other employer and thus had the right to dictate the terms of its employment of contractors. Any contractor unsatisfied with these terms need not bid on public works projects. The three sitting justices most sympathetic to Lochnerian jurisprudence —

Fuller, Brewer, and Peckham — dissented without opinion. The Court extended the *Atkin* holding to a *federal* eight-hour law in *Ellis v. United States* in 1907.[8]

Though *Atkin* dealt with a constitutional challenge by a contractor, state courts interpreted the opinion as foreclosing any successful federal constitutional challenge to public works labor statutes, including challenges by workers. Before *Atkin,* however, several state courts had held that such statutes violated *state* constitutional provisions. Courts held that the statutes unconstitutionally wasted taxpayer money, constituted class legislation benefiting union members and other highly paid and highly skilled workers at the expense of other workers, and/or improperly delegated legislative authority to labor unions. After *Atkin* courts continued to invalidate public works labor statutes on state grounds.[9]

The issue of regulation of labor on public works again reached the United States Supreme Court in 1915. This time the issue was the constitutionality of a state ban on the employment of aliens on public works. The Court ignored state court precedents holding that such bans violated the aliens' constitutional rights to liberty and to equal protection of the laws, and held, on the authority of *Atkin,* that the law in question passed constitutional muster.[10]

CONFLICT BETWEEN AFRICAN AMERICAN WORKERS AND CONSTRUCTION UNIONS

Aliens and other outsiders, including the relatively small number of African Americans then living outside the South, suffered because of northern and midwestern public works laws. Such laws, however, generally did not exist where the vast majority of African Americans lived, in the South. Southern locales did not need legislation to restrict African Americans from public works projects, because exclusion was accomplished through informal pressure by government officials.[11]

Meanwhile, beginning in the 1910s, thousands of African American construction workers moved to cities in both the North and the South. They quickly came into conflict with the building-trades unions. Construction unions had never treated African American workers well. Many of the unions excluded African Americans completely. Others, especially southern unions faced with many potential African American competitors, admitted African Americans but relegated them to second-class seg-regated locals. Because of grassroots resistance among white workers, however, the American Federation of Labor rarely expended energy try-ing to organize African American locals.[12]

Some northern and midwestern construction unions formally admitted African Americans on equal terms, but even those unions rarely treated African Americans fairly. For example, in 1903 white brickmasons work-ing on a federal government construction project in Indianapolis walked off the job rather than work with an African American member of their union, Robert Rhodes. The contractor fired Rhodes at the insistence of the strikers. Rhodes appealed for relief from his union local. Not only did the local deny Rhodes's appeal, it also fined him twenty-five dollars for working on a nonunion project before he joined the union![13]

By the 1920s most African American building-trades workers, includ-ing former union members, had given up on organized labor. They instead chose to compete with union members by taking jobs at subunion wages.[14] This decision improved African Americans' employment prospects. By 1926 a survey found only fourteen local unions of African American car-penters, compared with an estimated thirty-nine in 1912, and the figure dropped again by 1929. By the late 1920s, the 340,000-member carpen-ters' union had only about 600 or so African American members. Yet despite continuous large-scale migration to the North by African Ameri-cans in general and by craft workers in particular, by 1930 the percentage of carpenters in the South who were African American had edged up from 15 percent in 1910 to 17 percent.[15]

African Americans also retained their antebellum strength in the trowel trades — bricklaying, plastering, and cement finishing — composing, for example, 61 percent of the South's plasterers and 44 percent of the plas-terers and cement finishers. African Americans were numerous enough in those fields to create their own informal training programs and to allow their employers to withstand labor boycotts by white unionists. African Americans so dominated these fields that whites in unions such as the Hod Carriers and Common Building Laborers Union sometimes felt compelled to offer them equal status.[16]

Skilled construction unions, however, continued to exclude African Americans nationwide. In 1928 a survey of construction unions revealed the following:

Prevailing-Wage Laws

69

- "practically none" of the members of the electricians' union were African American
- the sheet metal workers' union had no African Americans among its twenty-five thousand members
- the plasterers' union had only one hundred African American members among its thirty thousand members, despite the presence of six thousand African Americans in the trade
- the plumbers and steamfitters had "a long history of successfully maneuvering to avoid Negro membership"[17]

The plumbers' and electricians' unions not only excluded African Americans from membership, but, as discussed in chapter 2, also used their control of state licensing boards to try to exclude African Americans from their fields.[18]

Despite the exclusion of African Americans from craft unions, more southern African Americans were employed in construction in 1930 than in any industry except agriculture and domestic service. Because the effects of union and educational discrimination were hardly felt in unskilled construction work, African Americans did most of that work. In at least six southern cities African Americans composed more than 80 percent of the unskilled construction force. Overall, approximately 150,000 African Americans worked in the construction industry in the late 1920s, mostly in the South. To protect white workers' jobs, several southern cities passed ordinances prohibiting African American contractors from working in white neighborhoods.[19]

Meanwhile, in the 1920s the demographics of northern union discrimination changed. During and after World War I, foreign immigration to the United States slowed. Aliens ceased to pose a serious threat to union dominance of the construction industry, particularly after the Immigration Act of 1924 substantially limited the influx of southern- and eastern-European immigrants. A new "threat" to northern unions, however, soon arose in the form of African American migrants from the South.[20]

As in the South, African Americans who migrated north managed to get a disproportionate share of unskilled construction jobs, while discriminatory union practices and a relative lack of skills forced African Americans to accept lower-paying nonunion employment to maintain a smaller presence in skilled construction work. By 1930 African Americans composed an overall proportion of the northern urban construction worker force that approximated their proportion of the total northern urban population.[21]

The steady increase in African American competitors unnerved union leadership, particularly because the construction industry went into depression several years before the rest of the economy. A contemporary source noted that "Negroes outside the South are a small factor in the building trades, yet they have been able to depress the market here and there, in Chicago, Pittsburgh, Cleveland, and elsewhere, to an extent sufficient to cause bitter complaint from the white unions which commonly bar them from membership. . . . [T]heir numbers, though small, were sufficient to create an oversupply of certain types of building labor and to depress established standards, even though no attempt was made to undercut prevailing rates."[22]

As one historian points out, "by 1930 black workers had obtained a foothold in the northern construction work force, but the low proportion of skilled construction workers who were Black suggests that the foothold was tenuous one."[23] The resentment white union members felt toward African Americans who were taking "their" jobs made African Americans' foothold even more tenuous.

THE ORIGINS OF THE DAVIS-BACON ACT

Competition between African American workers and exclusionary unions in New York led to the introduction of the bill that ultimately became the Davis-Bacon Act. By the late 1920s African Americans, who made up about 4.8 percent of New York City's total population, made up about 2.5 percent of the city's skilled construction workers and 7.3 percent of the unskilled.[24] Not only was the number of African American construction workers residing in New York growing rapidly, but construction contractors hired African Americans from the South to work in New York on federal public works projects. As one scholar notes, "The migration of Negro workers to the North created great resentment among Northern whites, especially when Negroes were transported North by employers to be used as . . . cheap labor."[25]

New York's building-trades unions were virtually impenetrable to African Americans. Powerful Local 3 of the electrical workers' union, like other electrical union locals nationwide, simply refused to admit African Americans. The plumbers' union resorted to a different tack, enforcing racial exclusiveness through control of the licensing process. The carpenters' union, meanwhile, relegated African Americans to a Jim Crow local. They assigned all African American union members to Local 1888, initially a mixed local based in Harlem. The white members gradually transferred membership to other locals. Once Local 1888 became segregated, the district council made Harlem the sole jurisdiction in which the local's members could work.[26]

New York overcame state constitutional barriers to prevailing-wage legislation with a constitutional amendment specifically permitting such legislation, and was one of the few states to have a prevailing-wage law in the 1920s. In 1926 the United States Supreme Court found that an Oklahoma prevailing-wage law unconstitutionally violated due process because its ill-defined terms were too vague for the employer to know what the law permitted him to pay his employees. A year later, however, the New York Court of Appeals rejected a claim — brought by taxpayers seeking to prevent "wasteful" spending — that New York's similar law was unconstitutional because it was "unintelligible."[27]

New York's law provided that "[t]he wages to be paid for a legal day's work, as hereinbefore defined, to laborers, workmen or mechanics upon such public works . . . shall be not less than the prevailing rate for a day's work in the same trade or occupation in the locality within the state where such public work on, about or in connection with which such labor is performed."[28] Though on its face the New York law might have appeared "unintelligible," common knowledge suggested that its prevailing-wage language was intended to establish the union wage on public works projects, and it was implemented in such a way as practically to guarantee this result. The law could not explicitly establish the union wage, because that would have left it constitutionally vulnerable to charges that it improperly delegated legislative power to the unions.

In his opinion for the Court of Appeals, Justice Benjamin Cardozo not only upheld New York's prevailing-wage law against constitutional challenge but defended the law's substance. Two decades earlier, the Court of Appeals had observed that prevailing-wage laws decreed that any worker who could not command the prevailing wage "must be deprived of all opportunity to secure employment on all public works in their respective callings, and so the tendency of such legislation is to check individual exertion and to suppress industrial freedom."[29] By contrast, Cardozo argued that the law prevented the "merciless exploitation of the indigent or the idle."[30] In Cardozo's view, then, the indigent or idle were apparently better off staying that way than accepting a job at less than the union wage.

No matter how one perceives its effects on the "indigent or idle," New York's prevailing-wage law protected union construction workers from wage competition on state public works projects. Federal projects, however, were not subject to the law's requirements.

The Bacon Bill

In 1927 Algernon Blair, a contractor from Alabama, received a federal contract to build a Veteran's Bureau hospital in Representative Robert Bacon's Long Island, New York, congressional district. The firm imported a crew of African American construction workers from Alabama to work on the project. Because this was a federal project, New York's prevailing-wage law did not cover it. Besieged with constituent complaints, Bacon submitted a bill that would require contractors working on federal public works projects to comply with state prevailing-wage laws.[31]

According to Bacon's statement to the House Committee on Labor, the workers brought into his district "were herded onto this job, they were housed in shacks, they were paid a very low wage, and the work proceeded. Of course, that meant that the labor conditions in that part of New York State where this hospital was to be built were entirely upset. It meant that the neighboring community was very upset."[32]

Congressmen William Upshaw of Georgia teased Representative Bacon about Bacon's apparent anti-Negro sentiment: "You will not think that a southern man is more than human if he smiles over the fact of your reaction to that real problem you are confronted with in any community with a superabundance or large aggregation of negro labor." At least publicly, Bacon denied any specific animus against African Americans. He responded: "I just merely mention that fact because that was true in this particular case, but the same thing would be true if you should bring in a lot of Mexican laborers or if you brought in any nonunion laborer from any other state."[33] But Upshaw's comment is revealing, because he clearly understood the racist subtext of Bacon's complaint.

Bacon provided evidence of his own racism later in the same hearing

Prevailing-Wage Laws

when he praised "caucasian" immigrants and argued that Asian immigrants were "unassimilable." His remarks also suggest that he thought that African Americans were "unassimilable," but could not be completely excluded from the polity because, unlike Asians, African Americans "came earlier and under different circumstances."[34]

Nor were those the only racist comments Bacon made while opposing nonwhite immigration. For example, he inserted into the *Congressional Record* the following statement by some "distinguished and learned Americans" opposing nonwhite immigration into the United States:

> We urge the extension of the quota system to all countries of North and South America from which we have substantial immigration and in which the population is not predominately of the *white race*. . . . [W]e have been admitting upwards of 75,000 immigrants from Mexico, the West Indies, Brazil, and elsewhere, who are for the most part not of the white race, and who, because of their lower standards of living, are able to compete at an advantage with American workers. . . . [O]nly by such a system of proportional representation in our future immigration could the racial status quo of the country be maintained or a reasonable degree of homogeneity secured. Without such basic homogeneity, we firmly believe, no civilization can have its best development.[35]

The 1928 Hearings

In 1928 Bacon proposed H.R. 11141, "A Bill to Require Contractors and Subcontractors Engaged on Public Works of the United States to Give Certain Preferences in the Employment of Labor."[36] The committee hearings on this bill give further insight into the racial bias that propelled forward the issue of the regulation of labor on public works. Bacon submitted a supportive letter to the Committee on Labor from Secretary of Labor James J. Davis.

In the letter Davis endorsed a memorandum written by Ethelbert Stewart, commissioner of labor statistics. The memorandum recounted that a contractor from the South brought an *"entire outfit of negro laborers from the South"* into Bacon's district, treated them poorly, and "employed no local labor." Stewart observed that the practice of bringing workers from the South "adds confusion to the question of workmen's compensation." "In addition to this," Stewart continued, "there is nothing to prevent the contractor having this class of labor from throwing an injured worker out of his gang upon the charity of the city of State of New York, since he is under no obligation to take care of or return the negro workmen to his home."[37]

Davis later became a senator from Pennsylvania and a Davis-Bacon cosponsor. Like Bacon, Davis was an avowed racist, which was clear when he expressed his strong support of racist immigration restrictions. In 1925, for example, Davis argued that United States immigration policy should take "the hereditary qualities which the individual brings to America" into account because "[t]he blood of a nation determines its history." He argued that Congress should do what it could to "purify the national stream of life, to dry up the sources of hereditary poisoning, and to keep America sound at the core." Davis was the Republicans' leading spokesman for immigration restrictions throughout the 1920s.[38]

Testimony by union representatives reveals a definite racial element to their support of the 1928 bill. William J. Spencer, secretary of the buildings-trades department of the American Federation of Labor told the committee, "There are complaints from all hospitals of the Veteran's Bureau against the condition of employment on these jobs. That is true whether the job is in the States of Washington, Oregon, Oklahoma, or Florida. The same complaints come in. They are due to the fact that a contractor from Alabama may go to North Port and take a crew of *negro* workers and house them on the site of construction within a stockade and feed them and keep his organization intact thereby and work that job contrary to the existing practices in the city of New York."[39]

Emil Preiss, business manager of Local 3, International Brotherhood of Electrical Workers, New York City, who was from Bacon's district, stated that "[t]here are thousands of skilled mechanics in [Long Island] today who are unable to obtain employment on [the Veteran's hospital], owing to the fact that poorly-paid labor is imported and being housed somewhat like cattle on the job and that labor is living under conditions that an American [apparently, as opposed to Negro] workman could not countenance." Preiss added that "the class of mechanics they are using out there today is an undesirable element of people. They are mixing with that community, but the community is refusing to house these people who can not be housed on the jobs."[40]

Prevailing-Wage Laws

In March 1930 the House Committee on Labor held hearings on H.R. 7995, "A Bill to Require Contractors and Subcontractors Engaged on Public Works of the United States to Give Certain Preferences in the Employment of Labor," and H.R. 9232, "A Bill to Regulate the Rates of Wages to Be Paid to Laborers and Mechanics Employed by Contractors and Subcontractors on Public Works of the United States and of the District of Columbia." Representative Bacon submitted the former bill, and Representative Elliott Sproul of Illinois the latter. The Sproul bill was the first to require that federal contractors and subcontractors pay the prevailing wage.

Representative Bacon stated during the hearings on his bill that he favored requiring contractors to pay the prevailing wage, but believed that such a provision would be unconstitutional because it was too vague. He again invoked Algernon Blair's presence in his district to explain why the federal public works legislation was necessary. Bacon complained that "[t]his contractor picked up Government work all over the United States simply because they [*sic*] could make a low bid by bringing in cheap labor from Alabama."[41]

Another interesting aspect of Bacon's testimony is that it refutes the oft-heard claim that Davis-Bacon legislation was promulgated to ensure quality work by favoring skilled union workers. Representative Charles Easterly of Pennsylvania asked Bacon whether Algernon Blair was "a good concern." Bacon responded, "Yes, they do good work; at least I am so informed."[42]

Later in his testimony, Representative Bacon submitted a letter he sent to a fellow congressman. In this letter, Bacon argued that his bill was "aimed, and the purpose of the bill is directed against, a monopoly of the benefits of labor by a special few, namely, those gangs of imported workmen, under the strict control of a contractor, who moves them from one part of the country to the other in chasing Federal construction work."[43]

Later in the March 1930 hearing, Representative Sproul discussed his reasons for a prevailing wage bill. He stated that "[i]t is manifestly unfair that a contractor who pays the prevailing rate of wages in the locality in which the Government's work is done, and who bases his bid for the work upon the prevailing wage scales, should be underbid by a contractor whose intent is, if he is awarded the contract, to import labor at a much lower scale of wages. . . . What follows? He imports labor to which he pays less than the prevailing wage."[44]

Sproul mentioned several such instances, at least one of which involved African American workers. Sproul complained that at St. Elizabeth's Hospital the contractor paid bricklayers only eight dollars a day, compared to a prevailing wage of thirteen dollars a day.[45] Later in the hearing, Representative John J. Cochran reported that he had "received numerous complaints in recent months about southern contractors employing low-paid *colored* mechanics getting the work and bringing the employees from the South. Just recently there was trouble at St. Elizabeth's Hospital."[46]

The 1931 Hearings

In January 1931 the House Committee on Labor held hearings on H.R. 16619, a prevailing-wage bill destined to become the Davis-Bacon Act. Representative Bacon, who submitted the bill, argued that it would prevent federal contractors from importing "cheap, bootleg labor" into a federal construction site and remove the temptation to import "cheap, bootleg, itinerant labor."[47]

The Senate hearings on Davis-Bacon in February 1931 were short. American Federation of Labor president William Green testified at the hearings and noted that "[c]olored labor is being brought in to demoralize wage rates" in a federal post office job in Kingsport, Tennessee.[48] T. A. Lane, of the Bricklayers Union, also alluded to the Kingsport case, noting that "wage reduction is taking place in Tennessee right to-day." Lane added that "cheap labor" was being imported from North Carolina to work on a post office in Alexandria, and that the Blair company (which, as we have seen, used itinerant African American workers) had within the last six weeks acquired the contracts for the office in Spartanburg, South Carolina, the post office at Kosciusko, the Memphis veterans' building, and the post office at Streator, Illinois.[49]

The 1931 Congressional Record Debate

The debate in the Senate over the Davis-Bacon bill, as recorded in the *Congressional Record,* was only a page long and contained no direct or indirect references to African Americans. The House, however, was a different matter. Several representatives made direct or implicit negative references to African American construction workers, including the following:

Prevailing-Wage Laws

Mr. Fiorello La Guardia — "A contractor from Alabama was awarded the contract for the Northport Hospital, a Veterans' Bureau hospital. I saw with my own eyes the labor that he imported there from the South and the conditions under which they were working. These unfortunate men were huddled in shacks living under most wretched conditions and being paid wages far below the standard. These unfortunate men were being exploited by the contract. Local skilled and unskilled labor were not employed. The workmanship of the cheap imported labor was of course very inferior."

Mr. Bacon — "The unscrupulous contractor who hitherto came in with cheap, bootleg labor must now come in and pay the prevailing rate of wages in the community where the building is to be built."

Mr. Bacon — "Members of Congress have been flooded with protests from all over the country that certain Federal contractors on current jobs are bringing into local communities outside labor, cheap labor, bootleg labor."

Mr. Cochran — "What would be the result if cheap labor was brought into my city? It would be resented, and trouble would result."

Mr. Miles Allgood — "Reference has been made to a contractor from Alabama who went to New York with bootleg labor. That is a fact. That contractor has *cheap colored labor* that he transports, and he puts them in cabins, and it is labor of that sort that is in competition with white labor throughout the country. This bill has merit, and with the extensive building program now being entered into, it is very important that we enact this measure."[50]

Congress overwhelmingly passed Davis-Bacon, and President Hoover signed it into law on March 3, 1931.[51] The mood of the times was quite favorable for the passage of this legislation. Davis-Bacon was not the only action taken by the federal government at the beginning of the depression to help whites receive priority in employment. Just a month before Davis-Bacon passed, the Department of Labor began to deport thousands of Mexican aliens, many of whom had been living legally in the United States for years, even decades.[52]

Besides playing to racist sentiment at a time of economic hardship, the legislative history of Davis-Bacon reveals that the law appealed to pro-union legislators, to congressmen who shared the popular (but foolish) view that unemployment could be lowered by the imposition of high wages in a deflationary environment,[53] and to congressmen who sought to ensure that pork barrel projects brought to their district in a time of mass unemployment benefited local constituents, not itinerant workers.

When Davis-Bacon became law early in the depression era, the federal government was about to embark on an ambitious public works program that would soon account for half of all money spent on construction work.[54] As intended, Davis-Bacon severely limited the ability of African Americans to compete for jobs on federal projects.

Immediate Discriminatory Effects

Davis-Bacon's discriminatory effects were subtle but real. The only recourse African Americans had in a labor market dominated by exclusionary unions that demanded above-market wages was their willingness to work for less money than the unionists. The act prohibited African American workers from exercising that advantage by establishing mandatory above-market wages based on the prevailing union wage.

The original Davis-Bacon Act had a significant drafting flaw, in that it did not provide for predetermination of the prevailing wage by the government. Instead, the law provided that all contracts for public construction must contain a clause requiring contractors to pay the prevailing wage. Any dispute between workers and contractors regarding the prevailing wage was to be settled by mandatory arbitration mediated by the secretary of labor. Contractors were extremely unhappy with this situation, because they could not be certain of what the prevailing wage would be when they started construction and, therefore, could not accurately estimate the profitability of their bids. Labor unions were also unhappy, because contrary to the clear intent of the statute, some contractors claimed that the prevailing wage was lower than the union wage.[55] The unions might also have been concerned that the vagueness and indeterminacy of the statute would lead to a successful due-process challenge.

To resolve these difficulties, in 1935 Congress amended Davis-Bacon to provide for predetermination of wages by the Department of Labor.[56] The Department of Labor, in turn, promulgated regulations for Davis-Bacon that required that wages be paid at union scale in any area in which construction labor was at least 30 percent unionized. This rule guaranteed that almost all Davis-Bacon wages would be set according to union wages.[57]

Because the union-wage rule meant that there was no economic benefit to hiring nonunion labor, contractors had every incentive to hire unionized workers for skilled positions. Union members were generally the best-trained workers, and they could be hired quickly and efficiently through union hiring halls.[58]

Contractors also faced political pressure to hire only union labor: if a contractor did not hire union labor, well-organized union locals could pressure the Department of Labor to investigate that contractor's labor practices, a costly diversion even for a law-abiding contractor. Local governments also exerted pressure on contractors to hire union labor.[59]

Faced with these incentives, the vast majority of Davis-Bacon contractors opted for union labor when hiring skilled workers. Because most construction craft unions had few or no African American members, federal contractors rarely hired skilled African Americans. Skilled African American workers in the South suffered somewhat because of Davis-Bacon,[60] and northern African Americans fared even worse. Of all northern skilled African American workers, construction workers were least likely to have found work in their field during the depression.[61] Ironically, considering that Davis-Bacon was purportedly passed to protect local workers, unions insisted that employers bring in union labor from distant cities rather than hire local nonunion African Americans.

Not all of skilled African American workers' troubles are attributable to Davis-Bacon; the virtual collapse of nongovernment construction would have harmed them in any event. However, as Robert Weaver concludes, "much of the government-financed construction involved use of union labor, and certain trades in almost every community did not include Negroes among union members, while many unions actually barred Negroes from participation. These factors were quickly reflected in the employment status of Negro skilled workers."[62] By giving significant extra power to exclusionary labor unions, Davis-Bacon made the situation far worse than it otherwise would have been.

Unskilled African American construction workers also fared poorly under Davis-Bacon during the depression. Faced with less union competition and discrimination, unskilled African Americans received some work as laborers on Davis-Bacon projects. In order to stem competition from laborers, however, skilled construction unions demanded that such jobs pay very high wages. As a result, laborers were severely underutilized on Davis-Bacon projects. African Americans were overrepresented as laborers in the general construction pool, so they suffered disproportionately from the relative underuse of laborers.

When African Americans did receive jobs as laborers, they found these to be dead-end positions. Because of discrimination in union and public vocational school training programs, the only way unskilled African Americans could become skilled workers was to accept unskilled employment on nonunion projects and learn on the job.[63] Under union rules, however, and therefore on Davis-Bacon projects, laborers received no training and were forbidden to use tools in any way.

Following general union practice, "apprentice" was the only category of unskilled workers in training for skilled positions recognized under Davis-Bacon. Unions rarely allowed African Americans into their apprenticeship programs, and African Americans faced discrimination in government-sponsored programs. Davis-Bacon regulations thus not only limited the employment opportunities of unskilled African Americans, but prevented those who did get jobs from gaining skills.

Long-Term Discriminatory Effects
World War II brought further hardship to African American construction workers. Discrimination in government contract work continued in the war industries, particularly in the South. To make matters worse, at the start of World War II federal agencies began signing "stabilization agreements," preserving the status quo with unions. These agreements were first promulgated in the construction industry and gave a closed shop to the Building Construction Trades Department of the AFL. The stabilization pacts often resulted in the disqualification of African American skilled and semiskilled workers from defense construction.[64]

Fortunately for African Americans, necessity dictated that they were not excluded completely from defense construction. Many army camps were built in the South, and there simply were not enough white workers to fill the available jobs, particularly since the residential type of construction involved was a specialty of African American carpenters. The federal government was therefore sometimes able to pressure unions to allow African Americans into their carpentry unions, or at least to form new segregated locals. In many other cases, however, African Americans were excluded from major construction projects and in some cities union policies barred them altogether from defense construction work.[65]

The standardization of wages and further unionization caused by Davis-Bacon during the war threatened the future of southern African American carpenters, who dominated small-scale construction jobs. The carpenters' union had previously not been well organized in this relatively nonlucrative area. However, the bonanza brought on by federal wartime construction of military housing and other small-scale projects, combined with high Davis-Bacon wages, attracted the union's attention. Labor shortages protected the jobs of African American carpenters in the short run, but after the war they were forced for the first time to compete with white unionized carpenters.[66]

In response to complaints of discrimination in public works and other federal projects during World War II, the federal government set up the Fair Employment Practices Committee (FEPC). At its worst, the FEPC was completely ineffective. At its best, it froze an unfavorable status quo. It was nevertheless unpopular among right-wing legislators, particularly in the South, and was not renewed after the war.[67]

Because of union discrimination, abetted by the monopoly power Davis-Bacon and state law equivalents granted unions, and by union control of apprenticeship programs, by 1950 African Americans constituted only a small percentage of skilled building-trades workers. By the late 1950s African Americans in the construction industry were limited almost entirely to unskilled jobs because of union discrimination. For example, only 3.24 percent of the carpenters in the United States were African American in 1950.[68] The figures on African American participation in apprenticeship programs were even bleaker; African American apprentices ranged from .6 to 4.1 percent of apprentices in various skilled trades.[69]

President Eisenhower tried to alleviate discrimination against African American workers in federal public works by establishing the President's Committee on Government Contracts (PCGC). However, the PCGC did not have jurisdiction over labor unions. This rendered it almost totally ineffective, because unions, not employers, were the primary source of discrimination against African American construction workers.[70] As one expert noted, "No one doubts that employers discriminate. Nevertheless, it is no less true that in innumerable cases it is the unions that, in effect, do the hiring and the discriminating while individual employers are often prepared to hire Negroes. That is the way it works in many of the building craft unions."[71]

As of January 1, 1959, complaints of discrimination were pending with the (helpless) PCGC against many of America's leading international unions. As of 1961 African Americans were still barred from the unions of the electrical workers, operating engineers, plumbers, plasterers, and sheet metal workers, among others. In one notorious incident, because the local union refused membership to nonwhites, African Americans were prevented from working on the construction of the Rayburn House of Representatives office building.[72]

President Kennedy's Committee on Equal Opportunity (PCEO), appointed in March 1961, took a more direct approach to union discrimination. An executive order gave the PCEO power to require contractors to submit compliance reports discussing the racial practices of unions dealt with by these contractors.[73] The effects on discrimination were minimal, however, because intransigent unions used their political power to protect themselves.

Throughout this period, craft unions pleaded innocent to charges of discrimination. Their lack of African American members, they claimed, was due to the fact that there was a shortage of skilled African American labor. They neglected to mention that this shortage was largely created by union exclusion of African Americans from government-funded apprenticeship programs. Meanwhile, in the mid-to-late 1960s, craft unions held work stoppages to prevent the employment of African Americans on such publicly funded construction projects as the Cleveland Municipal Mall (1966), the U.S. Mint in Philadelphia (1968), and the building site of the New York City Terminal Market (1964).[74]

Even federal efforts to insure compliance with the 1964 Civil Rights Act did not completely shield African Americans from the discriminatory effects of Davis-Bacon. A 1968 Equal Employment Opportunity Commission study found that "the pattern of minority employment is better for each minority group among employers who do not contract work for the government [and are therefore not subject to Davis-Bacon] than it is among prime contractors who have agreed to nondiscrimination clauses in their contracts with the federal government [and who are subject to Davis-Bacon]."[75]

According to Department of Labor statistics, as late as 1970 almost all African Americans in construction still held low-paying unskilled jobs. Yet because of Davis-Bacon, federal contractors were still allowed to train workers only if those workers were in bona fide apprenticeship programs.[76]

Top officials in the Nixon administration's Department of Labor believed that abolishing Davis-Bacon would be the most effective means of increasing minority employment on public works projects.[77] In a futile attempt to avoid offending the union voters Nixon was wooing, however, the department instead decided to launch affirmative action "city plans," which in effect amounted to quotas, to encourage the use of skilled minority workers in federal construction projects. The earliest decisions of the Second, Fifth, Sixth, Seventh, and Ninth Circuits upholding quotas all involved discriminatory craft unions that benefited from Davis-Bacon.[78]

A series of studies conducted in the 1970s and 1980s concluded that Davis-Bacon continued to have discriminatory effects on African Americans.[79] Despite decreased discrimination in the construction industry, and more lenient Davis-Bacon rules promulgated by the Reagan administration, many students of Davis-Bacon believe that it continues to reduce substantially African American participation in the construction industry, largely because it continues to favor skilled workers, who are disproportionately white, at the expense of the unskilled, who are disproportionately African American.[80]

FIVE ✳ New Deal Labor Laws

AS WE HAVE SEEN, New Deal–era amendments to the Railway Labor and Davis-Bacon acts significantly harmed particular segments of the African American workforce. Broader New Deal labor laws, including provisions of the National Industrial Recovery Act, the Fair Labor Standards Act, and the Wagner Act, damaged African American workers more generally. These laws at best failed to take account of the interests of African Americans, and at worst were enforced in a discriminatory manner.[1] Overall, their effect was to cartelize the labor marked to the disadvantage of African Americans.

Under constitutional standards extant when Franklin Roosevelt was elected in 1932, the New Deal labor laws both exceeded the federal government's power and violated the Lochnerian right to liberty of contract. By 1937, however, the Supreme Court acquiesced to the New Deal. While the New Deal Court expressed a newfound willingness to protect "discrete and insular minorities" from state-sponsored discrimination,[2] this did little to protect African Americans from New Deal labor legislation that had subtle discriminatory intent and indirect discriminatory effects. For the most part, African Americans were left at the mercy of political winds, which were not clearly blowing in their favor at the time.

Fortunately for African Americans, the political winds shifted in the ensuing thirty years sufficiently to permit them to salvage the tremendous civil rights victories of the 1950s and 1960s. Nonetheless, the discriminatory effects of the New Deal lingered.

THE NATIONAL INDUSTRIAL RECOVERY ACT

The National Industrial Recovery Act (NRA), passed during the famous first hundred days of the Roosevelt administration, had the potential to impair African American workers' ability to participate in the labor market permanently. The NRA redistributed employment and resources from African Americans — the most destitute Americans suffering from the depression — to whites. Of all the New Deal programs, the NRA was the most harmful to African American workers.[3] Had the Supreme Court not declared it unconstitutional in 1935, the NRA might have consigned African Americans to permanent second-class legal and economic status.

Two major components of the NRA — its wage provisions and its collective bargaining provisions — harmed African Americans.

The Discriminatory Effects of NRA Wage Provisions

The NRA required businesses to pay certain categories of workers a wage determined by joint labor-business panels, with labor generally represented by exclusionary unions.[4] The NRA wage provisions discriminated against African Americans in a variety of ways. First, the NRA did not establish codes for agricultural and domestic labor, fields in which African Americans were disproportionately represented. Wages in these fields were stagnant while other provisions of the NRA forced an increase in prices.[5]

Second, even within an industry generally covered by NRA, occupational classifications frequently were arranged so that minimum-wage scales did not cover work generally performed by African Americans. When occupations dominated by African Americans *were* covered, these occupations often received a lower classification than white-dominated occupations requiring similar or fewer skills. Thus, the NRA established implicit wage differentials between white and African American workers.[6]

The NRA also contained grandfather clauses providing that minimum-wage scales for some classes of labor should be based on wages received as of a certain date in the past. Many African American leaders believed that the way the government implemented the rule discriminated against unskilled African American workers.[7]

The maintenance of such official wage differentials would have been a disaster for African Americans in the long term by permanently relegating them to low-wage positions. In the short term, African Americans suffered from the NRA mostly because it raised wages for many jobs above sustainable market levels. The origins of this problem were more regional than racial. New Deal economists and other influential members of the

Roosevelt administration believed that the way to reduce southern poverty and industrial backwardness was to impose high wages on the region, despite southern industries' comparatively low productivity per worker. In effect, the administration turned economic logic on its head, believing that wage increases would raise productivity, which is a bit like asking the cart to pull the horse.[8]

Code wages were frequently far higher than market wages for southern industrial jobs. For example, because of the NRA, wages in the South's largest industry, textiles, increased by almost 70 percent in five months. Employers responded to such massive wage increases by investing in mechanization and dismissing their unskilled workers.[9]

The codes hit African Americans particularly hard because African Americans were disproportionately concentrated in unskilled jobs that paid salaries well below the codes' requirements. Code wages in Georgia for job categories dominated by African Americans, for example, were up to five times higher than market wages.[10]

Racism exacerbated the negative effects of the NRA on African American employment, as some employers dismissed their unskilled African American workers and replaced them with unskilled whites. Despite the clear authority to do so, NRA officials refused to prohibit the discharge of African Americans due to the codes. White employers also faced the possibility of private, anonymous violence if they hired African Americans while white unemployment remained high. The wage codes gave them one less reason to take the risk.[11]

Many employers of unskilled African Americans simply could not afford to pay NRA wages to workers of any race. Employers therefore eliminated menial jobs often held by African Americans, especially young African Americans, such as office boy and grocery deliverer. Industrial firms that used obsolete machinery and relied on low-paid, unskilled African American employees either shut down or bought modern machinery and replaced their African American laborers with skilled white workers — few African American workers in the Jim Crow South had the skills needed to operate the machines.[12]

The wage provisions of the NRA initially had broad support among African American leaders. One writer for the National Urban League's *Opportunity* declared that "a minimum wage ... will be of immeasurable benefit to ... Black workers who are unskilled and confined to the lowest

New Deal Labor Laws

paid jobs in the industrial system." This attitude was "widely held" in the African American community.[13]

Once the wage provisions went into effect, however, African Americans and others quickly recognized their harmful effects on African American workers. Southern industrialists called for the government to set a reduced minimum wage for African Americans to preserve their companies' competitiveness and their workers' jobs; with some merit, they accused northern industrialists of supporting a relatively high wage scale to retard the flight of low-wage industries to the South.[14]

Most African American leaders, and all national African American organizations, opposed racially based wage differential schemes, despite the short-term harm that high NRA wages caused African Americans. African American leaders believed that African Americans were better off temporarily suffering extra unemployment than excepting a government-endorsed wage differential.[15] The leaders reasoned that the long-term economic and political harm of accepting the precedent of de jure discrimination by the federal government would far outweigh whatever gains African Americans would receive from a wage differential. Also, African American socialists — an increasingly vocal and important segment of the African American leadership during the 1930s — were concerned that wage differentials based on race would inhibit needed solidarity between white and African American workers. Several major African American organizations formed the Joint Committee for Economic Recovery to monitor and protest discrimination in the NRA. Largely because of its pressure, the government never implemented explicit racial wage differentials.[16]

Nevertheless, as the disemployment effects of the NRA became apparent, growing numbers of African Americans, especially southern African Americans, endorsed wage differentials in order to stem the rising tide of African American unemployment. Richmond minister Gordon Blaine Hancock criticized African American opponents of wage differentials for putting abstract ideals of racial equality ahead of concrete economic needs. African American representatives from the Tuskegee Institute petitioned the National Recovery Administration to allow a plant that had shut down because of its inability to pay code wages to reopen and pay subcode wages. The Atlanta Black Chamber of Commerce supported wage differentials to help its constituency of African American small businessmen, who had an overwhelmingly African American workforce.[17]

Opponents of wage differentials regarded supporters as "black Judases," but the idea had mainstream appeal. As Robert Weaver, a critic of wage differentials, acknowledged: "Negroes have lost jobs as a result of the NRA, and a lower wage for them would counteract this tendency. It would assure Negroes of retaining their old jobs and perhaps it would lead to a few additional ones."[18]

In any event, many African American workers, fearful for their jobs, cooperated with their employers in schemes to circumvent the codes. Some employers paid lower wages than the law required by, for example, classifying African American automobile workers as lower-paid lumber workers, and some evaded the codes by classifying their African American employees as independent contractors or executives. Other employers demanded and received kickbacks.[19]

Although the NRA existed for only about two years, Charles Roos, an architect of the law, estimated that its minimum-wage provisions directly or indirectly put five hundred thousand African Americans out of work. Others consider such estimates excessive because of the law's short duration and the fact that it was widely circumvented. Regardless, it seems clear that the NRA's wage provisions had a significant negative effect on African American employment, and that African Americans' only respite from the law was the government's incompetence in enforcing it.[20]

The Discriminatory Effects of NRA Union Provisions
Before discussing the effects of NRA union provisions on African Americans, a brief digression into the history of relations between African Americans and labor unions is in order. By the late nineteenth century, and throughout the *Lochner* era, American Federation of Labor craft unions, along with the railroad brotherhoods, were the most powerful and significant American labor unions.[21] These unions generally served skilled and semiskilled workers.

The hostility exhibited toward African Americans by the railroad brotherhoods and many construction unions, discussed in previous chapters, reflected more general union hostility toward African Americans. By the early twentieth century, the AFL's member unions almost universally engaged in racial discrimination, ranging from complete exclusion of African Americans to segregation of African Americans into second-class Jim Crow locals. The few successful examples of interracial unionism in the AFL took place in fields "where blacks were so numerous that whites could not possibly organize a successful union without them." Even in those trades, African Americans and whites typically worked along racially separate lines.[22]

Unions excluded and segregated African Americans for three major reasons. First, union discrimination served an economic function; if unions could exclude African Americans — as well as other groups, such as women and immigrants — the supply of labor in their trades would decline significantly, leading to a significant rise in the price employers would pay for union labor. The skilled workers who dominated the AFL were especially concerned that an influx of skilled African American competitors would undermine their relatively favorable position in the labor force.[23]

Another reason labor unions discriminated is that they served a social function, much like a lodge or private club. Most white union workers simply refused to allow African Americans into their unions because their own perceived social status would decline if they associated with African Americans, and because mixing with African Americans would imply a degree of social equality that most whites belligerently refused to acknowledge.[24] Union leaders used whites' fear of "social equality" as a recruitment tool. They "pleaded with white workers to organize for protection against employer practices that threatened to place them on the same level as African-Americans at work and in the community."[25]

Finally, although craft unions were exclusionary by their very nature, their leaders sought to enhance the unions' political power by dispelling the public's impression that the unions' activities aided only self-interested, relatively well-paid, elite workers. By engaging in discrimination against African Americans and other minorities, and acting as leading advocates of racist public policies, craft unions positioned themselves as defenders of all white workers against attempts by capitalists to subvert the white American working man's standard of living. As one historian puts it, "White labor constructed an ideology of white supremacy to secure and to justify their power and status in their places of work and in the community."[26] Many rank-and-file union members adopted this ideology and came to believe that they were the white workingman's vanguard against incursions by the darker races.[27]

For all of these reasons, racist labor unions in both the South and North supported establishment of a caste system that reserved unskilled low-paying jobs for African Americans, and skilled high-wage jobs for whites. The ideology that supported this system held that African Americans were mentally inferior and therefore were incapable of performing these jobs.

Employers, like the rest of white society, typically believed in African American inferiority,[28] but experience frequently overcame ideology. Employers continued to hire African Americans for occupations where African American workers had proved themselves competent before the rise of labor unions, such as the railroad and construction occupations discussed in previous chapters. In those fields, even "race strikes" by white workers were usually ineffective, because, if necessary, employers' total labor requirements could be supplied by African Americans.[29]

Moreover, despite their racism, employers frequently had an economic incentive to try African American workers in new fields to reduce their wage costs.[30] Capitalism serves as a learning process, and once white employers found that African Americans could perform a skilled or semi-skilled job, African Americans often got a permanent foothold in that industry.

A major problem for African Americans in many skilled and semi-skilled professions was a lack of numbers. If employers tried to hire them, there were often not enough African Americans with the requisite skills to keep operations on-line if whites struck to protest the hiring of African Americans.[31] Few employers would risk a strike under such circumstances. On the other hand, when white workers went on strike for other reasons, employers were free to ignore their employees' racial preferences and filled the strikers' positions with whoever was available, including African Americans.

Although sometimes African American replacement workers were laid off when a strike ended — particularly if the strike had been successful — African Americans often made their strikebreaking positions into permanent employment. By 1909 African Americans had used strikebreaking to break into the building trades in Chicago, the mining industry in various locales, packinghouses, foundries in Birmingham and Decatur, and the steel industry in Pittsburgh and Youngstown. Years later African Americans broke into the meatpacking industry following a strike in 1921, the coal industry after a Pennsylvania strike in 1922, the metal trades in

Detroit after a strike in 1921, brickmaking after a New Jersey strike in 1923, and railway shop employment after a strike in 1922.[32] According to one expert, the list of industries opened to African Americans by strike-breaking "could be continued indefinitely."[33]

African Americans' willingness, even eagerness, to serve as strike-breakers increased AFL enmity toward them, even though, as one African American critic noted, "criticism of the Negro strikebreaker comes with poor grace from unionists who subscribe to a policy of excluding Negroes from their Union."[34] Labor leaders found themselves consistently in a conundrum: they refused even to consider granting African Americans equal union rights and privileges, but found achievement of their goals frequently undermined by African American workers. The only two possible solutions were to improve union treatment of African Americans, or to try to gain monopoly power and use it to exclude African American competitors. Between the 1890s and the New Deal, most American unions chose the latter strategy. Nevertheless, AFL officials consistently blamed the AFL's lack of cooperation with African Americans on African Americans themselves.[35]

Not surprisingly, African Americans reciprocated the AFL's hostility. African American leaders — ranging from moderates and conservatives such as Booker T. Washington, Professor (later Dean) Kelly Miller of Howard University, and Bishop Archibald J. Carey of Atlanta to nationalist Marcus Garvey and (at times) socialist W. E. B. Du Bois — advocated African American cooperation with industry against labor unions.[36] Fifty-two African American newspaper editors meeting in 1924 unanimously condemned "all forms of Unionism and economic radicalism."[37] African American workers, learning "that they stood to gain more by exploiting class divisions among whites than by uniting with white unions as separate and unequal allies," generally shared their leadership's anti-union attitudes.[38]

By 1933, before passage of the NRA, American unions claimed 2.25 million members. Historians estimate the number of African American union members in 1930 at fifty thousand, at most, a gross underrepresentation even given African Americans' concentration in agriculture. Furthermore, that figure had probably declined by 1933, after several years of economic depression.[39]

The NRA granted tremendous power to discriminatory unions by certifying them as exclusive bargaining agents for workers in various industries. In a two-month period after the passage of the NRA, AFL membership rose to almost four million.[40] This growth in union strength led to widespread displacement of African American workers as racist labor unions took advantage of the monopoly power granted to them by the NRA. A 1934 editorial in the NAACP's journal *The Crisis* noted: "Daily the problem of what to do about union labor or even about a chance to work, confronts the Negro workers of the country. . . . Seeking to avail itself of the powers granted under section 7A of the NRA, union labor strategy seems to be to form a union in a given plant, strike to obtain the right to bargain with the employers as the sole representative of labor, and then to close the union to black workers, effectively cutting them off from employment."[41]

Not surprisingly, the NAACP, National Urban League, and other African American organizations strongly opposed section 7a. Individual African American leaders across the political spectrum, including T. Arnold Hill, Kelly Miller, Roy Wilkins, W. E. B. Du Bois, and Harry E. Davis also opposed section 7a. Du Bois, for example, argued that the NRA reinforced the "sinister power" of the AFL.[42]

Despite complaints of union discrimination directed to the National Labor Relations Board, the federal government declined to intervene on behalf of African Americans. The only relief that African Americans received from section 7a was that many employers formed company unions that successfully competed with independent AFL unions. Unlike AFL unions, company unions, though not necessarily paragons of egalitarian virtue, ordinarily did not explicitly discriminate based on race and sometimes were conduits for corporate philanthropy for the African American community. African American workers were understandably much more favorably disposed than whites toward these unions.[43]

Because of the negative effects of the NRA on African Americans, the NRA was very unpopular among them. The African American press called the NRA "Negro Run Around," "Negroes Ruined Again," "Negroes Rarely Allowed," "Negro Removal Act," "Negroes Robbed Again," and "No Roosevelt Again."[44] A contemporary newspaper noted that for African Americans the symbolic NRA Blue Eagle "may be . . . a predatory bird instead of a feathered messenger of happiness."[45] Professor Herbert Hill notes that "[t]he legislation intended to be the keystone of President Roosevelt's program to protect and uplift the working class had . . . become a millstone around the Black worker's neck."[46]

Roosevelt administration spokesmen defended the NRA to African Americans by pointing out that it led to the acceptance of the forty-hour work week, the enactment of minimum-wage legislation, the swifter end of child labor, and the promotion of collective bargaining. Although the New Dealers may have had the best of humanitarian motives, none of these interferences in the labor market helped the average African American worker. Indeed, their primary effect was to increase unemployment among African Americans.[47]

THE DEMISE AND RESURRECTION OF THE NRA

Fortunately for African Americans, the Supreme Court declared the NRA unconstitutional on May 27, 1935, in *A.L.A. Schechter Poultry Corp. v. United States*.[48] While New Deal circles mourned this day as "Black Monday," the African American leadership celebrated.[49] The two most harmful parts of the NRA resurfaced, however, in subsequent legislation that left hundreds of thousands of African Americans unemployed.

The National Labor Relations Act

Section 7a of the NRA became section 9 of the National Labor Relations Act of 1935, popularly known as the Wagner Act.[50] The Wagner Act established labor unions as exclusive collective bargaining agents through a process of governmental certification by the National Labor Relations Board (NLRB).[51] Majority vote in each workplace in NLRB elections determined union representation; a minority of workers could not choose their own representative.

Like section 7a, section 9 gave organized labor a privileged place within the legal structure and increased its power enormously. Union membership rose to more than eight million by 1941. The Wagner Act also banned company unions and made it more difficult for companies to retain strikebreakers after a settlement was reached; thus the act was potentially even more harmful to African Americans than section 7a had been.[52]

As originally drafted, the Wagner Act contained a clause prohibiting unions from discriminating against African Americans or excluding them from unions. African American leaders thought this clause was crucial. For example, Kelly Miller predicted "the doom of the Negro in American industry" if the Wagner Act did not contain a clause protecting African Americans. Senator Wagner nevertheless succumbed to AFL pressure and dropped the clause.[53] The Roosevelt administration was undisturbed by this development. As Harvard Sitkoff explains, "The great majority of New Dealers accepted discrimination against blacks as an inevitable cost of economic recovery."[54]

African Americans initially viewed the Wagner Act with considerable hostility because it gave government sanction to racially biased labor agreements negotiated under it. Unions often used their newfound power to persuade employers to agree to a "closed shop," excluding nonunion members from employment. The closed union shop, Roy Wilkins of the NAACP argued, is really the white union shop.[55]

Moreover, to the extent that the Wagner Act raised wages and labor standards beyond market levels, it had the same effect as a minimum-wage law in eliminating marginal African American jobs.[56] In a memorandum to President Roosevelt, the National Urban League warned that the Wagner Act was a "serious threat to the job security of Negro workers."[57]

Most AFL craft unions, strengthened by the Wagner Act, continued their discriminatory practices. For example, as noted in chapter 4, construction craft unions recalcitrantly continued to discriminate against African Americans, despite pressure from federal and local civil rights authorities. American Federation of Labor unions that faced competition from the Congress of Industrial Organizations (CIO) treated African Americans better, at least until their certification was secure. Moreover, as the importance of labor unions grew, "black workers seemed to feel that organizing within the segregated confines of the AFL proved a better alternative than no union at all."[58] In the South, African American membership in the AFL rose to 450,000 by the end of World War II.[59]

Unions formed by the CIO organized other African American workers. By 1945, two hundred thousand southern African Americans belonged to the CIO. Much to the relief of African American leaders, few CIO unions overtly discriminated against African Americans, and some actively promoted racial brotherhood and equality, even in unfriendly southern territory. Unlike the AFL, moreover, the CIO had a progressive political plat-

New Deal Labor Laws

form, including support for civil rights laws, that appealed to many African Americans. Experience with CIO organizing also provided training to many southern African American activists who participated in the civil rights struggles of the forties, fifties, and sixties.[60]

On the other hand, CIO leaders, believing in the traditional socialist notion that economic progress for the working class was the best antidote for prejudice, rejected special internal measures to provide redress or opportunities for African Americans.[61] Worse yet, over time many CIO unions responded to pressure from the white rank and file and discriminated in subtle ways. These unions frequently excluded African Americans from apprenticeship programs that led to skilled jobs, and otherwise tried to relegate African Americans to unskilled positions.[62] Although disputes among historians still rage over the extent of the CIO's commitment to racial egalitarianism,[63] this commitment clearly diminished over time.

Some CIO leaders were ideologically committed to racial egalitarianism, certainly more so than the regular members. As was inevitable in such a large-scale organization, however, most leaders were more concerned with practical issues than with abstract ideological notions. The primary motivation for the CIO's support of racial equality, therefore, was practical — to prevent African Americans from undercutting union wages, and to get needed African American votes during organizing drives.[64] Although some CIO unions remained committed to egalitarianism, other unions, such as the steelworkers', lost their commitment to racial equality soon after they achieved government recognition and thus no longer needed African American support, and proceeded to discriminate against African American members.[65] Still other union activists were forced to choose between racial egalitarianism and victory in union elections over their Communist rivals, and chose the latter.

During World War II, Communist organizers, under orders from the Soviet Union, had opposed any measure, including antidiscrimination efforts, that could disrupt production and potentially harm the war effort.[66] Once the war was won, however, the Communists emphasized racial egalitarianism in their union organizing drives. Non-Communist union leaders sometimes responded with racist appeals to white workers.[67]

By the 1950s, an authority on the history of the CIO concludes, "the CIO relegated African American workers to the margins."[68] In 1955, when the AFL and CIO merged, the CIO failed to insist that the AFL enforce a nondiscrimination policy in its unions.[69] The early enthusiasm of African Americans for the CIO had substantially diminished by this point. Horace Cayton—who had praised the CIO's racial policies when he coauthored *Black Workers and the New Unions* in 1939—concluded in 1955: "In retrospect, the history of Negro workers and the CIO is a history of exaggerated hopes and broken promises. In the 1930's we very much wanted to believe that a great change was taking place, that the rise of the CIO would mean a real break with the racism of the old AFL, and that a new interracial labor movement was about to be born. . . . But it never happened."[70]

Ironically, to the extent that the CIO's nondiscrimination policy *was* enforced before the merger, it did little to protect African American workers and in some ways hurt them. Unlike the craft trades, where AFL unions served as their own employment agents, industrial employers were solely responsible for hiring unionized industrial workers; CIO unions rarely expended energy in preventing their employers from discriminating in hiring.[71]

In the absence of pressure on employers from either the government or the unions to institute a nondiscriminatory hiring policy, the CIO's equal-wage policy encouraged employers to favor whites for employment, particularly for skilled or supervisory employment.[72] Some employers, for racist reasons, were disinclined to hire African Americans, but even a nonprejudiced employer had incentives to prefer white workers if he had to pay all workers the same wage.

First, some economic historians believe that skilled African American workers were on average less productive than white workers with the same job title because African Americans had lower "human capital," as a result of discrimination in education and apprenticeship programs.[73] Moreover, "Conventional economic models have shown that rational employers will learn to segregate workers who do not share a common outlook, language, or any other characteristic that make integration costly."[74]

Integration of skilled and supervisory workers was costly because white workers had an ideological belief that such positions should be reserved for whites. Indulging this belief by hiring only white workers allowed employers to limit potentially costly racial strife at the workplace.[75] In theory some employers could have found an economic niche by hiring an all–African American skilled workforce. In practice, a shortage of skilled African American workers and the political problems that such a workforce would invite made that an unattractive strategy. Moreover, as a few bold employers discovered, to have an all–African American workforce that competed with white workers was to invite violence.[76]

The Wagner Act was widely thought to be unconstitutional at the time of its passage.[77] By 1937, however, a majority of the Supreme Court had decided to acquiesce to the New Deal and its vast expansion of the powers of government. The Court first held that, contrary to precedent distinguishing "labor" and "commerce," the Wagner Act was within Congress's authority to regulate commerce.[78] The Court next eviscerated the Lochnerian tradition of hostility to class legislation and laws interfering with free labor markets. The Court denied that the act interfered with a company's "right to conduct its business in an orderly manner without being subjected to arbitrary restraints." Rather, the act protected the worker's "right to organize for the purpose of securing the redress of grievances and to promote agreements with employers." This statement is disingenuous, because the right to organize was never in question, only the power of the government to encourage and even require organization.

The Court acknowledged the weight of the charge of class legislation; the Wagner Act had "been criticized as one-sided in its application; that it subjects the employer to supervision and restraint and leaves untouched the abuses for which employees may be responsible." Instead of attempting to rebut these charges, the Court held that they did not affect the constitutionality of the statute.[79]

In 1944 the Supreme Court issued a decision requiring unions granted exclusive bargaining rights under the Wagner Act to represent fairly all workers in the bargaining group.[80] Nevertheless, African Americans would have to wait until passage of the 1964 Civil Rights Act (and beyond) before they could get fair treatment from unions that benefited from privileges granted by the Wagner Act.

African Americans also had to wait until the 1960s for the NLRB to invalidate discriminatory union practices. The NLRB ruled in 1945 that the statutory bargaining agent must represent all employees without discrimination. The board also held, however, that segregation and exclusion of African Americans from membership did not constitute unfair representation. It was not until 1962 that the NLRB granted relief to a

Only One Place of Redress

claimant based on a union's failure to meet its duty of fair representation. In 1964 the board held that racial discrimination is an unfair labor practice under the Wagner Act.[81] As historian Paul Moreno concludes, "the Wagner Act created precisely the sort of anti-competitive economic structure that fostered discrimination. . . . its overall effect was to strengthen an interest group that had strong economic incentive to exclude African-Americans. . . . government and industry commitment to high wages for those employed meant unemployment for newcomers. . . . organized labor profoundly complicated progress toward fair employment."[82] Former NAACP labor counsel Herbert Hill adds that the "general result" of the Wagner Act, along with the Fair Labor Standards Act, "was to provide a series of legal protections and benefits to white workers and to make African-American workers more vulnerable to job discrimination."[83]

The Fair Labor Standards Act

While section 7a of the NRA metamorphosed into the Wagner Act, the minimum-wage provisions of the NRA were reincarnated as the Fair Labor Standards Act of 1938 (FLSA).[84] The initial wage floor under the FLSA was twenty-five cents, with a maximum work week of forty hours. The wage was increased in increments of five cents a year to a limit of forty cents.

The Supreme Court had held that minimum-wage laws violated the right to liberty of contract in 1923 and 1936, but reversed itself in a 5–4 decision in *West Coast Hotel Co. v. Parrish* in 1937, a case involving a state minimum-wage law.[85] *Parrish* marked the demise of Lochnerian jurisprudence under the Fourteenth Amendment. For the majority in *West Coast Hotel*, a government's failure to enact a minimum-wage law results in a subsidy for "unconscionable employers" who rely on public welfare to ensure that their workers have sustenance. The minimum-wage law, according to the Court, rather than being illicit class legislation or interference with free labor markets, as the Lochnerian dissenters argued, actually restored neutrality to the labor market.

Several Roosevelt appointees later, the Court ruled on the constitutionality of the FLSA in 1941. A unanimous Court stated that "it is no longer open to question that the fixing of a minimum wage is within the legislative power and that the bare fact of its exercise is not a denial of due process under the Fifth more than under the Fourteenth Amendment."

The Court also directly overturned *Lochner* by adding that it is no "longer open to question that it is within the legislative power to fix maximum hours."[86]

The FLSA imposed a national minimum wage, but productivity, wages, and the cost of living remained lower in the South than in the North. Thirteen percent of southern workers covered by the minimum-wage law earned less than twenty-five cents an hour, compared to less than one-tenth of 1 percent in the rest of the country. A more equitable FLSA would have created regional differentials in minimum-wage requirements, as allowed for in the original bills passed by the Senate and the House Labor Committee.[87] Such differentials were common in federal law. The Public Works Administration, for example, paid significantly lower wages in the South than elsewhere in the United States. The Davis-Bacon Act, as we have seen in chapter 4, required the payment of the local prevailing wage.

The FLSA contained no such differentials. The act was not intended to reflect the status quo, but to eliminate low-wage employment in the South. Standard economic theory suggests that wise investment in physical and human capital raises productivity. New Deal officials, by contrast, continued to believe that "improvements in physical well-being and morale," made possible by government-imposed higher wages, would lead to productivity gains.[88] Other New Dealers hoped that the FLSA would "break the political stranglehold of the planter and merchant-manufacturer oligarchy in the South" and improve long-term prospects for New Deal liberalism to thrive in southern politics.[89]

Meanwhile, labor union leaders, who by the late 1930s were an integral part of the New Deal coalition, supported a high, uniform national minimum wage partly out of labor solidarity, but also to limit competition between unskilled nonunionized southern workers and unskilled union members, and to increase the demand for highly skilled workers, who disproportionately belonged to labor unions.[90] As labor leaders understood, minimum-wage laws reduce the incentive of employers to hire unskilled workers, as the price of unskilled labor rises relative to the price of skilled labor and mechanization. Many northern industrialists, particularly those who had southern competitors, also supported a uniform minimum wage to reduce competition, as did a few high-wage southern employers.[91]

Like the NRA minimum wage, the FLSA discriminated against African

Americans in two ways. First, it failed to cover many African American workers.[92] This may have been a blessing in disguise, however, as the FLSA created massive unemployment for African Americans when it applied to jobs held by them.

The disemployment effects of the FLSA were mainly felt by unskilled African American workers in the South, who were most likely to work in jobs that paid less than the government-imposed minimum wage. The Labor Department reported in 1938 that between thirty thousand and fifty thousand workers, mostly southern African Americans, lost their jobs because of the minimum wage within *two weeks* of the Fair Labor Standards Act's imposition — and that was before the scheduled increases that were to raise the minimum wage by an additional 60 percent over three years. African Americans in the tobacco industry were particularly hard hit. In Wilson, North Carolina, for example, machines replaced two thousand African American tobacco stemmers in 1939.[93]

Because the burdens of the FLSA mainly fell on disenfranchised African American workers, political outrage in the South over its contribution to the unemployment problem was muted. Most southern white politicians nevertheless opposed the FLSA because they recognized that southern industry would suffer along with poor African Americans as high minimum wages limited the South's ability to compete with the North for factories.[94] The South in 1938 was backward economically, had a simmering race problem, poor schools, and generally lacked air conditioning, which was still in its commercial infancy. The only advantage the South could offer employers was the region's low wages.

Meanwhile, as with the NRA, most African American leaders unflinchingly opposed any flexibility in the FLSA's application. They opposed not only racial differentials, but regional differentials, for fear that any discrepancies in the required wage rates would ultimately be used to consign African Americans to lower-wage employment. Some African American leaders in the South, however, believed that the mostly northern-based African American leadership was neglecting the needs of southern African Americans.[95]

Ironically, northern African American leaders' enthusiasm for the FLSA was shared by racist southern whites such as Louisiana governor Richard Leche. He regarded the FLSA as an "emancipation proclamation" for southern whites because it would eliminate competition with low-paid

African American workers. Under the minimum-wage law, employers' racist preferences operated in white workers' favor, as did the fact that far fewer African Americans than whites had the education or experience to fill the higher-paid skilled or semiskilled positions that became more efficient with the mandated rise in wages for unskilled workers.[96]

African American supporters of the FLSA did not waver, however, perhaps because the act's medium-term disemployment effects on African American workers were masked by other factors. In 1939 the Public Works Administration provided temporary employment to about one million African Americans, some of whom would otherwise have been left unemployed by the FLSA. By the time the Supreme Court upheld the FLSA in 1941, a wartime labor shortage was about to replace the depression-era labor surplus, substantially increasing the employment opportunities for African Americans in the private sector. Indeed, the FLSA's wage requirements became superfluous as wages in southern industry skyrocketed on their own.[97]

By 1943, however, economist Gunnar Myrdal was able to predict the negative effects the FLSA was to have on postwar African American employment, particularly in the South:

> As low wages and sub-standard labor conditions are most prevalent in the South, this danger [of unemployment] is mainly restricted to Negro labor in that region. When the jobs are made better, the employer becomes less eager to hire Negroes, and white workers become more eager to take the jobs from the Negroes. There is, in addition, the possibility that the policy of setting minimum standards might cause some jobs to disappear altogether or to become greatly decreased. What has earlier been replaced by mechanization has often been cheap labor. If labor gets more expensive, it is more likely to be economized and substituted for by machines. Also inefficient industries, which have hitherto existed solely by the exploitation of labor, may be put out of business when the government sets minimum standards.

Moreover, as Myrdal noted, the South's main attraction to industry was cheap labor. The FLSA partially ruined this advantage, resulting in fewer opportunities for African Americans in southern industry.[98]

New Deal labor policies contributed to a persistent increase in African American unemployment. In 1930 the ratio of African American to white unemployment was 92:100; in 1940 it was 118:100; in 1949 it was 160:100; by 1954 it was 2:1 and has remained that way.[99]

A variety of factors caused this rise in African American unemployment, most of which relate to New Deal legislation. As historian Raymond Wolters notes, "[t]he New Deal was essentially an attempt to solve the nation's economic problems democratically, but such a 'democratic' system usually gives the greatest benefits to those who are best organized."[100] African Americans were among the politically worst organized groups in the United States and were mostly disenfranchised as well. African American workers therefore received disproportionately few benefits from New Deal economic regulations, but bore a disproportionate allocation of the burdens.

The Agricultural Adjustment Acts (AAAS) reimbursed white planters for taking land out of production, causing many owners to evict African American tenant farmers from their land. The AAAS also accelerated the mechanization of farmland that remained in production, throwing thousands more unskilled African American farm workers into the labor market. "All accounts of the impact of the [AAAS] on African-Americans," a recent survey concludes, "agree that it caused grave hardship and was the chief source of downward mobility for African-Americans in the South."[101]

The Fair Labor Standards Act had the negative effects Myrdal predicted, creating unemployment and making it particularly difficult for African American farmworkers left unemployed by the AAAS to find unskilled work. To take just one industry as an example of the disemployment effects of the FLSA on African Americans, the percentage of jobs in the tobacco industry held by African Americans declined from 67.9 percent in 1930 to 54.7 percent in 1940, to 37.2 percent in 1950, to 26.8 percent in 1960.[102]

In 1940, before the effects of minimum-wage laws and the second AAA were felt fully, white unemployment was 1.1 times as high as African

American unemployment in the South. By 1950 it was 59 percent as high, and it remained that way in 1960. Similar effects occurred in other regions of the country. Employment of African American teenagers, a prime indicator of their future access to the economic mainstream, dropped from 60 percent in 1956 to 30 percent in 1977, in part because of increased minimum-wage rates and coverage.[103] Meanwhile, the unemployment rate for white teens remained stable.[104]

Many southern African Americans who were put out of work by New Deal legislation went to the North during the Second Great Migration in the 1940s and 1950s. They disproportionately entered occupations and regions that had unemployment rates well above the national average. According to economic historian Gavin Wright, "As early as 1950, African-American unemployment rates were between 10 and 15 percent in almost all the major points of southern in-migration; and the unemployment rates for new immigrants were staggering."[105] Relative unemployment in the inner cities of the North continued to increase as African American workers poured in.[106]

The Wagner Act exacerbated the regional and cyclical unemployment problems faced by African Americans in the North. As discussed previously, the act granted monopoly power to discriminatory unions, particularly AFL craft unions. Industrial employers increasingly responded to the above-market wages that unions demanded by relocating factories overseas and mechanizing, in the process eliminating unskilled jobs disproportionately held by African Americans. The CIO unions expended their resources mainly in protecting skilled, predominantly white workers from these trends. In other words, the Wagner Act equalized white and African American wages for the same job but also drove the price of unskilled industrial workers beyond sustainable levels. Consequently, African American industrial workers were replaced by machines and cheaper foreign labor.[107]

Ironically, just when New Deal policies began to push African Americans into northern industrial areas, which were about to enter an era of steep relative economic decline,[108] per capita income in the South began to grow at a rate significantly higher than the national average, a trend that continued for decades.[109] Median African American incomes nevertheless rose substantially when they moved to the higher-wage North.[110] On the other hand, without New Deal pressures a more gradual migration would have caused less of the economic, cultural and social dislocation that inevitably accompanies the mass migration of millions of people. In sum, New Deal legislation contributed to a significant, persistent increase in African American unemployment, and therefore contributed to the development of the urban "underclass."

Historians have mostly neglected the harm New Deal legislation caused African Americans. In part, this neglect is a reflection of their focus on New Deal public works and welfare programs, which provided significant benefits to African Americans. More generally, however, this neglect is a result of the assumption that African Americans were "better off with an all-powerful national government, since most African-Americans lived in the South, and southern governments treated African-Americans worse than the national government did."[111]

In fact, however, New Deal laws that hurt African Americans regulated areas — wages, agricultural production, collective bargaining — that southern state governments generally left alone. Thus, contrary to the asserted dichotomy between national and state government regulation, the historical choice with regard to particular New Deal regulatory issues was often between federal government regulation and unregulated labor markets. Because of their lack of political influence, for most of the period after Reconstruction and before the modern civil rights era African Americans were better off with free labor markets than with federal regulation. Indeed, economist Harold Demsetz has argued that until the early 1960s all major federal regulatory legislation worsened the economic well-being of African Americans.[112]

Some would contend that whatever the sins of the New Deal with regard to African Americans, the rise of activist government during the 1930s, and the abandonment of Lochnerian jurisprudence it precipitated and required, was necessary to overcome federal indifference to the plight of African Americans, particularly those oppressed in the Jim Crow South. Clearly, however, the abandonment of liberty of contract was not necessary as a *logical* matter for the federal government to take decisive action against state-sponsored discrimination. There is no inherent conflict between judicial protection of liberty of contract and federal enforcement of the Fourteenth Amendment.

Bruce Ackerman nevertheless argues that the rise of federal regulatory power during the New Deal was a necessary prelude to government intervention on behalf of African Americans. He contends that the essence of the constitutional battles during the New Deal was over the federal government's authority to pursue "social" equality.[113] According to Ackerman, the New Dealers' success soon allowed the federal government to pursue a subset of social equality — racial equality.

However, the constitutional triumph of New Deal economic policies was less a triumph for social equality, and more a triumph for government power as such. At the time, the ultimate consequences for African Americans of this triumph were highly uncertain. Although African Americans had made some political progress by the late 1930s, and had a few friends in the Roosevelt administration, they still had little political power and lacked the support of white public opinion.[114] For example, in 1939 only 19 percent of residents of New England and the Middle Atlantic states, 12 percent of midwestern whites, and an even smaller percentage of southern whites, agreed that African Americans "should be able to live wherever they want to live, and there should be no laws or social pressure to keep them from it." As late as 1944, most whites agreed that "white people should have the first chance at any kind of job."[115] Little wonder, then, that the federal labor market interventions of the 1930s, when few African Americans could vote, were disastrous for African Americans.

Moreover, before the 1940s there was little if any historical correlation in the United States between support for government regulation of the economy and support for civil rights. Few of the Progressives who dominated left-wing politics before the New Deal evinced sympathy for civil rights, and many were hostile to African Americans. Indeed, many of the same regulatory impulses that inspired the New Deal motivated supporters of segregation laws earlier in the century.[116] The most statist postbellum presidential administration before FDR's, Woodrow Wilson's, was extremely hostile to African Americans. The Hoover administration, dominated by Progressive Republicans, including Hoover himself, also treated African Americans poorly.[117]

From a 1930s perspective, then, it was at least as likely that federal power was ultimately to be used against African Americans as in their favor. This danger was acknowledged by contemporary African American commentators. John Davis, an outspoken African American activist, wrote in 1936 that "[t]he present burdens we bear in a period of national economic hardship might find some excuse if there emerged promises of a more equitable treatment of the Negro in the future. But when we view future plans of the New Deal, the plight of the Negro is as dismal as it has been in the past." T. Arnold Hill of the National Urban League wrote that same year that "[i]f the present trend continues, there is slight question that the Negro will be gradually forced into a condition of economic peonage, every bit as devastating as plantation slavery ever was." On the other hand, widespread African American support for President Roosevelt and the New Deal suggests that most African Americans at the time perceived the risk-reward situation more favorably.[118]

What changed in African Americans' favor after the New Deal was not new federal power, but the newfound political will to use the powers granted by the Reconstruction amendments — will that had been sorely lacking since the defeat of the antidisenfranchisement "Force Bill" in Congress in 1890. Post–New Deal willingness to enforce civil rights did not result from the growth in federal regulatory power per se — for example, FDR steadfastly refused to support federal antilynching legislation throughout his tenure — but was a consequence of World War II, the cold war, and the migration of millions of African Americans to northern cities. These factors led to a fundamental shift in American social attitudes and political priorities.[119]

The European campaign of World War II was fought, at least rhetorically, in response to the racism of Nazi Germany, which made domestic racism seem like an anomaly. The war also created an egalitarian spirit across the country, which carried over to the postwar era. Public opinion began to shift dramatically against racism; the proportion of the population stating that African Americans should have the same job opportunities as whites gradually rose from 42 percent in 1944 (the first year the question was asked in a poll) to 87 percent in 1966.[120]

The cold war, and the accompanying competition for the hearts and minds of new Third World nations, made the end of officially sanctioned racism in the United States a foreign policy imperative.[121] Perhaps most important, the migration of African Americans from the South to cities in large industrial states made them an electoral power whose votes were of crucial importance. African American voting power persuaded the Democratic Party to adopt a civil rights plank in its platform in 1948 and provided the margin of victory in the critical and close presidential election of 1960.[122] As discussed previously, New Deal agricultural and labor policies in effect *forced* many African Americans to go north, where they exercised their newfound political muscle, but that is hardly what Ackerman means when he assigns the New Deal credit for federal action in favor of racial equality.

Ackerman also argues that, federal regulatory power aside, New Deal jurisprudence and the end of Lochnerism were necessary precursors to *Brown v. Board of Education,*[123] and the subsequent judicial battle against state-sponsored segregation. Ackerman reasons that *Brown* resulted from an ideological shift from a laissez-faire mentality to the view that state action can and should change private preferences. Ackerman neglects to note, however, that the parties that lost in *Brown* were local governments that enforced public school segregation. It is hard to see how a Supreme Court decision invalidating local segregation *laws* can be construed as a victory for New Deal statism.

Moreover, Lochnerian jurisprudence, had it survived the New Deal, could have been a potent weapon against segregation laws. Many of these laws, after all, restricted freedom of contract by preventing voluntary transactions between whites and African Americans. As Mark Tushnet has explained, segregation laws could be seen as illicit "class legislation" because they involved the "concentrated power of organized white racists" overbearing the "interests of less-organized African-Americans and whites uninterested in segregation."[124] Indeed, when segregation laws were spreading during the 1890s, civil rights activists argued that the laws constituted illicit class legislation. Justice John Harlan's *Plessy v. Ferguson* dissent argued that the segregation law at issue constituted class legislation.[125] Even the *Plessy* majority acknowledged that the segregation law at issue would be unconstitutional if it were enacted "for the annoyance or oppression of a particular class," but the Court disingenuously claimed the idea that the law did not fit that paradigm. Lochnerian jurisprudence's antisegregation potential was never fully realized, in part because the Supreme Court justices shared the era's racist views, and in part because the strong *Plessy* precedent was handed down before *Lochner,* at a time when the Court exhibited broad deference to the states' police power.[126]

Just as prosegregation decisions were not implicit in Lochnerism, *Brown* was not implicit in the New Deal's constitutional commitment to activist government. Rather, it resulted from the dramatic turn from racism among the legal and intellectual elite in the 1940s and 1950s.[127]

In earlier decades, by contrast, Progressive lawyers who were committed to activist government were generally hostile to the concept of judicial intervention on behalf of African Americans.[128] Indeed, law reviews in the 1900s and 1910s were filled with articles defending segregation laws from a statist, Progressive perspective, and attacking "conservative" judges who sometimes invalidated such laws on liberty of contract/property rights grounds.[129]

Although the triumph of New Deal statism had little directly to do with the victory of the civil rights movement, it did shape the form that victory took. The growth of the American state during and after the New Deal allowed the government to intervene more dramatically in the labor market on behalf of African Americans than classical liberal precepts of the sort that motivated Lochnerian courts would allow. Classical liberal principles, for example, caution against the type of government intervention into the workings of labor markets represented by many modern antidiscrimination laws that apply to private parties. A Lochnerian regime might even hold such laws to be unconstitutional restraints on liberty of contract. Certainly, it is difficult to imagine a Lochnerian Supreme Court holding, as the modern Court has held, that "eradicating discrimination" in the private sector is not only a proper goal of government, but that this goal overrides the Constitution's explicit limitations on government power.[130]

On the other hand, as Paul Moreno notes, "[f]ree market principles . . . contained their own set of antidiscrimination principles" — opposition to legislation benefiting particular groups and support for government neutrality in the operation of labor markets.[131] In fact, given the post–World War II historical trends favoring equal rights for African Americans discussed previously (which were, except for the increase in migration rates caused by the second AAA, independent of the rise of New Deal statism), one can imagine that but for the interruption of the Great Depression and the New Deal, and the concomitant demise of classical liberalism as a vital American ideology, entirely different forms of civil rights protections could have arisen. Civil rights protections could have been of the sort envisioned by Reconstruction-era Radical Republicans, including Frederick Douglass: a classical liberal combination of equal protection of the law/prohibitions on class legislation, liberty of contract and free labor markets, and freedom of association.[132] Instead, a more statist combina-

New Deal Labor Laws

tion ultimately prevailed: interest group liberalism, the welfare state, and government enforcement of nondiscrimination norms against private parties. The classical liberal vision of civil rights admittedly holds little utopian promise. It does not obligate the state to eradicate discrimination, or to guarantee "equal opportunity." On the other hand, unlike the modern regime, the classical liberal vision does not depend on granting the government massive regulatory powers, and hoping, despite a wealth of contrary historical experience from the United States and abroad, that those powers will never be grossly abused.

Conclusion

✣

LEGAL SCHOLARS AND historians have written a great deal about blatant, obvious examples of discriminatory state action against African Americans, such as segregation laws. By contrast, the literature on more subtle forms of discriminatory state action, such as facially neutral labor legislation that served to restrict African Americans' access to the labor market, is sparse.[1] Even facially neutral laws clearly intended to harm African American workers, such as emigrant agent laws and the Davis-Bacon Act, have received little attention from historians and legal scholars.

The neglect of the effects of facially neutral labor laws on African American welfare has led historians and legal scholars to underestimate the role of state action in the oppression of African Americans. The dominant view in legal and historical circles is that the economic subjugation of African Americans between Reconstruction and the modern civil rights era primarily resulted from irrational private discrimination and social custom in a free market environment.

Yet modern political economy, particularly public choice theory, suggests that downplaying the role of state regulation, including facially neutral regulations, in enforcing discriminatory norms is problematic. As Mancur Olson's classic work *The Logic of Collective Action* explains, large, diffuse interest groups have trouble enforcing mutually desired norms in the absence of coercion. In other words, it is very difficult for a cartel, including a cartel of racist whites, to operate effectively unless the government intervenes on its behalf.[2]

Moreover, politicians often supply legislation to meet the demands of important voter constituencies, rather than to serve the interest of the public at large.[3] To put it another way, as noted in the Preface to this book, legislation tends to benefit those with political power at the expense of those who lack it. Because of disenfranchisement, African Americans were rarely an important political constituency from the 1890s until after World War II, either locally or nationally. Southern planters, members of discriminatory labor unions, northern industrialists, and other organized white interest groups, however, were important constituencies. When these politically powerful groups turned to government to pass legislation on their behalf, the resulting laws at best failed to consider African Americans' interests, and at worst intentionally benefited the interest groups at the expense of African Americans.[4]

In 1992 Professor Richard Epstein, relying largely on economic theory, argued that as a historical matter, African Americans' economic predicament was mainly a result of a combination of Jim Crow laws, actual or threatened private violence, and laws that gave monopoly power to private actors who discriminated against African Americans. Epstein argued that had African Americans lived under a Lochnerian economic system, and been granted protection of their liberty and property, they would have had much greater economic success.[5]

Critics have taken Epstein to task for relying on economic theory without providing substantial historical evidence to support his thesis.[6] Ian Ayres, for example, responded with the traditional view that there is no evidence that African Americans faced an unfree labor market, aside from occasional violence. Ayres claimed that "the historical record does not come close" to supporting the "hypothesis that state coercion stifled market forces" or to supporting the claim that "market forces were never allowed to secure adequate employment opportunities for African-Americans." Ayres later partially retracted his argument, and acknowledged that Jim Crow laws, including emigrant agent laws, placed some restrictions on the southern labor market that harmed African Americans.[7] Nevertheless, he and others still assert that there is little evidence of detrimental government interference in the labor market in the North, where African Americans also fared poorly economically.

This book has shown that government interference with labor markets to the disadvantage of African Americans was far more prevalent than Epstein's critics — not to mention authors of standard works on African American and labor history — have acknowledged. The series of case studies presented in this book shows that in a wide range of fields, regulation was essential to limiting African American access to, and mobility in, the labor market.

Only One Place of Redress

One should not leap from this fact to the conclusion that labor market regulations were primarily responsible for African Americans' economic plight. The social and economic disadvantages resulting from slavery undoubtedly lingered for generations. State violence and state refusal to protect African Americans from private violence inhibited African Americans' economic success, as did other forms of state action and inaction that affected the labor market, such as gross inequality in the provision of publicly funded education.[8] Social mores, sometimes reinforced by state action, but sometimes, especially in the North, the product of purely voluntary social and market interactions, also played some role in the economic subjugation of African Americans.[9]

In assessing responsibility for relative African American poverty, disentangling the causal importance of culture, violence, social mores, and state action — all of which were mutually reinforcing — seems impossible. As economist Price Fishback concludes, "No one as yet has been able to assign definitive weight to each source." Economists have devoted very little attention to "modeling" government-sponsored discrimination, or to developing an explicitly political model of discrimination. Moreover, it's not at all clear that any models that economists may develop in the future will be of much assistance. For example, as Fishback notes, "The impact of most forms of governmental discrimination cannot generally be measured in straightforward labor market studies."[10]

Although the role of government regulations in harming African Americans economically cannot be accurately measured, the standard literature on African American legal and economic history typically assigns almost no weight to labor market regulation as a cause of the economic problems African Americans faced. This book should serve as a useful corrective to this literature. Ideally, it will also inspire legal scholars and historians to explore further the role that labor market regulation and other facially neutral government regulations played in harming African Americans economically.[11]

The fact that economic regulation generally clashed with the interests of African Americans when they lacked political power does not prove, or even necessarily suggest, that over the longer run African Americans would have benefited disproportionately from economic laissez-faire. Once African Americans were enfranchised by implementation of the 1965 Voting Rights Act, and became accepted by the public at large as part of the polity, they may have even started to benefit disproportionately from state action. African Americans are a discrete, identifiable, and relatively well-organized group, the type of group that public choice theory suggests often gains disproportionately from collective political action.[12]

Similarly, although Lochnerian jurisprudence disproportionately benefited African Americans before the modern civil rights era, such jurisprudence might disproportionately harm them today. Even if one can conclude that as a historical matter Lochnerian jurisprudence served an important antidiscrimination purpose, Lochnerian jurisprudence cannot presently be supported as sound policy based on the fact that it disproportionately benefited African Americans in the past when they were disenfranchised.[13]

Presentist concerns aside, the history recounted in this book calls into question the traditional view that Lochnerian jurisprudence represented "an unadorned endorsement of the strong and wealthy at the expense of the weak and poor." A recent review essay explains that "Progressive historians and New Deal constitutionalists have portrayed the jurisprudence of economic regulation from Reconstruction to 1937 as if it were designed to do little more than meet the needs of the Carnegies and Morgans at the expense of the people." Liberty of contract, a typical jeremiad proclaims, "meant freedom of the rich to impose terms." According to one prominent legal historian, "The result in *Lochner* was that the Constitution was virtually treated as a legal sanction of the Survival of the Fittest."[14]

This traditional view is based on the assumption that market outcomes were unfair to all but wealthy, corporate interests, which benefited at the expense of the rest of society. In fact, however, as elementary public choice economics suggests, because the wealthy as a class faced no fundamental disadvantages in the political market, there is no a priori reason to believe that economic regulation worked systematically to their disadvantage, nor has such disadvantage been shown empirically.

On the other hand, certain economically disadvantaged groups — including African Americans, women, and aliens — did face a fundamental obstacle to success in the political process: they were, to varying degrees, disenfranchised. As this book and a few other works have shown, Lochnerism, when used to invalidate legislation interfering with free contract, protected these disenfranchised groups from hostile political majorities.[15]

Only One Place of Redress

In addition to the African American workers discussed in this book, Chinese laundrymen, Italian immigrants seeking construction work in New York, and African Americans seeking housing in cities eager to legislate segregation and exclusion during the 1910s and beyond were among those who benefited from Lochnerian jurisprudence.[16] At the same time, as other scholars have shown, the public at large — which faces severe coordination and information problems in opposing "class legislation" benefiting powerful interest groups — gained from the invalidation of legislation that assisted special interests at the public's expense.[17]

Although the protection of despised and disenfranchised groups was frequently a fortuitous by-product of Lochnerism's hostility to special-interest legislation rather than a product of a conscious decision by the courts to protect these groups, that is part of Lochnerism's allure. Lochnerian free labor and anti-class-legislation doctrines provided neutral principles that shielded minority groups from harmful legislation without relying on judges to rise above the prejudices of their society. African American workers were able to benefit from Lochnerian jurisprudence when they were not even parties to the relevant cases. Well before the NAACP established an effective African American legal defense organization, the interests of African Americans were often indirectly represented by litigants arguing in favor of liberty of contract.

Lochnerism, of course, is dead and buried, and perhaps for good reason. Lochnerian courts were never able to articulate clearly how to distinguish class legislation from public-regarding legislation, or laws inappropriately interfering with free labor markets from reasonable police power regulations. Arguably, depending on one's view of the proper role of the judiciary in the American constitutional republic, the courts should never have tried.[18]

Resurrecting *Lochner* may not be wise, but legal scholars and historians should stop demonizing it. Ultimately, the primary complaint about *Lochner* has been that it inhibited the ability of government to regulate the economic marketplace, especially the labor market. As Justices Sandra Day O'Connor, Anthony Kennedy, and David Souter recently alleged, *Lochner*'s "interpretation of contractual freedom" is said to have "rested on fundamentally false factual assumptions about the capacity of a relatively unregulated market to satisfy minimal levels of human welfare." In response to the justices' claims about the limitations of free labor markets,

Conclusion

one must ask the classic economic question, "Compared to what?" The empirical basis for the purported social benefits of the modern regulatory state is dubious, at best.[19]

With regard to labor regulations of the type discussed in chapters 3–5 of this book, historians frequently assume that under a freedom of contract regime, corporations could hold all wages down, guaranteeing that no dependent workers could earn a decent wage.[20] Some readers will no doubt intuit that if freedom of contract gave African Americans a kind of equality with white Americans in industry, it was not equal economic power, but equality in "wage slavery." Some would suppose, for example, that legislation benefiting labor unions at least allowed the vast majority of workers who were white to improve their economic status, even if African Americans were left behind.[21]

This belief rests on the assumption that labor unions, abetted by government, were responsible for wage increases received by white workers; without unions "inequalities in bargaining power" purportedly would have ensured that workers received wages just above starvation levels. This is a powerful myth, one so pervasive that I remember learning it in my grade school social studies class. In fact, however, no historical correlation between union membership and wage growth exists.[22] Rather, as economic theory would predict, because a generally competitive labor market existed in the United States, wages during the *Lochner* era rose with productivity.[23] As one economist concludes, "wages must come from production and can rise on a sustained basis only from increased productivity."[24]

Labor unions can undoubtedly raise wages for specific groups of workers. But as Albert Rees notes in *The Economics of Trade Unions,* no one has demonstrated that labor unions increase all workers' overall share of the distribution of income at the expense of capital. Rather, "the likeliest effects of unions on the distribution of income is to redistribute it among workers." In other words, to the extent that unions raise wages for their members, these gains come "at the expense of nonunion labor."[25]

Visceral condemnation of *Lochner* by historians and legal scholars (not to mention Supreme Court justices) ultimately seems based on an ingenuous faith in the efficacy and fairness of political solutions to perceived market failures, and a concomitant unreasonable, almost pathological, distrust of markets. Yet the basic faith in the benevolent state that so characterized most of the twentieth century has been shaken, not only by economic insights, but by the many crimes of governments — including "democratic" governments — claiming to act in the name of equality and the public good. As we enter the twenty-first century, worldwide appreciation for the benefits of voluntary, peaceable market transactions is reaching a historical apex. While we should not necessarily disinter Lochnerism, the doctrine, and the judges who enforced it, should at least be allowed to rest in peace.

Notes

INTRODUCTION

1 83 U.S. (16 Wall.) 36 (1873).

2 Historians typically cite the following state cases: In re Jacobs, 98 N.Y. 98 (1885) (invalidating a law regulating the production of cigars), Ritchie v. People, 40 N.E. 454 (Ill. 1895) (invalidating a law that limited women to a maximum of eight hours of daily factory labor), and Godcharles v. Wigeman, 6 A. 354 (Pa. 1885) (invalidating a law requiring cash payment of wages). However, there were many other cases where the courts favored the principles expressed in the *Slaughter-House* dissent over those of the majority. E.g., Joseph v. Randolph, 71 Ala. 499, 508 (1882); State v. Moore, 18 S.E. 342, 345 (N.C. 1893).

  On cases involving the Chinese, see Charles J. McClain, *In Search of Equality: The Chinese Struggle against Discrimination in Nineteenth Century America* (1996); David E. Bernstein, "*Lochner,* Parity, and the Chinese Laundry Cases," 41 *Wm. & Mary L. Rev.* 211 (1999); Thomas Wuil Joo, "New 'Conspiracy Theory' of The Fourteenth Amendment: Nineteenth Century Chinese Civil Rights Cases and the Development of Substantive Due Process Jurisprudence," 29 *U.S.F. L. Rev.* 353 (1995).

3 198 U.S. 45 (1905).

4 See Planned Parenthood v. Casey, 505 U.S. 833, 959–61 (1992) (Scalia, J., dissenting); Dolan v. City of Tigard, 512 U.S. 374, 406–509 (1994) (Stevens, J., dissenting); United States v. Lopez, 514 U.S. 549, 605–7 (1995) (Souter, J. dissenting).

5 See Lochner, 198 U.S. at 75 (Holmes, J. dissenting) (criticizing Lochner majority for deciding the case based "upon an economic theory which a large part of the country does not entertain"); Raoul Berger, *Government by Judiciary: The Transformation of the Fourteenth Amendment* 249–82 (1977); Robert Bork, *The Tempting of America* 36–49 (1990); John Hart Ely, *Democracy and Distrust: A Theory of Judicial Review* 14–21 (1980); William G. Ross, *A Muted Fury: Populists, Progressives, and Labor Unions Confront the Courts, 1890–1937,* at 42 (1994); Aviam Soifer, "The Paradox of Paternalism and Laissez-Faire Constitutionalism: United States Supreme Court, 1888–1921," 5 *L. & Hist. Rev.* 249, 250 (1987).

6 For works attacking Lochnerian jurists for their purported Social Darwinism, see, e.g., Richard Hofstader, *Social Darwinism in American Thought* 5–6 (rev. ed. 1955); Clyde E. Jacobs, *Law Writers and the Courts: The Influence of Thomas E. Cooley, Christopher G. Tiedeman, and John F. Dillon upon American Constitutional Law* 24 (1954); Paul Kens, *Judicial Power and Reform Politics: The Anatomy of* Lochner v. New York 5 (1990); Arnold M. Paul, *Conservative Crisis and the Rule of Law: Attitudes of Bar and Bench, 1887–1895*

(1960); Benjamin Twiss, *Lawyers and the Constitution: How Laissez Faire Came to the Supreme Court* 154 (1942); Roscoe Pound, "The Scope and Purpose of Sociological Jurisprudence, Part II," 25 *Harv. L. Rev.* 489, 496–99 (1912).

7   Cass R. Sunstein, "*Lochner*'s Legacy," 87 *Colum. L. Rev.* 873, 873 (1987).

8   Holmes famously wrote that "the Fourteenth Amendment does not enact Mr. Herbert Spencer's *Social Statics.*" Lochner, 198 U.S. at 75 (Holmes, J. dissenting). A close reading of the context of the *Social Statics* remark reveals that Holmes was arguing that the *sic utere tuo ut alienum non lædes* principle — "use your own property in such a manner as not to injure that of another" — could not be the basis of American constitutional law. Holmes was simply using Spencer as an example of a prominent intellectual who believed the *sic utero* principle *should* be the basis of law. Holmes, however, was *not* accusing the Court of believing in Social Darwinism, or of otherwise being influenced by Spencer, whose works Holmes had never read. See Philip D. Wiener, *Evolution and the Founders of Pragmatism* 173 (1965).

9   The cases cited by Sunstein are West Coast Hotel v. Parrish, 300 U.S. 379 (1937), Nebbia v. New York, 291 U.S. 502 (1934), Adkins v. Children's Hospital, 261 U.S. 525 (1923), Bunting v. Oregon, 243 U.S. 426 (1917), and Muller v. Oregon, 208 U.S. 412 (1908); see generally Hebert Hovenkamp, "The Political Economy of Substantive Due Process," 40 *Stan. L. Rev.* 379, 382–83 (1988) (rejecting the thesis that Lochnerian judges were "formalists").

Contrary to Sunstein's assumption that the courts relied on the common law to favor market ordering, common law precepts were actually often used to deny liberty of contract claims. See, e.g., Muller v. Oregon, 208 U.S. 412 (1908); Patterson v. Bank Eudora, 190 U.S. 169 (1903); Holden v. Hardy, 166 U.S. 396 (1898). In general, the common law system gave wide scope to regulation under the police power. See William Novak, *The People's Welfare* (1996). Moreover, Sunstein assumes that laws establishing minimum wages and maximum hours served to redistribute income to the poor. Minimum-wage laws in fact price the unskilled out of the labor market to the benefit of other workers, whereas maximum-hours laws, by their very nature, do not redistribute income from employers to employees. To the extent that maximum-hours laws indirectly redistribute income among workers, the poorest workers are unlikely to be the beneficiaries, because they typically lack political power. In fact, the cases Sunstein cites involved protectionist legislation that applied to women only — legislation that was intended to protect male workers from female competitors.

10   For works discussing the natural rights and free labor influences on Lochnerian jurists, see, e.g., James W. Ely Jr., *The Chief Justiceship of Melville W. Fuller, 1888–1910,* at 141 (1995); Daniel R. Ernst, "Free Labor, the Consumer Interest, and the Law of Industrial Disputes, 1885–1900," 36 *Am. J. Legal Hist.* 19, 19 (1992); William E. Forbath, "The Ambiguities of Free Labor: Labor and the Law in the Gilded Age," 1985 *Wis. L. Rev.* 767, 782–86; Charles W. McCurdy,

"The Roots of 'Liberty of Contract' Reconsidered: Major Premises in the Law of Employment, 1867–1937," 1984 *Sup. Ct. Hist. Soc'y Y.B.* 20, 24–26; William E. Nelson, "The Impact of the Antislavery Movement upon Styles of Judicial Reasoning in Nineteenth Century America," 87 *Harv. L. Rev.* 513, 558–60 (1974).

For works discussing the influence of the anti-class-legislation tradition on Lochnerian jurists, see Ely, supra, at 76–77; Howard Gillman, *The Constitution Besieged: The Rise and Demise of Lochner Era Police Powers Jurisprudence* 33–44 (1993); Michael Les Benedict, "Laissez-Faire and Liberty: A Re-evaluation of the Meaning and Origins of Laissez-Faire Constitutionalism," 3 *L. & Hist. Rev.* 293 (1985); Charles W. McCurdy, "Justice Field and the Jurisprudence of Government-Business Relations: Some Parameters of Laissez Faire Constitutionalism, 1863–1897," 61 *J. Am. Hist.* 970, 973–74 (1975).

The framing of the Fourteenth Amendment is discussed in Earl Maltz, *Civil Rights, the Constitution and Congress, 1863–1869* (1990), and William Nelson, *The Fourteenth Amendment: From Political Principle to Judicial Doctrine* (1988).

11   On the general issue of judicial hostility to labor legislation, see Charles W. McCurdy, "The 'Liberty of Contract' Regime in American Law," in *The State and Freedom of Contract* 161, 167 (Harry Scheiber ed. 1998).

12   Lochner v. New York, 198 U.S. 45 (1905). See Editorial, "A Check to Union Tyranny," 86 *The Nation* 346 (1905); Richard A. Epstein, "The Mistakes of 1937," 11 *Geo. Mason L. Rev.* 5, 17 (1988); Sidney G. Tarrow, "*Lochner versus New York*: A Political Analysis," 5 *Labor Hist.* 275, 284 (1964). The Court at this time did not inquire into what motivated legislation, but the justices were probably aware that the hours provision was intended to benefit organized labor.

Many scholars have argued that the Court simply did not believe that legislation should redress inequalities in bargaining power. In part, this view relies on Coppage v. Kansas, 236 U.S. 1, 14 (1915), where the Court held that "inequalities of fortune" cannot be the basis for undermining liberty of contract. The Court went on to explain, however, that contracts are mutually beneficial, regardless of whether one party has more resources than the other. It is thus an error to suggest that the Court was against ameliorative legislation. Rather, the majority believed, consistent with classical (and neoclassical) economic theory, that preserving liberty of contract is in *everyone's* interest. Government interference in the labor market would not help workers as such, but would help the political class at the expense of others. See also Adkins v. Children's Hosp., 261 U.S. 525 (1923) (invalidating a minimum-wage law, and noting that the law in question resulted in unemployment among those it purported to help).

13   E.g., Paul, supra note 7; Soifer, supra note 6; Archibald Cox, *The Court and the Constitution* 135 (1987); Charles Grove Haines, *Revival of Natural Law Concepts* 179–80 (1958); Thomas Reed Powell, "Collective Bargaining before the

Notes to Introduction

Supreme Court," 33 *Pol. Sci. Q.* 396 (1918); Margaret Spahr, "Natural Law, Due Process and Economic Pressure," 24 *Am. Pol. Sci. Rev.* 332 (1930).

14   E.g., Derrick A. Bell Jr., *Race, Racism and American Law* 35 (2d ed. 1980); Harry N. Scheiber, "Original Intent, History, and Doctrine: The Constitution and Economic Liberty," *Am. Econ. Rev.,* May 1988, at 140, 142; see generally Gregory S. Alexander, "The Limits of Freedom of Contract in the Age of Laissez-Faire Constitutionalism," in *The Fall and Rise of Freedom of Contract* 103, 104 (F. H. Buckley ed. 1999); Christopher T. Wonnell, "The Influential Myth of a Generalized Conflict of Interests between Labor and Management," 81 *Geo. L.J.* 39 (1992).

15   See Daniel Shaviro, "The Minimum Wage, the Earned Income Tax Credit, and Optimal Subsidy Policy," 64 *U. Chi. L. Rev.* 405, 453 (1997). The directors of more mechanized businesses in the South also supported minimum-wage laws in order to reduce competition from businesses that relied on cheap labor. Bruce J. Schulman, *From Cotton Belt to Sunbelt* 86 (1991). For more on the origins of high, uniform national minimum-wage laws, see chapter 5.

16   Raymond Wolters, "Section 7a and the Black Worker," 10 *Lab. Hist.* 459, 466 (1969) (quoting Roy Wilkins).

17   E.g., Arthur F. McEvoy, "Freedom of Contract, Labor, and the Administrative State," in *The State and Freedom of Contract* 198, 218 (Harry Scheiber ed., 1998). One historian, reflecting common sentiment, decries judicial protection of liberty of contract during the *Lochner* era as a "perversion" of the Fourteenth Amendment, which was meant to aid African Americans. William Brock, *An American Crisis: Congress and Reconstruction 1865–1867,* at 288, 300 (1967). Derrick Bell even purports to find an implicit connection between Lochnerian ideology and racism. Derrick Bell, "Does Discrimination Make Economic Sense?" *Hum. Rts.,* fall 1988, at 38, 41–42; see also Bruce Ackerman, *1 We the People: Foundations* 147* (1991) (mentioning what he regards as *Plessy v. Ferguson*'s "deep intellectual indebtedness to laissez-faire").

Lochnerian jurists and their allies in the bar and academy can justifiably be criticized for having a mixed record, at best, on civil rights issues. The blame should not be placed on Lochnerism, however, but on the racism that infected Americans across political boundaries. See generally Mark Tushnet, "*Plessy v. Ferguson* in Libertarian Perspective," 16 *Law and Philosophy* 245 (1997). The Lochnerians' contemporary Progressive rivals were, as a rule, even less support- ive of civil rights than were the Lochnerians, and more inclined to enforce racism through public policy. See David E. Bernstein, "Philip Sober Controlling Philip Drunk: *Buchanan v. Warley* in Historical Perspective," 51 *Vand. L. Rev.* 797 (1998). *Lochner*-era Supreme Court justices sometimes defended African Amer- ican rights in Lochnerian terms. E.g., Buchanan v. Warley, 245 U.S. 60, 76 (1917); McCabe v. Atchison, Topeka & Santa Fe Ry, 235 U.S. 151, 161–66 (1914); Berea College v. Kentucky, 211 U.S. 45, 67 (1908) (Harlan, J., dissent- ing). Justice Holmes, darling of the Progressives, was the least sympathetic justice to African American claims during the *Lochner* era. See Bernstein, supra. At least through the New Deal era, the battle historically was not between the Lochnerian jurisprudence and something resembling modern liberal jurisprudence, but between a jurisprudence that sought to put some limits on government power, and the statist views of the Progressive/sociological school. Id.

I. EMIGRANT AGENT LAWS

1   Plantation owners lost ownership of their slaves, and land prices fell dramatically as a result. For example, Steelman notes that the loss of slave labor was said to have caused a 50 percent decline in the value of land in North Carolina. Joseph Flake Steelman, "The Immigration Movement in North Carolina, 1865–1890," at 44 (Ph.D. diss., University of North Carolina 1947).

2   William Cohen, *At Freedom's Edge: Black Mobility and the Southern White Quest for Racial Control, 1861–1915* (1991); Neil Fligstein, *Going North: Migration of Blacks and Whites from the South, 1900–1950,* at 24 (1981); Thomas Jackson Woofter Jr., *Negro Migration: Changes in Rural Organization and Population in the Cotton Belt* 117 (Negro Univ. Press reprint ed. 1969) (1920).

In part, these labor shortages were the result of a significant decline in the labor force participation of African American women and children after the Civil War. Roger L. Ransom & Richard Sutch, *One Kind of Freedom: The Economic Consequences of Emancipation* 6–7, 44–47, 55, 232–36 (1977); Woofter, supra, at 34–35; Gerald David Jaynes, *Branches without Roots: Genesis of the Black Working Class in the American South, 1862–1882,* at 88 (1986).

3   Theodore B. Wilson, *The Black Codes of the South* (1965); see generally Gilbert Thomas Stephenson, *Race Distinctions in American Law* 36, 41–63 (Mnemosyne 1969) (1910); Donald G. Nieman, Introduction to 3 *From Slavery to Sharecropping: White Land and Black Labor in the Rural South, 1865–1900,* at vii, viii (Donald G. Nieman ed., 1994).

4   Civil Rights Act of 1866, 42 U.S.C. § 1981 (1994).

5   Robert Higgs, *Competition and Coercion: Blacks in the American Economy, 1865–1914,* at 117 (1977); Richard K. Vedder, "The Slave Exploitation (Expropriation) Rate," 12 *Explorations in Econ. Hist.* 453 (1975).

6   Woofter, supra note 2, at 34; see also Fligstein, supra note 2, at 24; Jaynes, supra note 2, at 116; Peter Kolchin, *First Freedom: The Responses of Alabama's Blacks to Emancipation and Reconstruction* 22 (1972); William Pickens, *Bursting Bonds: The Heir of Slaves* 8 (rev. ed. 1929); Jacqueline Jones, "Work Now, Get Paid Much Later: 'Free Labor' in the Postbellum South," 15 *Revs. Am. Hist.* 265, 267 (1987); George Alfred Devlin, "South Carolina and Black Migration 1865–1940: In Search of the Promised Land" 76 (Ph.D. diss., University of South Carolina 1984).

Notes to Chapter 1

7   See generally Jacqueline Jones, *The Dispossessed* (1992); Leon Litwack, *Trouble in Mind* (1998).

8   Higgs, supra note 5.

9   Cohen, supra note 2, at 42–43; Jennifer Roback, "Southern Labor Law in the Jim Crow Era: Exploitative or Competitive?" 51 *U. Chi. L. Rev.* 1161, 1161 (1984); cf. Harold D. Woodman, *New South — New Law: The Legal Foundations of Credit and Labor Relations in the Postbellum Agricultural South* 90 (1995); Jonathan M. Wiener, "Class Structure and Economic Development in the American South, 1865–1955," 84 *Am. Hist. Rev.* 970, 973–74 (1979).

10 Violence was used against African Americans caught trying to migrate. "Testimony Taken by the Joint Select Comm. to Inquire into the Condition of Affairs in the Late Insurrectionary States," H.R. Rep. No. 42–22, pt. 10, at 1466 (1872) (testimony of William B. Jones, planter); Frederick Douglass, "The Nation's Problem: Speech Made upon the Twenty-Seventh Anniversary of Abolition in the District of Columbia (Apr. 16, 1889)," in *Negro Social and Political Thought, 1850–1920*, at 323 (Howard Brotz ed., 1966).

    For other examples of how violence was used to stifle market forces, see Higgs, supra note 5, at 10; 7 *African American Life in the Post-Emancipation South, 1861–1900: Black Freedom/White Violence, 1865–1900* (Donald G. Nieman ed., 1994); Aremona G. Bennett, "Phantom Freedom: Official Acceptance of Violence to Personal Security and Subversion of Proprietary Rights and Ambitions Following Emancipation, 1865–1910," 70 *Chi.-Kent L. Rev.* 439, 461–69 (1994); William F. Holmes, "Whitecapping: Agrarian Violence in Mississippi, 1902–1906," 35 *J. S. Hist.* 165 (1969).

11 Cohen, supra note 2, at 4; James R. Grossman, *Land of Hope: Chicago, Black Southerners, and the Great Migration* 26–27 (1989); Jaynes, supra note 2, at 63–64.

12 Cohen, supra note 2, at 35, 220, 227–28. According to Cohen, laws that survived Reconstruction included: Ala. Code § 4468 (1876); Ga. Code §§ 4814–15 (1882); Act of Aug. 21, 1876, 15th Leg., R.S., ch. 138, §§ 1, 3, 1876 Tex. Gen. Laws 228, *reprinted in* 8 H.P.N. Gammel, *The Laws of Texas 1822–1897*, at 1064 (Austin, Gammel 1898); and Va. Code tit. 56, ch. 206, § 22 (Munford 1873). For more on the history of these peonage laws, and the use of convict labor more generally, see Pete Daniel, *The Shadow of Slavery: Peonage in the South, 1901–1969* (1972); Alex Lichtenstein, *Twice the Work of Free Labor: The Political Economy of Convict Labor in the New South* (1996); Daniel Novak, *The Wheel of Servitude: Black Forced Labor after Slavery* 45–62 (1978).

13 Cohen, supra note 2, at 31–34.

14 Id. at 35; Act of Mar. 12, 1866, ch. 30, 1866 Ga. Laws 234; Act of Mar. 2, 1866, ch. 42, 1866 N.C. Sess. Laws 111; Act approved Nov. 8, 1866, 11th Leg., R.S., ch. 111, 1879 Tex. Gen. Laws 51, reprinted in 5 Gammel, supra note 12, at 1020, 1020–22; Va. Code tit. 16, ch. 28, §§ 884–85 (1887).

On lack of enforcement of vagrancy laws, see Peter Gottlieb, *Making Their Own Way* 14 (1987); Donald G. Nieman, "From Slaves to Citizens: African-Americans, Rights Consciousness, and Reconstruction," 17 *Cardozo L. Rev.* 2115, 2131 (1996).

15 Edward L. Ayers, *The Promise of the New South: Life After Reconstruction* 151 & n.56 (1992); Grossman, supra note 11, at 26; Neil R. McMillen, *Dark Journey, Black Mississippians in the Age of Jim Crow* 259 (1989); Pickens, supra note 6, at 8, 16, 21–22; William Edward Vickery, *The Economics of the Negro Migration, 1900–1960*, at 27 (1977); Charles H. Wesley, *Negro Labor in the United States: 1850–1925*, at 213 (1927); Carter G. Woodson, *A Century of Negro Migration* 120 (1918); Gavin Wright, *Old South, New South: Revolutions in the Southern Economy since the Civil War* 74–75, 77–78 (1986); Oscar Zeichner, "The Transition from Free Agricultural Labor in the Southern States," 12 *Agric. Hist.* 22, 29 (1939).

16 George Frederickson, *White Supremacy* 214 (1981); Grossman, supra note 11, at 22; Higgs, supra note 5, at 3; Ransom & Sutch, supra note 2, at 195; Vickery, supra note 15, at 34–35 (1977); Wright, supra note 15; William Cohen, "Negro Involuntary Servitude in the South, 1865–1940: A Preliminary Analysis," 42 *J. S. Hist.* 31, 39–40 (1976); Richard Vedder et al., "Demonstrating Their Freedom: The Post-Emancipation Migration of Black Americans," 10 *Res. Econ. Hist.* 213, 215 (1986); Ronald L. Lewis, "From Peasant to Proletarian: The Migration of Southern Blacks to the Central Appalachian Coalfields," 55 *J. S. Hist.* 77, 83 (1989); Roback, supra note 9, at 1169; Wiener, supra note 9, at 983.

17 Cohen, supra note 2, at 257; Daniel M. Johnson & Rex R. Campbell, *Black Migration in America* 62 (1981); Pickens, supra note 6, at 8.

18 Cohen, supra note 2, at 254–56 (attributing the migration of 100,000 African Americans to Oklahoma between 1890 and 1910 to a quest for autonomy from whites); Henderson H. Donald, *The Negro Migration of 1916–1918*, at 33 (1921) (finding that during World War I African Americans were more likely to migrate from areas where lynchings had occurred); Higgs, supra note 5, at 76 (noting that hundreds of African Americans fled violence in southwestern Mississippi in 1892–93 and 1902–6, and, encouraged by labor agents, migrated to the Delta); Robert A. Margo, *Race and Schooling in the South, 1880–1950: An Economic History* 48–49 (1990) (finding that African Americans would migrate from areas that did not offer adequate public schools); Arthur F. Raper, *Preface to Peasantry: A Tale of Two Black Belt Counties* 208 (2d ed. 1968) (describing African American migration from Greene County, Georgia, in response to lynching); Wesley, supra note 15, at 213 (reporting that in 1872 emigrant agents met with an especially "ready response" in "those places where there were cruelties and oppression"); Frenise A. Logan, "The Movement of Negroes from North Carolina, 1876–1894," 33 *N.C. Hist. Rev.* 45, 46–47, 54 (1956) (attributing large-scale migrations of African Americans from 1877 to

1880 and in 1889 to political discontent); Devlin, supra note 6, at 122–33 (describing the "Edgefield Exodus" in which thousands of African Americans deserted Edgefield County, South Carolina, from 1881 to 1882 in response to unfavorable legislation and generally unbearable conditions); id. at 133–34 (detailing the migration of hundreds of African Americans from Greenwood County, South Carolina, in 1898 in response to a series of lynchings); id. at 172–82 (discussing the lynching of a prominent African American man in Abbeville County, South Carolina, in 1916 and the subsequent African American migration from the county).

19 Jeannie M. Whayne, *A New Plantation South* 7 (1996); see also Woofter, supra note 2, at 117; Price V. Fishback, "Can Competition among Employers Reduce Governmental Discrimination? Coal Companies and Segregated Schools in West Virginia in the Early 1900s," 32 *J.L. & Econ.* 318, 324 (1989).

20 See, e.g., Grossman, supra note 11, at 29; George Brown Tindall, *South Carolina Negroes, 1877–1900,* at 176 (1952); Robert L. Brandfon, "The End of Immigration to the Cotton Fields," 50 *Mississippi Valley Hist. Rev.* 591, 611 (1964).

21 See, e.g., Florette Henri, *Black Migration* 75 (1975); Higgs, supra note 5, at 152–53 n.37; Woofter, supra note 2, at 166; Fishback, supra note 19; Nan Elizabeth Woodruff, "African-American Struggles for Citizenship in the Arkansas and Mississippi Deltas in the Age of Jim Crow," 55 *Radical Hist. Rev.* 33, 45 (1993); Edward Aaron Gaston Jr., "A History of the Negro Wage Earner in Georgia, 1890–1940," at 133–34 (Ph.D. diss., Emory University 1957).

22 August Meier, *Negro Thought in America, 1880–1915: Racial Ideologies in the Age of Booker T. Washington* 161 (1969) (concluding that African Americans' economic well-being improved from 1895 to 1915, even though their political and social status was declining; cf. Ayers, supra note 15, at 429–30 (noting rise in African American standard of living in first decade of twentieth century, but suggesting that long-term prospects were more negative); Eli Ginzberg & Alfred S. Eichner, *The Troublesome Presence: American Democracy and the Negro* 230–31 (1964) (discussing declining African American political and social fortunes between 1890 and 1915); Woofter, supra note 2, at 28 (finding increase in economic well-being among Georgia African Americans between 1900 and 1910, despite lynchings and discrimination).

23 Woodman, supra note 9, at 91 & n.47. Much to the aggravation of white planters, African Americans rarely agreed to contracts lasting more than one year. Alfred Holt Stone, "The Negro in the Yazoo-Mississippi Delta," 1902 *Am. Econ. Ass'n* 235, 259–60 (hereafter Stone, *Yazoo-Mississippi Delta*); cf. Alfred Holt Stone, "A Plantation Experiment," 19 *Q.J. Econ.* 270, 271–72 (1905) (hereafter Stone, *Plantation Experiment*).

24 Cohen, supra note 2, at 232.

25 Va. Code §§ 54, 359 (Munford 1873).

26 Cohen, supra note 2, at 233; Zeichner, supra note 15, at 29.

27 1876 Ga. Laws 17; Charles Nordhoff, *The Cotton States in the Spring and Summer of 1875,* at 105 (1876).

28 Shepperd v. County Comm'rs, 59 Ga. 535 (1877).

29 Plaintiff's Bill of Exceptions at 3–4, Shepperd v. County Comm'rs, 59 Ga. 535 (1877).

30 59 Ga. 535 (1876).

31 Ga. Code § 4598(a) (Lester 1882).

32 McMillen, supra note 15, at 259–61; Vickery, supra note 15, at 161.

33 1876–87 Ala. Acts 225; Cohen, supra note 2, at 233–34.

34 Cohen, supra note 2, at 169–70; Nell Irvin Painter, *Exodusters: Black Migration to Kansas after Reconstruction* 146, 191–97 (1977); Joe Louis Caldwell, "Any Place but Here: Kansas Fever in Northeast Louisiana," 21 *N. La. Hist. Ass'n J.* 51 (1990); John G. Van Deusen, "The Exodus of 1879," 21 *J. Negro Hist.* 105, 122 (1936); Sharon L. Woodson, "Exodus to Kansas," 82 *Crisis* 239 (1975); Douglass, supra note 10, at 323; see generally Robert G. Athearn, *In Search of Canaan: Black Migration to Kansas, 1879–80* (1978).
In practice, Reconstruction ended earlier in many states, as Democrats took control of southern states throughout the late 1860s and early 1870s. Ayers, supra note 15, at 8.

35 1880–81 Ala. Acts 162, 163; 1878–79 Ala. Acts 205, 205.

36 Joseph v. Randolph, 71 Ala. 499, 501–503 (1882) (stating the argument of the appellant).

37 Id. at 503–04 (stating the argument of the appellee). In fact, only approximately seven hundred African Americans from Alabama ultimately settled in Kansas. Many more settled in other southern states. Vickery, supra note 15, at 161.

38 Joseph, 71 Ala. at 508.

39 *Journal of the Senate of the General Assembly of the State of North Carolina* 130 (1881); see also Cohen, supra note 2, at 234; Frenise A. Logan, *The Negro in North Carolina 1876–1894,* at 132–33 (1964); see generally Eric Anderson, *Race and Politics in North Carolina 1872–1901,* at 80 (1981); Joseph H. Taylor, "The Great Migration from North Carolina in 1879," 31 *N.C. Hist. Rev.* 20 (1954).

40 Anderson, supra note 39, at 166; Ayers, supra note 15, at 150; Otto Klineberg, *Negro Intelligence and Selective Migration* 6 (1935); Logan, supra note 39, at 125; John Haley Hamilton III, "The Carolina Chameleon: Charles N. Hunter and Race Relations in North Carolina 1865–1931," at 155–58 (Ph.D. diss., University of North Carolina, Chapel Hill 1981).

41 "Peg Leg Williams: The Redoubtable Emigrant Agent Goes through Atlanta," *Atlanta Const.,* Mar. 1, 1890, at 5; "Peg-Leg Williams Arrested," *Atlanta Const.,* Feb. 25, 1890, at 1; "Advised to Stay Home," *Tarboro Southerner,* Jan. 2, 1890, at 3; "The Emigration Movement," *Tarboro Southerner,* Jan. 23, 1890, at 2; "Exodusters in Pitt," *Tarboro Southerner,* Feb. 27, 1890, at 3; "Notified to Leave," *Tarboro Southerner,* Feb. 20, 1890, at 3; *Tarboro South-*

erner, Jan. 30, 1890, at 4. Other agents recruited workers as well. See, e.g., "Escorted Away," *Tarboro Southerner*, Feb. 13, 1890, at 3; "Exodusting," *Tarboro Southerner*, Feb. 20, 1890, at 3.

42 "To Test the Law that Puts a Prohibition Tax upon Emigrant Agents," *Atlanta Const.*, Mar. 9, 1890, at 20.

43 Logan, supra note 39, at 133 (quoting *Fifth Annual Report of the North Carolina Bureau of Labor Statistics* 81 [1891]); *Tarboro Southerner*, Jan. 16, 1890, at 2); "Bearing Fruit," *Tarboro Southerner*, Feb. 13, 1890, at 2; "Notified to Leave," supra note 41; "Peg-Leg Williams Arrested," supra note 41; " 'Peg-Leg' Williams Arrested," *Tarboro Southerner*, Mar. 6, 1890, at 3; "Peg Leg Williams: The Redoubtable Emigrant Agent Goes through Atlanta," supra note 41.

44 1891 N.C. Sess. Laws 77, 77; Cohen, supra note 2, at 233–34; Logan, supra note 18, at 63; Letter from W. A. Guthrie, Durham, North Carolina, to the Editors of the *American Law Review*, in 38 *Am. L. Rev.* 144, 144–45 (1904).

South Carolina, the source of the second-largest number of Williams's recruits, also passed an emigrant agent law in 1891. Act of Dec. 24, 1891, No. 697, § 3, 1891 S.C. Acts 1084.

45 A "Bruce Williams" signed the bail bond for Moore, the arrested agent. Bail Bond, State v. Moore, 18 S.E. 342 (N.C. 1893) (No. 210). Whether this was a pseudonym of Peg Leg's, a relative of his, or someone unrelated and coincidentally named "Williams" is not known. Williams later claimed to have "whipped this [emigrant agent] law in Alabama and North Carolina," which implies he played a role in this case. "Guarding Jail in Madison," *Augusta Chron.*, Jan. 16, 1900, at 1.

46 Record of Criminal Court of New Haven County at 3–4, State v. Moore, 18 S.E. 342 (N.C. 1893) (No. 210). An arcane procedure, not relevant to this discussion, was involved.

47 State v. Moore, 18 S.E. 342 (N.C. 1893).

48 "To Test the Law that Puts a Prohibition Tax upon Emigrant Agents," supra note 42.

49 Id.

50 Id.; William F. Holmes, "Labor Agents and the Georgia Exodus, 1899–1900," 79 *S. Atlantic Q.* 436, 439 (1980).

51 Cohen, supra note 2, at 264; Alfred W. Reynolds, "The Alabama Negro Colony in Mexico, 1894–1896" (pt. 1), 5 *Ala. Rev.* 243, 247 (1952); "A Negro Colony: 'Peg' Williams Proposes to Establish One in Mexico," *Atlanta Const.*, Jan. 2, 1895, at 8.

52 *Birmingham News*, Feb. 20, 1899; Cohen, supra note 2, at 265; "Judge Hart Signs Order Placing Williams in Greene County Jail: State Emigrating Act Which Defendant Is Fighting Is Declared Constitutional," *Atlanta Const.*, Jan. 17, 1900, at 3 (hereafter "Williams in Greene County Jail"); " 'Gwine to Mississippi," *Atlanta Const.*, Nov. 26, 1899, at 16.

53 Holmes, supra note 50, at 438; "Mad Rush of Negroes from Middle Georgia,"

Augusta Chron., Jan. 15, 1900, at 1 (hereafter "Mad Rush"); "Williams in Greene County Jail," supra note 52.

In 1900 Morgan County had 5,207 whites and 10,606 African Americans. R. P. Brooks, "A Local Study of the Race Problem: Race Relations in the Eastern Piedmont Region of Georgia," 26 *Pol. Sci. Q.* 193, 195 (1911).

54 Ayers, supra note 15, at 195.

55 Id.; Carl Kelsey, "Some Causes of Negro Migration," *Charities*, Oct. 1905, at 15, 17; Sydney Nathans, " 'Gotta Mind to Move, A Mind to Settle Down': Afro-Americans and the Plantation Frontier," in *A Master's Due* 204, 207–12 (William J. Cooper et al. eds., 1985); Brandfon, supra note 20, at 592–93; Stone, "Yazoo-Mississippi Delta," supra note 23, at 235, 238–39, 250, 262; Stone, "Plantation Experiment," supra note 23, at 270.

56 "From Georgia to Mississippi," *Augusta Chron.*, Dec. 3, 1899, at 1; "Georgia Negroes Mississippi-Mad," *Augusta Chron.*, Dec. 10, 1899, at 12; "Mad Rush" supra note 53; "R. A. Williams Arrested," *Greenesboro Herald-J.*, Jan. 19, 1900, at 1.

57 Holmes, supra note 50, at 439; " 'Gwine to Mississippi," supra note 52; "Mad Rush," supra note 53.

58 Arthur Raper, *Tenants of the Almighty* 132 (1943); Holmes, supra note 50, at 440; "Cotton Hurt by Drouth," *Greenesboro Herald-J.*, Sept. 1, 1899, at 1; "Williams in Greene County Jail," supra note 52; "Georgia Negroes Mississippi-Mad," supra note 56; "Mad Rush," supra note 53; " 'Peg-Leg' Arrested," *Greenesboro Herald-J.*, Dec. 22, 1899, at 1.

59 Raper, supra note 58, at 132, 133; "Arrest of Peg-Leg Williams," *Atlanta Const.*, Dec. 20, 1899, at 3; " 'Peg-Leg' Arrested," supra note 58; " 'Peg Leg' Williams's Arrest," *Atlanta Const.*, Dec. 26, 1899, at 3; "Williams in Greene County Jail," supra note 52.

60 "Mad Rush," supra note 53; " 'Peg Leg' Williams's Arrest," supra note 59.

61 "Mad Rush," supra note 53; Williams had refused to pay the five-hundred-dollar fee in other counties, and charges were brought against him in four other counties at about this time. Raper, supra note 58, at 133.

62 Raper, supra note 58, at 130–31; "State Political Gossip: Stick a Peg Here," *Atlanta Const.*, Jan. 14, 1900, at 6; "Emigration Fever in Newton," *Atlanta Const.*, Jan. 16, 1900, at 3.

Williams was not the only agent active in Georgia at this time. Varner v. State, 36 S.E. 93, 93 (Ga. 1900) (overturning, on nonconstitutional grounds, the conviction of an agent arrested in Decatur County for recruiting workers for jobs in Florida).

63 "R. A. Williams Arrested," supra note 56; see also "Angry with 'Peg-Leg,' " *Greenesboro Herald-J.*, Jan. 12, 1900, at 1.

On the population of Greene County, see Thaddeus B. Rice & Carolyn W. Williams, *History of Greene County, Georgia* 374 (1961); Raper, supra note 58, at 365.

Notes to Chapter 1

64 Holmes, supra note 50, at 441.

65 "Mad Rush," supra note 53; "Peg Leg Is in Trouble Again," *Atlanta Const.*,
    Jan. 15, 1900, at 3; "R. A. Williams Arrested," supra note 56.

66 Holmes, supra note 50, at 441–42; "Guarding Jail in Madison," supra note 45;
    "R. A. Williams Arrested," supra note 56.

67 "Angry Mob in Madison," *Greenesboro Herald-J.*, Jan. 19, 1900, at 1; "Guard-
    ing Jail in Madison," supra note 45. Groups of African Americans also milled
    around the jail, and rumors floated that they were going to try to liberate
    Williams. Id.

68 Id.; see also Holmes, supra note 50, at 442; "Peg Leg Is in Trouble Again," supra
    note 65.

69 "Guarding Jail in Madison," supra note 45.

70 This statement is quoted in "Williams in Greene County Jail," supra note 52.

71 "The Act Is Constitutional," *Augusta Chron.*, Jan. 17, 1900, at 1.

72 Id. Williams's case was transferred from superior court to county court. Wil-
    liams and La Vitte were indicted together in county court during its March term.
    Letter from Marshall W. Williams, Morgan County Records Archivist,
    Madison, Ga., to David E. Bernstein, Assistant Professor, George Mason Uni-
    versity School of Law (May 7, 1996) (hereafter Letter from Marshall W.
    Williams).

73 Holmes, supra note 50, at 442; "'Peg Leg' Williams Will Not Have Hear-
    ing until Next Friday," *Atlanta Const.*, Jan. 26, 1900, at 10; "Peg and Jim,"
    Greenesboro Herald-J., Feb. 9, 1900, at 4.

74 Holmes, supra note 50, at 443; Woodson v. State, 40 S.E. 1013 (Ga. 1902)
    (overturning the conviction of the agent, Woodson, on nonconstitutional
    grounds, and noting that he was an employee of "one Williams").

75 Holmes, supra note 50, at 443.

76 Id. at 443–44.

77 "Negro Exodus from Athens," *Augusta Chron.*, Mar. 12, 1900, at 1; "Vagrant
    Act Read to Negroes," *Augusta Chron.*, Mar. 13, 1900, at 1.

78 Id.

79 Ray Stannard Baker, *Following the Color Line: An Account of Negro Citi-
    zenship in the American Democracy* 80 (Corner House 1973) (1908) (repeat-
    ing Williams's claims that many of his recruits found success in Mississippi);
    "Georgia Negroes Mississippi-Mad," supra note 56; "A Penitent Exoduster,"
    Greenesboro Herald-J., Feb. 16, 1900, at 4; *Greenesboro Herald-J.*, Mar. 2,
    1900, at 1.

80 Baker, supra note 79 at 79 (noting that Mississippi planters often paid better
    wages and provided better contractual terms than those in Georgia); John M.
    Barry, *Rising Tide: The Great Mississippi Flood of 1927 and How It Changed
    America* 123 (1997) ("the Delta did offer blacks at least relative promise").

81 James C. Cobb, *The Most Southern Place on Earth: The Mississippi Delta and
    the Roots of Regional Identity* 90, 107 (1992); John C. Willis, "On the New

South Frontier: Life in the Yazoo-Mississippi Delta, 1865–1920," at 345 n.40 (Ph.D. diss., University of Virginia 1991); see generally Nathans, supra note 55, at 207–12.

82 McMillen, supra note 15, at 269.

83 See Williams v. Fears, 35 S.E. 699, 703 (Ga.), aff'd, 179 U.S. 270 (1900).

84 Raper, supra note 58, at 134.

85 Id. at 133.

86 He did, however, analogize the emigrant agent law to a California law that prohibited corporations from hiring Chinese workers. That law was invalidated by a federal court. Brief of Counsel for Plaintiff in Error at 15, Williams (citing In re Tribucio Parrott, 1 F. 481 (C.C.D. Cal. 1880)).

87 Brief of Counsel for Plaintiff in Error at 4, 12, 16, Williams v. Fears, 179 U.S. 270 (1900).

88 Charles Warren, "A Bulwark to the State Police Power—The United States Supreme Court," 13 *Colum. L. Rev.* 667, 669 (1913).

89 Brief of Counsel for Plaintiff in Error at 5–12, Williams.

90 James W. Ely Jr., *The Chief Justiceship of Melville W. Fuller, 1888–1910,* at 141 (1995); McCall v. California, 136 U.S. 104 (1890).

91 Williams, 179 U.S. at 276, 278.

92 Id. at 275.

93 As one reporter noted, if an agent sought to do business in the entire state of Georgia, the total license fee would amount to approximately sixty-eight thousand dollars. The reporter commented: "That looks rather prohibitory—don't it?" "Peg and Jim," supra note 73.

94 Williams v. Fears, 179 U.S. 270, 275–76 (1900).

95 Id. at 276–77, 278.

96 Id. (Harlan, J., dissenting).

97 See generally James W. Ely Jr., "Judicial Liberalism in the Gilded Age: Appraising John Marshall Harlan," 21 *Revs. Am. Hist.* 57 (1993).

98 Raper, supra note 58, at 134–35.

99 Baker, supra note 79, at 80.

100 Cohen, supra note 2, at 238.

101 See, e.g., State v. Roberson, 48 S.E. 595 (N.C. 1904); State v. Hunt, 40 S.E. 216 (N.C. 1901); State v. Napier, 41 S.E. 13 (S.C. 1902). For other cases upholding emigrant agent laws, see Hanley v. Moody, 39 F.2d 198 (N.D. Tex. 1930); Kendrick v. State, 39 So. 203 (Ala. 1905); In re Craig, 20 Haw. 483 (1911); Garbutt v. State, 77 So. 189 (Miss. 1918); State v. Bates, 101 S.E. 651 (S.C. 1919); State v. Reeves, 99 S.E. 841 (S.C. 1919); McMillan v. City of Knoxville, 202 S.W. 65 (Tenn. 1918); Cole v. Commonwealth, 193 S.E. 517 (Va. 1937).

102 Baker, supra note 79, at 80.

103 Holmes, supra note 50, at 448.

104 Ayers, supra note 15.

105 Carole Marks, *Farewell—We're Good and Gone: The Great African Ameri-*

can Migration 44 (1989); Woodson, supra note 15, at 162–63; Wright, supra note 15, at 203–04; see also Robert A. Margo, *Schooling and the Great Migration* 109 (National Bureau of Econ. Research Working Paper No. 2697, 1988) (arguing that better-educated African Americans were far more likely to migrate to the North).

Some historians have argued that the disparity in migration rates reflects the better opportunities urban and educated African Americans had in the North relative to their country cousins. This argument may have some weight, but it neglects the relative advantages educated and urban southern African Americans enjoyed relative to their rural counterparts if they stayed in the South.

106 Marks, supra note 105, at 20–21, 44. The negative economic effects of emigrant agent laws and the limits they placed on interstate migration may have been somewhat mitigated by growing African American migration from rural areas to nearby, in-state cities. See, e.g., Marks, supra, at 44; R. P. Brooks, "A Local Study of the Race Problem: Race Relations in the Eastern Piedmont Region of Georgia," 26 *Pol. Sci. Q.* 193, 202–03, 219 (1911) (discussing a rise in rural wages due to African American migration from certain Georgia counties to cities). The information and economic costs of such migration were substantially lower than the costs of interstate migration.

107 Gottlieb, supra note 14, at 40–43; Marks, supra note 105, at 20–21; Gunnar Myrdal, *An American Dilemma: The Negro Problem and Modern Democracy* 194 (1944).

108 Marks, supra note 105, at 29; see generally Alan D. DeSantis, *Selling the American Dream: The Chicago Defender and the Great Migration of 1915–1919* (1994); James R. Grossman, "Blowing the Trumpet: The *Chicago Defender* and Black Migration during World War I," 78 *Ill. Hist.J.* 82 (1985); Carolyn A. Stroman, "The *Chicago Defender* and the Mass Migration of Blacks, 1916–1918," *J. Popular Culture,* fall 1981, at 62, 63.

Some white-owned newspapers also published advertisements from out-of-state employers. See, e.g., Devlin, supra note 6, at 196 (discussing consideration by South Carolina officials of prosecuting a Charleston newspaper for publishing a Pennsylvania company's advertisement for workers).

109 Marks, supra note 105, at 30; James R. Grossman, "Black Labor Is the Best Labor," in *Black Exodus* 51, 57 (Alferdteen Harrison ed., 1991).

110 Marks, supra note 105, at 36; see generally Tera W. Hunter, *To 'Joy My Freedom: Southern Black Women's Lives and Labors after the Civil War* 235 (1997) (discussing an Atlanta woman who wanted to migrate but could not afford a train ticket).

111 1923 Ala. Acts 208 (instituting a $5,000 annual agent fee for each county in which the agent operated); 1927 Ga. Laws 56, 72 (instituting a $1,000 per county fee); 1930 Miss. Laws 146, 148, 177 (establishing a $500 annual agent tax per county in which the agent operated); 1929 Tex. Gen. Laws 16 (enacting a $1,000 annual tax in addition to a $100 to $300 tax for every county in

which the agent operated), 1949 Tex. Gen. Laws 434, 436; 1928 Va. Acts 35, 117–18 (instituting a $5,000 per county fee). In 1922, South Carolina raised its emigrant agent fee from $500 to $2,000 per county. Devlin, supra note 6, at 250. On local laws banning agents entirely see Wesley, supra note 15, at 292–93. In Georgia there was a failed legislative attempt to ban labor agents statewide. "The Exodus and a Bill," 1 *Opportunity* 317 (1923).

2. LICENSING LAWS

1 Herbert Northrup, *Organized Labor and the Negro* 38 (reprint ed. 1971) (1944).

2 See Lawrence Friedman, "Freedom of Contract and Occupational Licensing 1890–1910: A Legal and Society Study," 53 *Cal. L. Rev.* 487, 497 n.41 (1965).

3 Stephen Young, *The Rule of Experts* 75 (1987); Richard B. Freeman, "The Effect of Occupational Licensing on Black Occupational Attainment," in *Occupational Licensing and Regulation* (Simon Rottenberg, ed. 1980); Herbert Hill, "Black Labor and Affirmative Action: An Historical Perspective," in *The Question of Discrimination* 190, 213 (Steven Shulman & William Darity Jr. eds., 1989).

4 The Maryland Supreme Court upheld the law on the strength of *Slaughter-House*. In re Taylor, 38 Md. 28 (1877); see David S. Bogen, "The Transformation of the Fourteenth Amendment: Reflections from the Admission of Maryland's First Black Lawyers," 44 *Md. L. Rev.* 939, 943 (1985). The law was invalidated a few years later in an unreported decision. Id. at 1038–39.

5 118 U.S. 356 (1886).

6 Id. at 370.

7 Id.

8 Id. at 373.

9 Id. at 373–74.

10 129 U.S. 114 (1888).

11 Watson v. Maryland, 218 U.S. 173 (1910); Reetz v. Michigan, 188 U.S. 505 (1903); Hawker v. New York, 170 U.S. 189 (1898); Richard Reaves, *The Law of Professional Licensing and Certification* 1 (1984); Friedman, supra note 2, at 511.

12 175 U.S. 578, 589 (1897).

13 Lochner v. New York, 198 U.S. 45, 63 (1905), citing Bessette v. People, 62 N.E. 215 (Ill. 1901); People v. Beattie, 96 App. Div. 383, 89 N.Y. Supp. 193 (1904); In re Aubry, 78 P. 900 (Wash. 1904).

14 Friedman, supra note 2, at 494.

15 Douglas v. Noble, 261 U.S. 165 (1921).

16 Under *Yick Wo* and general considerations of equal protection, courts would still restrain licensing boards from denying licenses based on prejudice if the applicant had met the boards' criteria. For example, the Florida Supreme Court

ordered that a license be given to an applicant who proved discrimination, and wrote: "Ours is still a government of laws and not one of men actuated by caprice and arbitrary power. The highest duty of the man or board whose duty is to administer laws, rules, or regulations is to see that they bear equally on all persons or groups." York v. State ex rel. Jones, 197 So. 766, 767 (Fla. 1940).

17 Note, "Restriction of Freedom of Entry into the Building Trades," 38 *Iowa L. Rev.* 556, 557 (1953).

18 Cf. Walter Gellhorn, *Individual Freedom and Government Restraints* 114–15 (1968); Friedman, supra note 2, at 497 n.41.

19 Ira D.A. Reid, *Negro Membership in American Labor Unions* 38 (1930); 3 Philip Foner, *History of the Labor Movement of the United States: The Policies and Practices of the American Federation of Labor, 1900–1909*, at 240 (1964); Rayford Logan, *The Betrayal of the Negro* 155 (1965); Northrup, supra note 1, at 230–34; Sterling Spero & Abram Harris, *The Black Worker* 58–59 (1931); Charles S. Johnson, "Negro Workers and the Unions," *The Survey*, Apr. 15, 1928, at 113.

20 Winkler v. Benzenberg, 76 N.W. 345 (Wis. 1898).

21 People ex rel. Nechamcus v. Warden, 144 N.Y. 529, 534 (1895).

22 Id. at 539.

23 Id. at 543.

24 State v. Gardner, 51 N.E. 136 (Ohio 1898).

25 David H. Gerber, *Black Ohio and the Color Line: 1860–1915*, at 303 (1976); Lorenzo Greene & Carter G. Woodson, *The Negro Wage Earner* 192 (1928); Herbert Hill, *Black Labor and the American Legal System* 22 (1977); Michael K. Honey, *Southern Labor and Black Civil Rights: Organizing Memphis Workers* 50 (1993); Hill, "Affirmative Action," supra note 3, at 214.

26 Letter from C. H. Perry to the *Plumbers' Journal*, Mar. 1905, at 16, quoted in Spero & Harris, supra note 19, at 478–79; see also *Plumbers, Gas and Steam Fitters Official Journal*, Jan. 1905, at 10, quoted in Spero & Harris, supra note 19, at 481 ("There are about ten Negro skate plumbers working around here [Danville, Va.] doing quite a lot of jobbing and repairing, but owing to the fact of not having an examining board it is impossible to stop them, hence the anxiety of the men here to organize.").

27 Spero & Harris, supra note 19, at 59.

28 Douglas v. People ex rel. Ruddy, 80 N.E. 341 (Ill. 1907); Rock v. Philadelphia, 191 A. 669 (Pa. Super. 1937); Spero & Harris, supra note 19, at 160; Hill, supra note 25, at 22; National Interracial Congress, *Toward Interracial Cooperation* 123 (1926).

29 Replogle v. Little Rock, 267 S.W. 353, 356–57 (Ark. 1924).

30 Dewell v. Quarles, 181 S.E. 159, 160–61 (Ga. 1935).

31 People v. Brown, 95 N.E.2d 888, 894 (Ill. 1950).

32 See F. Ray Marshall, *The Negro and Organized Labor* 135 (1965); Reid, supra note 19, at 134; Florence Peterson, *American Labor Unions* 88–89 (1945);

Northrup, supra note 1, at 24; Robert C. Weaver, *Negro Labor: A National Problem* 42–43 (1948); F. Ray Marshall, "The Negro in Southern Unions," in *The Negro and the American Labor Movement* 128, 145 (Julius Jacobson ed., 1968).

33   Benjamin Shimberg, Barbara F. Esser, & Daniel H. Kruger, *Occupational Licensing: Practices and Policies* 116 (1972); Marshall, supra note 32, at 145.

34   Herman D. Bloch, "Craft Unions and the Negro in Historical Perspective," 43 *J. Negro Hist.* 10, 23 (1958).

35   Walter E. Williams, *The State against Blacks* 94–95 (1982).

36   Northrup, supra note 1, at xb, 116; Shimberg et al., supra note 33, at 112–13; Zachary Dyckman, "An Analysis of Negro Employment in the Building Trades" 73 (Ph.D. diss., Yale University 1971).

37   Hill, supra note 25, at 15; William Scott, *The Journeyman Barbers' International Union of America*, 44 n.27 (1936) (citing *Eleventh Census of the United States* 354–55 (1890)); Edward A. Gaston, "A History of the Negro Wage Earner in Georgia" 270 (Ph.D. diss., Emory University 1957).

38   See, e.g., R. Wright, *The Negro in Pennsylvania: A Study in Economic History* 75–76 (1911) (African American barbers lost most of their white customers, but retained their African American customers).

      The period from approximately 1890 to 1915 was marked by a significant increase in societal racism and a concomitant decline in the social standing of African Americans. Eli Ginzberg & Alfred S. Eichner, *The Troublesome Presence: American Democracy and the Negro* 230–31 (1964); August Meier, *Negro Thought in America, 1880–1915: Racial Ideologies in the Age of Booker T. Washington* 161 (1963).

39   Reid, supra note 19, at 155; Scott, supra note 37, at 43–44; Spero & Harris, supra note 19, at 76 (table 1).

40   C. Vann Woodward, *The Strange Career of Jim Crow* 116 (3d ed. 1974); Gaston, supra note 37, at 293–95.

41   Chaires v. Atlanta, 139 S.E. 559 (Ga. 1927).

42   "The Proposed Barbers Licensing Law," *Norfolk J. & Guide*, Aug. 3, 1929 (editorial page). The editors note that the discriminatory aspects of this law "are basically similar to the provisions employed by organized labor to bar members of the colored race from many skilled trades." Id.; see also Workers of the Writers' Program of the Work Projects Administration in the State of Virginia, *The Negro in Virginia* 351 (reprint ed. 1994) (1940).

43   Id.

44   *The Negro in Virginia*, supra note 42, at 151; Virginius Dabney, "Negro Barbers in the South," *The Nation*, July 16, 1930, at 64.

45   David Fellman, "A Case Study in Administrative Law: The Regulation of Barbers," 26 *Wash. U.L.Q.* 213, 214–15 n.1 (1941).

46   See Scott, supra note 37, at 80–84.

47   Id. at 87.

Notes to Chapter 2

48 W. Va. Code § 1409(41) (1936); Gerber, supra note 25, at 335–36 & n.44.

49 Fulton v. Ives, 167 So. 394 (Fla. 1936).

50 Id. at 404 (Brown, J., concurring).

51 Friedman, supra note 2, at 518; see "Constitutionality of Statute Regulating Barbers," 20 A.L.R. 1111; "Validity of Statute or Ordinance Regulating Barbers," 98 A.L.R. 1088; Fellman, supra note 45.

52 State v. Walker, 92 P. 775, 778 (Wash. 1907).

53 Freeman, supra note 3, at 168 (table 1).

54 Stuart Dorsey, "Occupational Licensing and Minorities," 7 *L. & Human Behavior* 171, 173, 177, 179 (1983).

55 Stuart Dorsey, "The Occupational Licensing Queue," 15 *J. Human Resources* 420 (1980).

56 Reuben Kessel, "The A.M.A. and the Supply of Physicians," 35 *Law & Contemp. Probs.* 267, 270 (1970).

57 Abraham Flexner, *Medical Education in the United States and Canada* 18, 25–26 (1910); see also Henry S. Pritchett, Introduction, id. at xiv.

58 Flexner, supra note 57, at 180–81.

59 Francis Delancy, *The Licensing of Professions in West Virginia* 111–12 & n.76 (1938); Herbert Wall, *Occupational Restrictions: A Study of the Laws of Eighteen Selected States, Covering the Requirements for Entering Occupations Therein* 30 (1929); Ronald Hamowy, "The Early Development of Medical Licensing Laws in the United States, 1875–1900," 3 *J. Libertarian Studies* 73 (1979).

60 Herbert M. Morais, *The History of the Afro-American in Medicine* 90 (rev. ed. 1976); James Summerville, *Educating African-American Doctors: A History of Meharry Medical College* 54 (1983); Kessel, supra note 56; Todd Savitt, "The Education of African-American Physicians at Shaw University, 1882–1918," in *Black Americans in North Carolina and the South* 160, 181–85 (Jeffrey J. Crow & Flora J. Hatley eds. 1984); Darlene Clark Hine, "The Anatomy of Failure: Medical Education Reform and the Leonard Medical School of Shaw University, 1882–1920," *J. Negro Educ.* 512 (1985).

61 Id. at 60–65; Savitt, supra note 60, at 183.

62 Delancy, supra note 59, at 111–15; Todd L. Savitt, "Entering a White Profession: African-American Physicians in the New South, 1880–1920," 61 *Bull. Hist. Med.* 507 (1987); see generally J. Burrow, *Organized Medicine in the Progressive Era: The Move toward Monopoly* (1977).

63 Darlene Clark Hine, *Black Women in White: Racial Conflict and Cooperation in the Nursing Profession 1890–1950*, at 92–93 (1989); Leon F. Litwack, *Trouble in Mind* 339–40 (1998); Summerville, supra note 60, at 51.

64 Morais, supra note 60, at 94; Gunnar Myrdal, *An American Dilemma* 32, 319, 419 (1943); Kessel, supra note 56, at 270.

Discrimination in medicine enforced through licensing laws was also extremely harmful to Jews. Reuben Kessel, "Price Discrimination in Medicine," 1

J.L. & Econ. 21, 47 n.82 (1958); Thomas G. Moore, "The Purpose of Licensing," 4 *J.L. & Econ.* 93 (1961).

65 Price Van Meter Fishback, "Employment Conditions of Blacks in the Coal Industry, 1900–1930," at 308–09 (Ph.D. diss., University of Washington 1983).

3. RAILROAD LABOR REGULATIONS

1 Malcolm Ross, *All Manner of Men* 122 (1948); see also Howard W. Risher Jr., *The Negro in the Railroad Industry* 1 (1971) ("the relatively high compensation and stable employment available on the railroads have meant better housing, improved educational opportunities, and increased status in the Negro community").

2 Walter E. Williams, "Freedom to Contract: Blacks and Labor Organizations," *Gov't-Union Rev.*, summer 1981, at 28, 31.

3 Risher, supra note 1, at 26.

4 Eric Arnesen, " 'Like Banquo's Ghost, It will Not Down': The Race Question and the American Railroad Brotherhoods, 1880–1920," *Am. Hist. Rev.* 1601, 1628 (1994).

5 Sterling Spero & Abram Harris, *The Black Worker* 22 (1931); F. Ray Marshall, *The Negro and Organized Labor* 89–96 (1965).

6 Marshall, supra note 5, at 91; Arnesen, supra note 4, at 1629.

7 Arnesen, supra note 4, at 1629; Paul Michel Taillon, "Culture, Politics, and the Making of the Railroad Brotherhoods, 1863–1916," at 464 (Ph.D. diss., University of Wisconsin 1997).

8 Spero & Harris, supra note 5, at 284; John G. Van Deusen, *The Black Man in White America* 60 (1944); William A. Sundstrom, "Half a Career: Discrimination & Railroad Internal Labor Markets," 29 *Industrial Relations* 423, 427 (1990). On licensing, see Smith v. Texas, 233 U.S. 630 (1914) (invalidating a law prohibiting any individual from acting as a railway conductor without having first had two years' experience as a brakeman or freight conductor); Smith v. Alabama, 124 U.S. 465 (1888) (upholding Alabama licensing statute for locomotive engineers).

9 William H. Harris, *The Harder We Run: Black Workers since the Civil War* 41 (1982); Arnesen, supra note 4, at 1608.

10 Spero & Harris, supra note 5, at 284, 315; Taillon, supra note 7, at 467.

11 Arnesen, supra note 4, at 1621–22; Sundstrom, supra note 8, at 429.

12 Arnesen, supra note 4, at 1622.

13 Spero & Harris, supra note 5, at 288.

14 Herbert Hill, *Black Labor and the American Legal System* 15 (1977); Spero & Harris, supra note 5, at 291–92; John Michael Matthews, "The Georgia 'Race Strike' of 1909," 40 *J. S. Hist.* 613, 617–21 (1974).

15 Harris, supra note 9, at 46; Arnesen, supra note 4, at 1630–31.

16 Harris, supra note 9, at 46–47.

Notes to Chapter 3

17   Id. at 48; Matthews, supra note 14, at 622; "Georgia Firemen Satisfied: Feel That with Equal Pay Whites Will Get Jobs from Negroes," *N.Y. Times,* June 29, 1909.

18   Taillon, supra note 7, at 515.

19   Spero & Harris, supra note 5, at 482.

20   Edward A. Gaston, "A History of the Negro Wage Earner in Georgia" 240 (Ph.D. diss., Emory University 1957); Matthews, supra note 14.

21   Herbert Northrup, *Organized Labor and the Negro* 52 (reprint ed. 1971) (1944); Risher, supra note 1, at 39; Sumner H. Slichter, *Union Policies and Industrial Management* 187 (1940).

22   St. Louis, Iron Mountain & S. Ry. v. Arkansas, 240 U.S. 518, 520–21 (1916); Chicago, Rock Island & Pac. Ry. v. Arkansas, 219 U.S. 453, 466 (1911); David A. Gerber, *Black Ohio and the Color Line, 1860–1915,* at 302–03 (1976); Northrup, supra note 21, at 52; Risher, supra note 1, at 39–40; William G. Thomas, *Lawyering for the Railroad* 194 (1999); Workers of the Writers' Program of the Work Projects Administration in the State of Virginia: *The Negro in Virginia* 349 (reprint ed. 1994) (1940); August Meier & Elliot Rudwick, "Attitudes of Negro Leaders toward the American Labor Movement from the Civil War to World War I," in *The Negro and the American Labor Movement* 27, 45 (Julius Jacobson ed., 1968).

23   Lorenzo Greene & Carter G. Woodson, *The Negro Wage Earner* 102–03 (1930); Sundstrom, supra note 8, at 427.

24   Spero & Harris, supra note 5, at 294–95.

25   Risher, supra note 1, at 38; Laurence Scott Zakson, "Railway Labor Legislation 1888 to 1930: A Legal History of Congressional Railway Labor Relations Policy," 20 *Rutgers L.J.* 317, 341 (1989).

26   John D. Finney Jr., "A Study of Negro Labor during and after World War I" 185, 189–90 (Ph.D. diss., Georgetown University 1967).

27   Spero & Harris, supra note 5, at 296–300.

28   Id. at 301.

29   See Northrup, supra note 21, at 51.

30   Spero & Harris, supra note 5, at 299–300.

31   James R. Grossman, *Land of Hope* 214–15 (1989); Spero & Harris, supra note 5, at 284–85. On union opposition to the end of federal control of the railroads, see Ruth O'Brien, *Workers' Paradox: The Republican Origins of New Deal Labor Policy, 1886–1935,* at 8, 76 (1998).

32   Northrup, supra note 21, at 50–54; John P. Frey, "Attempts to Organize Negro Workers," *American Federationist,* March 1929, at 296, 303.

33   Risher, supra note 1, at 26; Colin J. Davis, "The 1922 Railroad Shopmen's Strike in the Southeast: A Study of Success and Failure," in *Organized Labor in the Twentieth Century South* 117 (Robert H. Zieger ed., 1991); William E. Forbath, "The Shaping of the American Labor Movement," 102 *Harv. L. Rev.* 1111, 1152 (1989).

34   Spero & Harris, supra note 5, at 287–90; Ray Marshall, "The Negro in South-
     ern Unions," in *The Negro and the American Labor Movement* 128, 134–36
     (Julius Jacobson ed., 1968); Northrup, supra note 21, at 78–79; Risher, supra
     note 1, at 45; see generally Davis, supra note 33, at 113.

35   Risher, supra note 1, at 46.

36   158 U.S. 564 (1895).

37   Philip S. Foner, *Organized Labor and the Black Worker 1619–1973,* at 104
     (1974).

38   Id.; Harris, supra note 9, at 41.

39   In re Debs, 158 U.S. at 599–600. Although this injunction was obviously the
     most important event contributing to the strike's failure, thirty years after the
     strike Debs contended that had the union admitted African Americans, "there
     would have been a different story of the strike, for it would certainly have had a
     different result." Foner, supra note 37, at 105.

40   Derrick A. Bell Jr., *Race, Racism and American Law* 37 & n.9 (2d ed. 1980).

41   Osmond K. Fraenkel, "Recent Statutes Affecting Labor Injunctions and Yellow
     Dog Contracts," 30 *Ill. L. Rev.* 854 (1936).

42   Adair v. United States, 208 U.S. 161, 173–80 (1908). The law in question was
     (Erdman) Act of June 1, 1898, ch. 370, § 10, 30 Stat. 424, 428 (1898).

43   Blaine F. Moore, *The Supreme Court and Unconstitutional Legislation* 116
     (1913).

44   Hitchman Coal Co. v. Mitchell, 245 U.S. 229 (1917) (upholding injunction); see
     Coppage v. Kansas, 236 U.S. 1, 26 (1915) (permitting employers to condition
     employment on entry into yellow dog contract); see also Montgomery v. Pacific
     Elec. Ry., 293 R. 680, 689 (9th Cir. 1923) (holding California anti-yellow-dog-
     contract law unconstitutional and upholding injunction against railroad union).

45   Daniel Ernst, "The Yellow-Dog Contract and Liberal Reform, 1917–1932," 30
     Lab. Hist. 251, 254 (1989).

46   Matthews, supra note 14.

47   Willis v. Local No. 106, Hotel and Restaurant Employees International Alliance
     (Court of Common Pleas Cuyahoga County, July 27, 1927).

48   Id.

49   "Limiting Scope of Injunctions in Labor Disputes: Hearings on S. 1482 before a
     Subcomm. of the Senate Comm. on the Judiciary," 70th Cong., 1st Sess. 603–09
     (1928) (statement of Charles W. Chesnutt, Member, Ohio Bar); id. at 609–14
     (statement of Harry E. Davis, Member, Ohio House of Representatives); see
     "Spokesman for Negroes Condemns Anti-Injunction Bill," *Law and Labor,* Feb.
     1929, at 24. For the political context of the Shipstead Bill, see Robert H. Zieger,
     Republicans and Labor, 1919–1929, at 278–80 (1969). On the defeat of the
     yellow dog bill in Ohio, see Ernst, supra note 45, at 253.

50   "Limiting Scope of Injunctions in Labor Disputes," supra note 49, at 605, 607.

51   Id. at 607–09.

52 Id. at 609–14 (statement of Harry E. Davis).

53 William E. Forbath, *Law and the Shaping of the American Labor Movement* 36 (1991).

54 Railway Labor Act of 1934, ch. 691, 48 Stat. 1185 (codified as amended at 45 U.S.C. §§ 151–88 (1988)); Railway Labor Act of 1926, ch. 347, 44 Stat. 577 (amended 1934).

55 Ernst, supra note 45, at 267.

56 See Texas & N.O.R.R. v. Brotherhood of Ry. & S.S. Clerks, 281 U.S. 548, 567–71 (1930).

57 Richard A. Epstein, *Forbidden Grounds* 122 (1992).

58 "To Amend the Railway Labor Act . . . Providing for Union Membership and Agreements for Deduction from Wages of Carrier Employees for Certain Purposes: Hearings before a Subcomm. of the Comm. on Labor and Public Welfare on S. 3295," 81st Cong., 2d Sess. 251 (1950) (statement of Joseph C. Waddy, General Counsel, International Association of Railway Employees) (quoting *Proceedings of 32nd Convention of Brotherhood of Locomotive Firemen and Enginemen,* 1932).

    The 1926 quote is cited in Ira De A. Reid, "Negro Firemen," *The Nation,* Sept. 6, 1933, at 273.

59 Id.; Hill, supra note 14, at 343.

60 T. Arnold Hill, "Railway Employees Rally to Save their Jobs," 12 *Opportunity* 346 (1934).

61 Hill, supra note 14, at 345–46; Northrup, supra note 21, at 54–55; Kate Born, "Memphis Negro Workingmen and the NAACP," 28 *W. Tenn. Hist. Soc'y Papers* 90, 100–11 (1974).

62 G. E. Patterson, vice president of the Illinois Central Railroad, quoted in Hilton Butler, "Murder for the Job," *The Nation,* July 12, 1933, at 44.

63 Railway Labor Act of 1934, ch. 691, 48 Stat. 1185, 1187 (1934) (codified at 45 U.S.C. §§ 151–88 (1988)).

64 Williams, supra note 2, at 31; Railway Labor Act of 1934, § 2(a), 48 Stat. at 1187 ("[I]t shall be unlawful for any carrier . . . to use the funds of the carrier in maintaining or assisting or contributing to any labor organization.").

65 300 U.S. 515 (1937).

66 Note, "Judicial Regulation of the Railway Brotherhoods' Discriminatory Practices," 1953 *Wis. L. Rev.* 516, 517. The Norris-LaGuardia Act was drafted by Donald Richberg, counsel for the railroad brotherhoods. Despite concerns by its supporters at the time of its passage that Norris-LaGuardia was unconstitutional, the Supreme Court upheld it in Lauf v. E. G. Shinner & Co., 303 U.S. 323, 330 (1938). For state bans on labor injunctions, see Forbath, supra note 53, at app. B, n.1.

67 See Railway Labor Act of 1934, § 3(b), 48 Stat. at 1189–97 (establishing NRAB and NMB and delineating their authority); see also Northrup, supra note 21, at 55.

68 Northrup, supra note 21, at 66; Railway Labor Act of 1934, § 3(i), 48 Stat. at 1189–91.

69 Brotherhood of R.R. Trainmen v. A.T. & Santa Fe Ry., N.R.A.B. Award No. 6640 (1st Div. 1942).

70 Railway Labor Act of 1934, § 2, 48 Stat. at 1188.

71 Northrup, supra note 21, at 55–61.

72 T. Arnold Hill, *The Negro and Economic Reconstruction* 56 (1937); Northrup, supra note 21, at 66; National Mediation Board, Case No. R-621 (Apr. 30, 1940), cited in Northrup, supra note 21, at 66.

73 137 F.2d 817 (D.C. Cir.), rev'd, 320 U.S. 715 (1943).

74 Brotherhood of Ry. & S.S. Clerks, 137 F.2d at 818.

75 Brotherhood of Ry. & S.S. Clerks v. United Transp. Serv. Employees, 320 U.S. 715, 719 (1943).

76 Williams, supra note 2, at 32.

77 *Brotherhood of Locomotive Firemen and Enginemen: Proceedings of the Thirty-third Convention* 22, 584–85 (1937); "The Elimination of Negro Firemen on American Railways: A Study of the Evidence Adduced at the Hearing before the President's Committee on Fair Employment Practices," *Lawyers Guild Rev.,* March–April 1944, at 32, 35–36.

78 *The Negro in Virginia,* supra note 22, at 349; Northrup, supra note 21, at 62–65; Charles H. Houston, "Foul Employment Practice on the Rails," *Crisis,* Oct. 1949, at 269, 269.

79 Brotherhood of Locomotive Firemen v. Tunstall, 163 F.2d 289, 291 (4th Cir. 1947).

80 Id.

81 Alexa B. Henderson, "FEPC and the Southern Railway Case: An Investigation into the Discriminatory Practices of Railroads during World War II," 61 *J. Negro Hist.* 173, 181 (1976).

82 Northrup, supra note 21, at 62–65; Henderson, supra note 81, at 178.

83 Henderson, supra note 81, at 192.

84 Ross, supra note 1, at 127; *Lawyers Guild Rev.,* supra note 77, at 33.

85 Ross, supra note 1, at 130.

86 323 U.S. 192 (1944).

87 Risher, supra note 1, at 64; Ross, supra note 1, at 136–37.

88 16 So.2d 416 (Ala. 1943).

89 J. I. Case Co. v. National Labor Relations Bd., 321 U.S. 332, 339 (1944); Epstein, supra note 57, at 120.

90 Id.

91 Ross, supra note 1.

92 Epstein, supra note 57, at 124.

93 Risher, supra note 1, at 149; Williams, supra note 2, at 31; see Rolax v. Atlantic Coast Line R.R., 186 F.2d 473, 480 (4th Cir. 1951) (holding agreement discriminatory and void).

94 Northrup, supra note 21, at xc, 53 (tbl. IIa); Herbert Hill, "The AFL-CIO and the Black Worker: Twenty-Five Years after the Merger," 10 *J. Intergroup Rel.* 5, 20 (1982); Williams, supra note 2, at 33.

95 Edward Berman, "The Pullman Porters Win," *The Nation,* Aug. 21, 1935, at 217. Previously, the union had been ignored by the Pullman company, the government, and the AFL. Harvard Sitkoff, *A New Deal for Blacks: The Emergence of Civil Rights as a National Issue* 25 (1971). For a discussion of the immediate benefits received by African American porters, see T. Arnold Hill, *The Negro and Economic Reconstruction* 56–57 (1937). While then-employed African American sleeping car porters benefited, the rise in wages and benefits may have led the Pullman company to reduce its future hiring of sleeping car porters. African American station porters lost many jobs after the Supreme Court ruled that their positions were covered by the Fair Labor Standards Act. Risher, supra note 1, at 53.

96 Northrup, supra note 21, at 76; Sitkoff, supra note 95, at 175; "Statement of A. Philip Randolph," *Proceedings of the Fifty-fifth Annual Convention of the American Confederation of Labor* 829 (1933).

97 Northrup, supra note 21, at 100; see id. at 93–94.

98 Id. at xc.

4. PREVAILING-WAGE LAWS

1 40 U.S.C. 276a-c (1988).

2 See Ex Parte Kuback, 85 Cal. 274 (1890) (invalidating a law that banned Chinese labor on public works projects, and establishing an eight-hour day); Elmer C. Sandmeyer, *The Anti-Chinese Movement in California* 47–48 (1939) (noting that the Plumbers' and Carpenters' Eight Hour Leagues were leading advocates of anti-Chinese legislation).

3 E.g., Ex Parte Kuback, 85 Cal. 274 (1890).

4 Ex Parte Kuback, 85 Cal. 274 (1890); Baker v. Portland, 2 F. Cas. 472 (D. Ore. 1879); New York Laws of 1894, ch. 622. Grace H. Stimson, *Rise of the Labor Movement in Los Angeles* 100 (1955); 1 *Thirteenth Annual Report of the Bureau of Statistics of Labor of the State of New York* 522, 527, 543–44 (1895); "Employment of Labor on Federal Construction Work: Hearings on H.R. 7995 and H.R. 9232 before the House Comm. on Labor," 71st Cong., 2d Sess., at 15 (1930).

5 Ex Parte Kuback, 85 Cal. 274 (1890); Baker v. Portland, 2 F. Cas. 472 (D. Ore. 1879); People v. Warren, 34 N.Y. Supp. 942 (Sup. Ct. 1895).

6 See City of Chicago v. Hulbert, 68 N.E. 786 (Ill. 1903); see generally Irwin Yellowitz, *Labor and the Progressive Movement in New York State, 1897–1916,* at 29, 149 (1965).

7 Atkin v. Kansas, 191 U.S. 207 (1903). The contrary precedents were City of

Cleveland v. Clements Bros. Constr. Co., 65 N.E. 885 (Ohio 1902); People v. Orange County Road Const. Co., 67 N.E. 129 (N.Y. 1903).

8   Ellis v. United States, 206 U.S. 246 (1907).

9   Holden v. City of Alton, 53 N.E. 556 (Ill. 1899); Fiske v. People, 58 N.E. 985 (Ill. 1900); Street v. Varney Electrical Supply, 66 N.E. 895 (Ind. 1903); Lewis v. Board of Educ., 102 N.W. 756 (Mich. 1905); Wright v. Hoctor, 145 N.W. 704 (Neb. 1914); Wagner v. Milwaukee, 188 N.W. 487 (Wis. 1922).

10   Heim v. McCall, 239 U.S. 175 (1915). The contrary state precedents were Ex Parte Case, 116 P. 1037 (Idaho 1911); People v. Coler, 59 N.E. 716, 721 (N.Y. 1901).

11   Workers of the Writers' Program of the Work Projects Administration in the State of Virginia, *The Negro in Virginia* 352 (reprint ed. 1994) (1940) (discrimination by Richmond); Michael K. Honey, *Southern Labor and Black Civil Rights: Organizing Memphis Workers* 50 (1993); National Conference of Social Work, *The Negro Industrialist* 460 (1928) (Houston government discriminates in public works employment); Raymond Wolters, *Negroes and the Great Depression* 114–15 (1970) (discrimination by various southern governments during the depression); John D. Finney Jr., "A Study of Negro Labor during and after World War I" 193–96 (Ph.D. diss., Georgetown University 1967) (discrimination in various cities relating to World War I construction projects); Lester B. Granger, "Negro Workers and Recovery," *Opportunity,* May 1934, at 153 (discrimination in St. Louis).

12   Charles S. Johnson, "Negro Workers and the Unions," *The Survey,* Apr. 15, 1928, at 113, 114; "Whites Withdraw from Federation Because of Negro Members," *The Birmingham Reporter,* Feb. 7, 1920.

13   William H. Harris, *The Harder We Run: Black Workers since the Civil War* 40 (1982).

14   Herbert Northrup, *Organized Labor and the Negro* 28, 339–40 (reprint ed. 1971).

15   Northrup, supra note 14, at 21; Johnson, supra note 12, at 114; Mark W. Kruman, "Quotas for Blacks: The Public Works Administration and the Black Construction Worker," *Lab. Hist.,* winter 1975, at 38.

16   Northrup, supra note 14, at xc, 7, 44; F. Ray Marshall, "The Negro in Southern Unions," in *The Negro and the American Labor Movement* 128, 145 (J. Jacobson ed., 1968); T. Arnold Hill, "The Plight of the Negro Industrial Worker," 5 *J. Negro Educ.* 40, 43 (1936); Kruman, supra note 15, at 38.

     Northrup exaggerates the extent to which trowel trade unions actually granted African Americans equal status. The plasterers' union, for example, had fewer than one hundred African American members out of thirty thousand union members. Johnson, supra note 12, at 114.

17   Johnson, supra note 12, at 114.

18   See generally W. E. B. Du Bois, *The Negro Artisan* 94–95 (1902); David H.

Gerber, *Black Ohio and the Color Line: 1860–1915,* at 303 (1976); Herbert Hill, *Black Labor and the American Legal System* 22 (1977); Northrup, supra note 14, at 26; Sterling D. Spero & Abram L. Harris, *The Black Worker: The Negro and the Labor Movement* 478–81 (1931); Marshall, supra note 16, at 145.

19 Johnson, supra note 12, at 114; Kruman, supra note 15, at 38–39; Jesse O. Thomas, "The Negro Industrialist," *Nat'l Conf. Social Work Proceedings* 455, 459–60 (1928).

20 F. Ray Marshall, *The Negro and Organized Labor* 21 (1965); see also St. Clair Drake, *Race Relations in a Time of Rapid Social Change* 10 (1966) (discussing rapid increase in African American population in New York and other northern cities).

21 Kruman, supra note 15, at 39.

22 Spero & Harris, supra note 18, at 178 (emphasis added); see also Abraham Epstein, *The Negro Migrant in Pittsburgh* 41 (reprint ed. 1969).

23 Id.; see also T. Arnold Hill, "The Negro in Industry," 32 *American Federationist* 915, 916 (1925).

24 Id.

25 Marshall, supra note 20, at 21.

26 David E. Bernstein, "Licensing Laws: A Historical Example of the Use of Government Regulatory Power against African-Americans," 31 *San Diego L. Rev.* 89, 96 (1994); David E. Bernstein, "The Shameful, Wasteful History of New York's Prevailing Wage Law," 7 *George Mason Civ. Rts. L.J.* 1 (1997); Roger Waldinger & Thomas Bailey, "The Continuing Significance of Race: Racial Conflict and Racial Discrimination in Construction," 19 *Pol. & Soc'y* 291, 301 (1991).

27 Connally v. General Construction Co., 269 U.S. 285 (1926); Campbell v. City of New York, 244 N.Y. 317 (1927).

28 Campbell, 244 N.Y. at 322.

29 People v. Coler, 166 N.Y. 1, 16–17 (1901).

30 Campbell, 244 N.Y. at 329.

31 H.R. 17069, "A Bill to Require Contractors and Subcontractors Engaged on Public Works of the United States to Comply with State Laws Relating to Hours of Labor and Wages of Employees on State Public Works."

32 "Hours of Labor and Wages on Public Works: Hearings on H.R. 17069 before the House Comm. on Labor," 69th Cong., 2d Sess. (1927). It is interesting to compare Representative Bacon's comments with the statements of Mr. Victor Olander, secretary of the Illinois State Federation of Labor, explaining the causes of the 1917 East St. Louis antiblack race riot, which was provoked in large part by the federation: the railroads developed "a general propaganda in East St. Louis to bring them [Negroes] there and dump them there, and to let them run wild in the city without any place to sleep or live after they were through with them. At the time of the riot, every shed and shack in that town

was filled." "Testimony before the Chicago Commission on Race Relations," Aug. 16, 1920, at 8–9.

33   "Hours of Labor and Wages," supra note 32, at 3–4.

34   68 *Cong. Rec.* 5902–03 (1927).

35   68 *Cong. Rec.* 1904 (1927).

36   The bill would have required federal contractors to give preference to residents of the state where the work is performed who are veterans, nonveteran residents, American citizens, and aliens, in that order.

37   68 *Cong. Rec.* 1904 (1927).

38   James J. Davis, *Selective Immigration* 49–50 (1925); Robert H. Zieger, *Republicans and Labor, 1919–1929,* at 84 (1969); Robert H. Zieger, "The Career of James J. Davis," 98 *Penn. Mag. Hist. & Biography* 67, 83 (1973).

39   Id. at 17 (emphasis added).

40   Id. at 21. This testimony also appears in the March 1930 hearings discussed below, at 55.

41   "Employment of Labor," supra note 4, at 5–6.

42   Id. at 6.

43   Id. at 8.

44   Id. at 18.

45   Id.

46   Id. at 26–27 (emphasis added).

47   "Regulation of Hours Paid to Employees by Contractors Awarded Government Building Contracts: Hearings on H.R. 16619 before the Comm. On Labor," 71st Cong., 3d Sess. 20 (1931).

48   "Wages of Laborers and Mechanics on Public Buildings, Hearing on S. 5904 before the Comm. on Manufactures, United States Senate," 71st Cong., 3d Sess. 10 (1931).

49   Id. at 15.

50   74 *Cong. Rec.* at 6510–13.

51   Davis-Bacon Act, ch. 411, 46 Stat. 1494 (1931).

52   Abraham Hoffman, "Stimulus to Repatriation: The 1931 Federal Deportation Drive and the Los Angeles Mexican Community," 42 *Pac. Hist. Rev.* 205 (1973).

53   See Murray Rothbard, *America's Great Depression* 236–37 (3d ed. 1975).

54   Armand J. Thieblot, *The Davis Bacon Act* 11 (1975).

55   For some of the litigation these uncertainties spawned, see United States v. W.S. Barstow & Co., 79 F.2d 496 (4th Cir. 1935); Alliance Const. Co. v. U.S., 79 Ct. Cl. 730 (1934); United States v. Murphy, 11 F. Supp. 572 (W.D. Mich. 1934).

56   Pub. L. No. 403, 74th Cong.

57   Armand J. Thieblot Jr., *Prevailing Wage Legislation* 39–43 (1986). The secretary of labor established a structure for selecting a rate from those collected by a survey of the existing workforce. This method was the secretary's own creation, and a regulatory rather than statutory provision. It remained informal until it

was codified in 1952. Procedures for Predetermination of Wage Rates, 29 C.F.R. §§ 1.1–1.9 (1985).

58 Robert C. Weaver, *Negro Labor: A National Problem* 12 (1948).

59 Id.

60 Id. at 10; William A. Sundstrom, "Down or Out: Unemployment and Occupational Shifts of Urban Black Men during the Great Depression," 16 *Research in Econ. Hist.* 127, 149 (1996).

61 Sundstrom, supra note 60, at 152; Robert C. Weaver, "Negro Labor since 1929," 35 *J. Negro Hist.* 20, 23 (1950); see generally T. Arnold Hill, "The Plight of the Negro Industrial Worker," 5 *J. Negro Educ.* 40, 44 (1936) (noting that African Americans were rarely hired as "wreckers" on slum clearance projects in New York, even though "wrecking" had been a lucrative job source for African Americans).

62 Weaver, supra note 61, at 23.

63 Northrup, supra note 14, at 38.

64 Id. at 21; Weaver, supra note 58, at 16–40; John Payton, "Redressing the Exclusion of and Discrimination against Black Workers in the Skilled Construction Trades: The Approach of the Washington Lawyers' Committee for Civil Rights under Law," 27 *How. L.J.* 1397, 1403–04 (1984).

65 Weaver, supra note 58, at 18–19, 28–32, 35.

66 Northrup, supra note 14, at 34.

67 See generally Merl Elwyn Reed, *Seedtime for the Modern Civil Rights Movement: The President's Committee on Fair Employment Practice, 1941–1946* (1991); Louis Ruchames, *Race, Jobs, & Politics: The Story of the FEPC* (1953).

68 Philip S. Foner, *History of the Labor Movement in the United States: The Politics and Practices of the American Federation of Labor, 1900–1909*, at 238 (1981); Herman D. Bloch, "Craft Unions and the Negro in Historical Perspective," 43 *J. Negro Hist.* 10, 24 (1958).

69 Marshall, supra note 20, at 171 (table A-6).

70 Id. at 219–22; Julius Jacobson, "Union Conservatism: A Barrier to Racial Equality," in *The Negro and the American Labor Movement* 1, 17 (Julius Jacobson ed., 1968).

71 Jacobson, supra note 70.

72 Herbert Hill, "Labor Unions and the Negro," *Commentary,* Dec. 1959, at 479, 486; Herbert Hill, "Racism within Organized Labor: A Report of Five Years of the AFL-CIO, 1955–1960," 30 *J. Negro Educ.* 109, 113 (1961).

73 Marshall, supra note 20, at 226.

74 Herbert Hill, "Black Labor and Affirmative Action: An Historical Perspective," in *The Question of Discrimination* 190, 238, 258 n.181 (Steven Shulman & William Darrity, eds. 1989). On apprenticeships see Marshall, supra note 20, at 123 (table 6-1) (discrimination in New York); Herbert Hill, "Racial Discrimination in the Nation's Apprenticeship Training Programs," *Phylon,* fall 1962, at 215; *Advisory Committees to the United States Commission on Civil Rights,*

Reports on Apprenticeships (1964) (discrimination in California; Connecticut; Washington, D.C.; Florida; Maryland; New Jersey; New York; Tennessee & Wisconsin); Irving Kovarsky, "Apprenticeship Training Programs and Racial Discrimination," 50 *Iowa L.J.* 755 (1965); George Strauss & Sidney Ingerman, "Public Policy and Discrimination in Apprenticeship," 16 *Hastings L.J.* 285 (1965).

75 Quoted in Hill, supra note 18, at 389 n.*.

76 Thieblot, supra note 57, at 59; Payton, supra note 64, at 1411.

77 Paul Craig Roberts & Larry M. Stratton, *The New Color Line* 102 (1995).

78 United States v. Ironworkers Local 86, 443 F.2d 544 (9th Cir. 1971); United States v. Lathers Local 46, 471 F.2d 408 (2d Cir. 1972); International Ass'n Heat & Frost Insulators Local 53 v. Vogler, 407 F.2d 1047 (5th Cir. 1969); United States v. International Bhd. Elec. Workers Local 212, 472 F.2d 634 (6th Cir. 1973); United States v. Carpenters Local 169, 457 F.2d 210 (7th Cir. 1972); Herbert Hill, "The AFL-CIO and the Black Worker: Twenty-Five Years after the Merger," 10 *J. Intergroup Relations* 5, 20 (1982); Payton, supra note 64, at 1407. The Philadelphia Plan was upheld by the Third Circuit in Contractors Ass'n of E. Pa. v. Secretary of Labor, 442 F.2d 159 (3d Cir. 1971).

79 Thieblot, supra note 54, at 157; Comptroller General of the United States, Report to the Congress HRD-79-18: The Davis-Bacon Act Should Be Repealed 32 (April 27, 1979); John P. Gould & George Billingmayer, *The Economics of the Davis-Bacon Act* 62 (1980); William Keyes, "The Minimum Wage and the Davis-Bacon Act: Employment Effects on Minorities and Youth," 3 *J. Lab. Res.* 398, 407 (1982); see also Morgan O. Reynolds, *Power and Privilege: Labor Unions in America* 137 (1984); Kenneth A. Kovatch, "Should the Davis-Bacon Act Be Repealed?" *Bus. Horizons*, Sept.–Oct. 1983, at 33, 33.

80 E.g., "Testimony of Harry C. Allford, President & CEO, Nat'l Black Chamber of Commerce before the House Educ. Comm.," July 25, 1999.

The Reagan administration regulations are published at 29 C.F.R. 21 1.2(a) (July 1, 1989 ed.). These rules were challenged but upheld in Building and Constr. Trades Dept., AFL-CIO v. Donovan, 712 F.2d 611 (D.C. Cir. 1983).

5. NEW DEAL LABOR LAWS

1 Cf. James S. Olsen, "Race, Class, and Progress," in *Black Labor in America* 153, 153–55 (Milton Cantor ed., 1970) (detailing how New Deal legislation maintained racial barriers).

2 United States v. Carolene Prods. Co., 304 U.S. 144, 153 n.4 (1938).

3 Douglas Carl Abrams, "Irony of Reform: North Carolina Blacks and the New Deal," 66 *N.C. Hist. Rev.* 149, 150 (1989); John P. Davis, "NRA Codifies Wage Slavery," 41 *The Crisis* 298, 301–02 (1934).

4 National Industrial Recovery Act, ch. 90, 48 Stat. 195 (1933); Raymond Wolters, *Negroes and the Great Depression* 124–25 (1971); Davis, supra note 3, at

Notes to Chapter 5

298; see also John G. Van Deusen, *The Black Man in White America* 82 (rev. ed. 1944).

5   Harvard Sitkoff, *A New Deal for Blacks: The Emergence of Civil Rights as a National Issue* 54 (1971); Wolters, supra note 4, at 149–51.

6   Sitkoff, supra note 5, at 54; Wolters, supra note 4, at 124–25; Davis, supra note 3, at 301–02.

7   Wolters, supra note 4, at 130–31.

8   Bruce J. Schulman, *From Cotton Belt to Sunbelt: Federal Policy, Economic Development, and the Transformation of the South, 1938–1980,* at 23–25 (1991). Of course, if employers are required to pay higher wages, they will hire better workers and make more and better use of technology. In that sense, requiring higher wages increases the average productivity of employed workers. But the New Dealers claimed that forcing employers to give workers higher wages would raise *existing workers'* productivity by making them happier and healthier, which is quite another matter.

This theory was not unique to the Roosevelt administration. Similar arguments had been used by Progressive economists to justify earlier minimum-wage schemes. Robert E. Prasch, "American Economists and Minimum Wage Legislation during the Progressive Era: 1912–1923," 22 *J. Hist. Econ. Thought* 161 (1998).

9   Schulman, supra note 8, at 22, 29. It should be noted, however, that the textile codes were frequently circumvented. Bryant Simon, *A Fabric of Defeat: The Politics of South Carolina Millhands, 1910–1948* ch. 5 (1998).

10 Edward Aaron Gaston Jr., "A History of the Negro Wage Earner in Georgia, 1890–1940" (1957) (Ph.D. diss., Emory University).

11 Michael K. Honey, *Southern Labor and Black Civil Rights: Organizing Memphis Workers* 25 (1993); Wolters, supra note 4, at 117–18, 141; Abrams, supra note 3, at 151; Gaston, supra note 10, at 404, 407; Arthur F. Raper, "The Southern Negro and the NRA," 64 *Ga. Hist. Q.* 128, 135 (1980). On violence, see Patricia Sullivan, *Days of Hope: Race and Democracy in the New Deal Era* 20–21 (1997); Wolters, supra note 4, at 114–19.

12 Schulman, supra note 8, at 29; Sitkoff, supra note 5, at 54; Wolters, supra note 4, at 118; Gaston, supra note 10, at 406–12; Henry P. Guzda, "Frances Perkins' Interest in a New Deal for Blacks," *Monthly Lab. Rev.,* April 1978, at 31, 34; Michael S. Holmes, "The Blue Eagle as 'Jim Crow Bird': The NRA and Georgia's Black Workers," 57 *J. Negro Hist.* 276, 279 (1972); Raper, supra note 11, at 138.

13 Robert Bell, "Minimum Wage and the Black Worker," 11 *Opportunity* 199, 202 (1933); Wolters, supra note 4, at 94.

14 See Honey, supra note 11, at 26; Sullivan, supra note 11, at 45; Wolters, supra note 4, at 147; Davis, supra note 3, at 303; Gaston, supra note 10, at 405–06; Julian Harris, "Whites Oust Negro under N.R.A. in South," *N.Y. Times,* Aug. 27, 1933, at E6; Ira D. A. Reid, "Black Wages for Black Workers," 12

Opportunity 72, 73–74 (1934) (stating that NRA wage scale destroyed economic incentive to hire blacks); Robert C. Weaver, "A Wage Differential Based on Race," 41 *The Crisis* 236, 242–43 (1934) ("The minimum wage regulations of the NRA . . . resulted in wholesale discharges [of African American workers] in certain areas").

15 Herbert Hill, *Black Labor and the American Legal System* 284 (1977); Schulman, supra note 8, at 24–25. For a contemporary view, see Weaver, supra note 14, at 236–44.

16 Schulman, supra note 8, at 24, 112–13; Wolters, supra note 4, at 104, 112–13. In this context, "socialists" refers to people who favored socialism ideologically, including Communists.

17 Schulman, supra note 8, at 24; Wolters, supra note 4, at 121–22; Roger Biles, "The Urban South in the Great Depression," 56 *J. So. Hist.* 71, 97–98 (1990); Gaston, supra note 10, at 406.

18 Gaston, supra note 10, at 406; Weaver, supra note 14, at 238; see also Wolters, supra note 4, at 102–03.

19 Honey, supra note 11, at 27; Biles, supra note 17, at 97–98; Holmes, supra note 12, at 279–80.

20 Charles F. Roos, *NRA Economic Planning* 173 (1937); Schulman, supra note 8, at 29; Wolters, supra note 4, at 147, 214; Raper, supra note 11, at 134, 139–41.

21 3 Philip Foner, *History of the Labor Movement of the United States: The Policies and Practices of the American Federation of Labor, 1900–1909*, at 27 (1964).

22 Id. at 233–55; Charles Wesley, *Negro Labor in the United States* ch. 9 (1927); Frank Wolfe, *Admission to American Trade Unions* ch. 6 (1912); Eric Arnesen, "Following the Color Line of Labor: Black Workers and the Labor Movement before 1930," 55 *Radical Hist. Rev.* 53, 58 (1993); cf. "Limiting Scope of Injunctions in Labor Disputes: Hearings on S. 1482 before a Subcomm. of the Senate Comm. on the Judiciary," 70th Cong., 1st Sess. 605 (1928) (statement of Charles W. Chesnutt, member, Ohio Bar). In one case, a white steel union helped a company break a strike by an all–African American union. Harry M. McKiven Jr., *Iron and Steel: Class, Race, and Community in Birmingham, Alabama, 1875–1920*, at 125 (1995).

23 Abraham Epstein, *The Negro Migrant in Pittsburgh* 41 (reprint ed. 1969); McKiven, supra note 22, at 4; Sterling D. Spero & Abram L. Harris, *The Black Worker* 21 (1931); Van Deusen, supra note 4, at 56; Price V. Fishback, "Operations of Unfettered Labor Markets," 36 *J. Econ. Lit.* 722, 740 (1998); Bruno Lasker, "Race and the Job," *The Survey*, Oct. 15, 1925, at 77, 77; Robert J. Norrell, "Caste in Steel: Jim Crow Careers in Birmingham, Alabama," 73 *J. Am. Hist.* 669, 670 (1986).

24 W. E. B. Du Bois, *The Negro Artisan* 155 (1902) ("[T]he industrial up-building of the South has brought to the front a number of white mechanics, who from birth have regarded Negroes as inferiors and can with the greatest difficulty be

Notes to Chapter 5

brought to regard them as brothers in this battle for better conditions of labor."); F. Ray Marshall, *The Negro and Organized Labor* 12 (1965) ("the belief was prevalent that Negroes would 'degrade' a trade or occupation"); Herbert R. Northrup, *Organized Labor and the Negro* 50 (rev. ed. 1971); Ira D.A. Reid, *Negro Membership in American Labor Unions* 45 (1930); Spero & Harris, supra note 23, at 287; Lasker, supra note 23, at 77.

25 McKiven, supra note 22, at 170.

26 Id. at 168; see Michael Kazin, *Barons of Labor: The San Francisco Building Trades and Union Power in the Progressive Era* 146–47 (1987); Eric Arnesen, " 'Like Banquo's Ghost, It Will Not Down': The Race Question and the American Railroad Brotherhoods, 1880–1920," *Am. Hist. Rev.* 1601, 1608 (1994). Thus, throughout the late nineteenth and early twentieth centuries, labor unions led the battle against Asian immigrants to the United States, even when these immigrants ceased to compete with union workers to any meaningful degree. Herbert Hill, "Anti-Oriental Agitation and the Rise of Working-Class Racism," *Society,* Jan./Feb. 1973, at 43, 46; see also Roger Daniels, *Asian America: Chinese and Japanese in the United States since 1850,* at 29–30 (1988); Kazin, supra, at 163. This gave unions "far more legitimacy and influence in some of the industrial regions of the Far West than in most other sections of the country." George Frederickson, *White Supremacy* 225 (1981).

27 McKiven, supra note 22, at 170; Arnesen, supra note 26; Norrell, supra note 23, at 691; see generally David Roediger, *The Wages of Whiteness* 10 (1991).

28 Hill, supra note 15, at 21; McKiven, supra note 22 at 30; Gunnar Myrdal, *An American Dilemma* 222–23 (1944).

29 Marshall, supra note 24, at 101.

30 An early 1950s study of employers in North Carolina, for example, concluded that "Employers' attitudes toward labor are largely conditioned by self-interest; firms will use Negro workers when they believe that at a given wage rate Negroes give more satisfactory service than White workers and that their employment will not lead to racial friction." 4 National Planning Association Committee of the South, *Studies of Negro Employment in the Upper South* 212 (1953).

31 McKiven, supra note 22, at 168.

32 Id. at 104; Van Deusen, supra note 4; W. Trotter Jr., "Class and Racial Inequality: The Southern West Virginia Black Coal Miners' Response, 1915–1932," in *Organized Labor in the Twentieth Century South* 60, 62, 74–75 (Robert H. Zieger ed., 1991); Richard Robert Wright, "The Negro Skilled Mechanic in the North," 38 *Southern Workman* 155, 164–65 (1909).

33 Charles S. Johnson, "Negro Workers and the Unions," *The Survey,* Apr. 15, 1928, at 113, 114.

34 Van Deusen, supra note 4, at 59.

35 For example, an AFL official had the chutzpah to write in 1929 that as a rule "the American trade-unionist is more eager to organize the negro than the negro is to

become a member." John P. Frey, "Attempts to Organize Negro Workers," *American Federationist,* March 1929, at 296, 304.

36 Spero & Harris, supra note 23, at 135; W. E. B. Du Bois, "The Denial of Economic Justice to Negroes," *The New Leader,* Feb. 9, 1929, at 43, 46; Kelly Miller, "The Negro as a Workingman," 6 *Am. Mercury* 310, 313 (1925); Booker T. Washington, "The Negro and the Labor Unions," *Atlantic Monthly,* June 1913, at 753, 756.

37 Sitkoff, supra note 5, at 170.

38 McKiven, supra note 22, at 127; see also Paul Street, "The Logic and Limits of 'Plant Loyalty': Black Workers, White Labor, and Corporate Racial Paternalism in Chicago's Stockyards, 1916–1940," 29 *J. Social Hist.* 659 (1996).

39 Wolters, supra note 4, at 172; Julius Jacobson, "Union Conservatism: A Barrier to Racial Equality," in *The Negro and the American Labor Movement* 1, 4 (Julius Jacobson ed., 1968); see also Marc Karson & Ronald Radosh, "The American Federation of Labor and the Negro Worker, 1894–1949," in *The Negro and the American Labor Movement,* supra, at 155, 162.

40 Horace R. Cayton & George S. Mitchell, *Black Workers and the New Unions* 123 (1939).

41 "Union Labor Again," *The Crisis,* Nov. 1934, at 300.

42 Editorial, "The A.F. of L.," 40 *The Crisis* 292 (1933); Hill, supra note 15, at 101; Raymond Wolters, "Section 7a and the Black Worker," 10 *Lab. Hist.* 459, 471 (1969).

43 William H. Harris, *Keeping the Faith* 162 (1977); Wolters, supra note 4, at 182; Broadus Mitchell, *Depression Decade: From New Era through New Deal* 273–74 (1974); Jesse T. Moore Jr., *A Search for Equality: The National Urban League, 1910–1961,* at 82 (1981); Rick Halpern, "The Iron Fist and the Velvet Glove: Welfare Capitalism in Chicago's Packinghouses, 1921–1933," 26 *J. American Stud.* 159, 160 (1992); Street, supra note 38; Wolters, supra note 42, at 469.

44 Sitkoff, supra note 5, at 55.

45 Leslie H. Fishel Jr., "The Negro in the New Deal Era," in *The Negro in Depression and War* 7, 11 (Bernard Sternsler ed., 1969).

46 Hill, supra note 15, at 100. As one historian observes, "[F]ew blacks gained much more than a raise in their cost of living from the NRA." Sitkoff, supra note 5, at 54–55; see also Gaston, supra note 10, at 404; Steve Valocchi, "The Racial Basis of Capitalism and the States, and the Impact of the New Deal on African Americans," 41 *Social Problems* 347, 353 (1994).

47 See John P. Davis, "A Survey of the Problems of the Negro under the New Deal," 5 *J. Negro Educ.* 3 (1936); Lawrence W. Oxley, "Occupations, Negroes, and Labor Organizations," 14 *Occupations* 520, 523 (1936).

48 295 U.S. 495 (1935).

49 Hill, supra note 15, at 100.

50 National Labor Relations (Wagner) Act, ch. 372 § 9, 49 Stat. 449, 453 (1935)

(codified as amended at 29 U.S.C. §§ 151–69 (1988)). For histories of the Wagner Act, see Christopher L. Tomlins, *The State and the Unions: Labor Relations, Law and the Organized Labor Movement in America, 1880–1960* (1985); Mark Barenberg, "The Political Economy of the Wagner Act: Power, Symbol and Workingplace Cooperation," 106 *Harv. L. Rev.* 1379 (1993).

51 See Barenberg, supra note 50.

52 Wolters, supra note 4, at 184; Edna Bonacich, "Advanced Capitalism and Black/White Race Relations in the United States: A Split Labor Market Interpretation," 41 *Am. Soc. Rev.* 34, 46 (1976); Wolters, supra note 42, at 469.

53 Foner, supra note 21, at 215; Raymond Wolters, "Closed Shop and White Shop: The Negro Response to Collective Bargaining, 1933–1935," in *Black Labor in America* 137, 149 (Milton Cantor ed., 1969).

54 Sitkoff, supra note 5, at 52.

55 Hill, supra note 15, at 100; Wolters, supra note 42, at 41.

56 Myrdal, supra note 28, at 398.

57 Nancy J. Weiss, *The National Urban League, 1910–1940,* at 273 (1974) (quoting National Urban League memorandum).

58 Honey, supra note 11, at 85; Jacobson, supra note 39, at 6–7.

59 Judith Stein, "The Ins and Outs of the CIO," 44 *Int'l J. Lab. & Working Class Hist.* 53, 56 (1993).

60 Id. at 56; Rick Halpern, "Organized Labor, Black Workers, and the Twentieth Century South: The Emerging Revision," in *Race and Class in the American South since 1890,* at 43 (Melvyn Stokes and Rick Halpern eds., 1994); Jacobson, supra note 39, at 6.

61 Robert H. Zieger, *The CIO 1935–1955,* at 160 (1995).

62 William B. Gould, *Black Workers in White Unions: Job Discrimination in the United States* 21, 263, 371–72 (1977); Hill, supra note 15, at 190; Kevin Boyle, " 'There Are No Sorrows That the Union Can't Heal': The Struggle for Racial Equality in the United Automobile Workers, 1940–1960," 36 *Lab. Hist.* 5 (1995); Herbert Hill, "The Importance of Race in American Labor History," 9 *Int'l J. Pol. Culture & Soc'y* 317, 325–27 (1995) (hereafter Hill, "Importance"); Herbert Hill, "Myth-Making as Labor History: Herbert Gutman and the United Mine Workers of America," 2 *Int'l J. of Pol., Culture, & Soc'y* 132, 134–36 (1988); Sumner M. Rosen, "The CIO Era, 1935–1955," in *The Negro and the American Labor Movement,* supra note 39, at 188, 200–02; Thomas J. Sugrue, "Segmented Work, Race-Conscious Workers: Structure, Agency and Division in the CIO Era," 41 *Int'l Rev. Social Hist.* 389, 403 (1996).

63 For a recent review of the literature that is highly critical of the CIO, see Herbert Hill, "The Problem of Race in American Labor History," 24 *Revs. Am. Hist.* 189 (1996).

64 See Alan Draper, *Conflict of Interests: Organized Labor and the Civil Rights Movement in the South, 1954–1968,* at 10 (1994); Eric Arnesen, "Up from Exclusion," 26 *Revs. Am. Hist.* 147, 152–53 (1998); Hill, "Importance," supra

note 62, at 326; Rosen, supra note 62, at 200–01; Sugrue, supra note 62, at 392 (noting that African Americans would otherwise fill jobs and work for market wages rather than artificially high union wages).

65 Robin D. G. Kelly, *Race Rebels: Culture, Politics, and the Black Working Class* 80 (1994); Norrell, supra note 23, at 680; Michael Goldfield, "Race and the CIO: The Possibilities for Racial Egalitarianism during the 1930s and 1940s," 44 *Int'l Lab. & Working Class Hist.* 1, 11 (1993).

66 Arnesen, supra note 64, at 155; Jacobson, supra note 39, at 7. Harvey Klehr et al., eds., *The Secret World of American Communism* (1995), documents the dependence of American Communists on orders from the Soviet Union.

67 Goldfield, supra note 65, at 15.

68 Zieger, supra note 61, at 345.

69 Sumner M. Rosen, "The CIO Era, 1935–1955," in *The Negro and the American Labor Movement,* supra note 39, at 190.

70 Herbert Hill interview with Horace Cayton, Nov. 1957, quoted in Hill, "Importance," supra note 62, at 327.

71 *National Planning Association,* supra note 30, at 211; Northrup, supra note 24, at 232–33; Honey, supra note 11, at 280; Goldfield, supra note 65, at 10; Rosen, supra note 62, at 200–01.

72 Robert C. Weaver, *Negro Labor: A National Problem* 139 (1948).

73 See Robert Higgs, *Competition and Coercion: Blacks in the American Economy, 1865–1914,* at 87–89 (1977); Fishback, supra note 23, at 742–43; Robert Higgs, "Black Progress and the Persistence of Racial Economic Inequalities, 1865–1940," in *The Question of Discrimination* 9, 18 (William Darity Jr. & Steven Shulman eds., 1989).

74 Warren C. Whatley, "Getting a Foot in the Door: 'Learning,' State Dependence, and the Racial Integration of Firms," 50 *J. Econ. Hist.* 43, 44 (1990).

75 See, e.g., Wolters supra note 4, at 177.

76 For example, a northern man trying to run a mill near Tuscaloosa, Alabama, with African American employees was threatened by local whites. He was ordered to fire his workers or the whites would take matters into their own hands and "clean them out." Jacqueline Jones, *The Dispossessed* 40 (1992).

77 Cletus E. Daniel, *The ACLU and the Wagner Act* 11 (1980); Morgan O. Reynolds, *Power and Privilege* 125 (1984).

78 NLRB v. Jones & Laughlin Steel Corp., 301 U.S. 1, 30 (1937).

79 Id. at 46; see also Phelps Dodge v. NLRB, 313 U.S. 177 (1941).

80 J. I. Case Co. v. NLRB, 321 U.S. 332, 338 (1944).

81 Atlanta Oak Flooring Co., 62 N.L.R.B. 973, 975 (1945); Larus & Brother Co., 62 N.L.R.B. 1075, 1083 (1945); Veneer Prods., Inc., 81 N.L.R.B. 492, 494 (1948); Miranda Fuel Co., 140 N.L.R.B. 181, 190 (1962), enforcement denied, NLRB v. Miranda Fuel Co., 326 F.2d 172 (2d Cir. 1963); Independent Metal Workers Union, Local No. 1, 147 N.L.R.B. 1573, 1594 (1964); see generally Michael Jordan, "The NLRB Racial Discrimination Decisions, 1935–1964: The

Empiric Process of Administration and the Inner Eye of Racism," 24 *Conn. L. Rev.* 55 (1991).

82   Paul D. Moreno, *From Direct Action to Affirmative Action* 60–61 (1997).

83   Hill, supra note 15, at 97.

84   Fair Labor Standards Act of 1938, ch. 676, 52 Stat. 1060 (1938) (codified as amended at 29 U.S.C. §§ 201–19 (1988)).

85   West Coast Hotel Co. v. Parrish, 300 U.S. 379 (1937); Morehead v. New York ex rel. Tipaldo, 298 U.S. 587 (1936); Adkins v. Children's Hospital, 261 U.S. 525 (1923).

86   300 U.S. at 462.

87   Schulman, supra note 8, at 66; Andrew J. Seltzer, "The Political Economy of the Fair Labor Standards Act," 103 *J. Pol. Econ.* 1302, 1308 (1995).

88   Bureau of Labor Statistics, Bulletin No. 898, at 102, quoted in Schulman, supra note 8, at 64; see also Schulman, supra, at 51, 54, 60, 66.

89   Steve Fraser, "The Labor Question," in *The Rise and Fall of the New Deal Order, 1930–1980,* at 55, 75 (Steve Fraser & Gary Gerstle eds., 1989).

90   Schulman, supra note 8, at 55–56, 59, 71. The AFL took credit for the failure of the FLSA to provide for a lower minimum wage in the South. Elizabeth Brandeis, "Organized Labor and Protective Labor Legislation," in *Labor and the New Deal* 195, 228 (Milton Derber & Edwin Young eds., 1957).

91   Schulman, supra note 8, at 59, 70; Seltzer, supra note 87. Although the minimum-wage proposal was popular with the public at large, the importance of these groups' support for the FLSA should not be discounted. The South's congressional representatives were unable to stop the FLSA or to enact regional wage differentials, but they did manage to ensure that agricultural workers were not covered by the minimum wage. Schulman, supra, at 55. The difference, it seems, is that northern industry and labor unions did not compete with southern agricultural businesses or workers, so no lobbying force counteracted the South's resistance in the agricultural sphere.

92   Myrdal, supra note 28, at 398; Gaston, supra note 10, at 413; Marc Linder, "Farm Workers and the Fair Labor Standards Act: Racial Discrimination in the New Deal," 65 *Tex. L. Rev.* 1335, 1336 (1987).

93   Myrdal, supra note 28, at 398; Gavin Wright, *Old South New South* 219 (1986); Abrams, supra note 3, at 156; William A. Keyes, "The Minimum Wage and the Davis-Bacon Act: Employment Effects on Minorities and Youth," 3 *J. Lab. Res.* 399, 401 (1982).

94   Schulman, supra note 8, at 55–58; Wright, supra note 93, at 225.

95   Schulman, supra note 8, at 56.

96   Id. at 65–66.

97   Eli Ginzberg & Alfred S. Eichner, *The Troublesome Presence: American Democracy and the Negro* 297 (1964); John B. Kirby, *Black Americans in the Roosevelt Era* 223 (1980); Schulman, supra note 8, at 72, 102. The Supreme Court upheld the FLSA in United States v. Darby, 312 U.S. 100, 111 (1941).

Notes to Chapter 5

98 Myrdal, supra note 28, at 397, 398.

99 Richard K. Vedder & Lowell E. Gallaway, *Out of Work: Unemployment and Government in Twentieth Century America* 8 (tbl. 1.3) (1993); Bonacich, supra note 52, at 34; James J. Heckman & J. Hoult Verkerke, "Racial Disparity and Employment Discrimination Law: An Economic Perspective," 8 *Yale L. & Pol'y Rev.* 276, 282 (1990).

100 Wolters, supra note 4, at xi.

101 Valocchi, supra note 46, at 352; see also Ralph J. Bunche, *The Political Status of the Negro in the Age of FDR* 610 (1973); William H. Harris, *The Harder We Run: Black Workers since the Civil War* 100–01 (1982); Schulman, supra note 8, at 20; Sitkoff, supra note 5, at 52–54; Wolters, supra note 4, at 33–34; Wright, supra note 93, at 228–30; John Cogan, "The Decline in Black Teenage Employment: 1950–1970," 72 *Am. Econ. Rev.* 621 (1982).

102 Bunche, supra note 101, at 610; Wright, supra note 93, at 225.

103 Harold Demsetz, "Minorities in the Marketplace," 43 *N.C. L. Rev.* 271, 288 (1965).

104 Reynolds, supra note 77, at 143.

105 Wright, supra note 93, at 246; see also William A. Sundstrom, "Explaining the Racial Unemployment Gap: Race, Region, and the Employment Status of Men," 1940, 50 *Industrial & Lab. Relations Rev.* 460, 475 (1997).

106 Robert W. Fairlie & William A. Sundstrom, "The Emergence, Persistence and Recent Widening of the Racial Unemployment Gap" 20 (draft of May 1988) forthcoming, *Industrial and Labor Relations Review;* Richard Vedder & Lowell Galloway, "Racial Differences in Unemployment in the United States, 1890–1990," 52 *J. Econ. Hist.* 696 (1992); see also Thomas J. Sugrue, *The Origins of the Urban Crisis* 7 (1996).

107 Norrell, supra note 23, at 669, 685, 691; Robert H. Zieger, *The CIO 1935– 1955,* at 349 (1995); Bonacich, supra note 52, at 47–49; Keyes, supra note 93, at 400; Herbert R. Northrup, "Equal Opportunity and Equal Pay," in *The Negro and Employment Opportunity* 85, 87 (Herbert R. Northrup & Richard L. Rowan eds., 1965); Ralph K. Winter Jr., "Improving the Economic Status of Negroes through Laws against Discrimination: A Reply to Professor Sovern," 34 *U. Chi. L. Rev.* 817, 850 (1967).

108 Wright, supra note 93, at 245.

109 Id. at 239.

110 For a discussion, see id. at 247.

111 Letter from Michael J. Klarman, quoted in David E. Bernstein, "The Law and Economics of Post–Civil War Restrictions on Interstate Migration by African-Americans," 76 *Tex. L. Rev.* 781, 847 (1998) (quoted with permission).

112 See Demsetz, supra note 103, at 302.

113 1 Bruce Ackerman, *We the People: Foundations* 146 (1993).

114 Only eighty to ninety thousand of the more than 3.5 million adult African Americans in nine southern states voted in the 1940 presidential election, with

Notes to Chapter 5

a majority of those in Texas. Even worse, the South then was a one-party Democratic system, with primaries in which African Americans could not participate. Abigail & Stephen Thernstrom, *America in Black and White* 66–67 (1998).

115 Id. at 13, 60.

116 Moreno, supra note 82, at 27–28; Donald G. Nieman, *Promises to Keep: African-Americans and the Constitutional Order, 1776 to Present* 101 (1991); David E. Bernstein, "Philip Sober Controlling Philip Drunk: *Buchanan v. Warley* in Historical Perspective," 51 *Vand. L. Rev.* 797, 822 n.113 (1998); Charles Crowe, "Racial Violence and Social Reform: Origins of the Atlanta Riot of 1906," 53 *J. Negro Hist.* 234, 245 (1968); Christopher Silver, "The Racial Origins of Zoning: Southern Cities from 1910–1940," 6 *Planning Perspective* 189, 190 (1991).

117 On Wilson, see Henry Blumenthal, "Woodrow Wilson and the Race Question," 48 *J. Negro Hist.* 1 (1963); Cleveland M. Green, "Prejudices and Empty Promises: Woodrow Wilson's Betrayal of the Negro, 1910–1919," 87 *Crisis* 380 (1980); George C. Osborn, "The Problem of the Negro in Government, 1913," 23 *Historian* 330, 338–39 (1961); Nancy J. Weiss, "The Negro and the New Freedom: Fighting Wilsonian Segregation," 84 *Pol. Sci. Q.* 61, 61 (1969). On Hoover, see George F. Garcia, "Black Disaffection from the Republican Party during the presidency of Herbert Hoover, 1928–1932," 45 *Annals of Iowa* 462 (1980).

118 John P. Davis, "A Survey of the Problems of the Negro under the New Deal," 5 *J. Negro Educ.* 3, 11 (1936); T. Arnold Hill, "The Plight of the Negro Industrial Worker," 5 *J. Negro Educ.* 40, 40 (1936).

Abrams suggests that the following factors motivated African American support for the New Deal:

> As meager as the government's material assistance was, it was more than they might have expected otherwise. The New Deal, moreover, did not exclude African-Americans, and that in itself was progress. Although no important Civil Rights legislation was adopted during Roosevelt's terms as president, he did denounce lynching, appointed Afro-Americans to more important posts than they ever held, and sponsored New Deal policies that at least broke the pattern of racial discrimination. The Republicans had no sympathy for direct relief, and under President Herbert Hoover they had sought to build a lily-white GOP in the South.

Abrams, supra note 3, at 176; see also Nancy J. Weiss, *Farewell to the Party of Lincoln: African-American Politics in the Age of FDR* (1983).

However, when Republican presidential candidate Wendell Willkie campaigned for black votes, many African Americans returned to the GOP. Id. According to one source, almost 50 percent of African Americans voted for Willkie. James J. Kenneally, "Black Republicans during the New Deal: The

Role of Joseph W. Martin, Jr.," 55 *Rev. Pol.* 117, 120 (1993). Because most African American voters at the time lived in the North where Democratic machines actively solicited their votes, it is possible that a clear majority of African Americans nationwide preferred Willkie.

119   "Historians, seeking a nascent civil rights movement in the 1930s, have given perhaps too much credit to the New Deal." Abrams, supra note 3, at 178.

120   Paul Burstein, *Discrimination, Jobs, and Politics* 46 (1998); J. R. Pole, *The Pursuit of Equality in American History* 256 (1978); Sugrue, supra note 106, at 9.

121   Mary L. Dudziak, "Desegregation as a Cold War Imperative," 41 *Stan. L. Rev.* 61, 62 (1988).

122   See Sugrue, supra note 106, at 9; Michael J. Klarman, "*Brown,* Racial Change, and the Civil Rights Movement," 80 *Va. L. Rev.* 7, 30–39, 133–40 (1994).

123   Cf. Ackerman, supra note 113, at 110.

124   Mark V. Tushnet, "Progressive Era Race Relations Cases in Their 'Traditional' Context," 51 *Vand. L. Rev.* 993, 995–96 (1998).

125   Plessy, 163 U.S. at 559. Harlan also emphasized that the segregation law at issue in *Plessy* was "caste legislation," a particularly pernicious subset of class legislation. Id. For other examples of arguments that Jim Crow laws were "class legislation," see Bernstein, supra note 116.

126   But cf. Buchanan v. Warley, 245 U.S. 60 (1917) (invalidating residential segregation law on Lochnerian grounds).

127   Michael J. Klarman, "Constitutional Fact/Constitutional Fiction: A Critique of Bruce Ackerman's Theory of Constitutional Moments," 44 *Stan. L. Rev.* 759 (1992).

128   See Bernstein, supra note 116.

129   William G. Ross, *A Muted Fury: Populists, Progressives, and Labor Unions Confront the Courts, 1890–1937,* at 66 (1994); Bernstein, supra note 116, at 832–33, 836–40.

130   E.g., Roberts v. United States Jaycees, 468 U.S. 609, 614 (1984); Bob Jones University v. United States, 461 U.S. 574 (1983).

131   Moreno, supra note 82, at 29.

132   Eric Foner, *Reconstruction: America's Unfinished Revolution* (1989); David Montgomery, *Beyond Equality: Labor and the Radical Republicans 1862–72* (1967). Douglass argued that African Americans needed no special assistance from the government. When asked, "What shall we do with the Negro?" he responded: "Do Nothing with us! . . . if the Negro cannot stand on his own legs let him fall." Douglass did not want African Americans to "become wards of the state or the object of 'class legislation.' " George Frederickson, *Black Liberation* 29 (1995).

   Some historians argue that classical liberal ideology was to blame for the failure of Reconstruction. E.g., Foner, supra at 507; Montgomery, supra, at 446–47; John G. Sproat, *"The Best Men": Liberal Reformers in the Gilded*

Age 15 (1968); Bertram Wyatt-Brown, Introduction to Moorefield Storey, *Charles Sumner* at xvi (Arthur M. Schlesinger Jr. ed., 1983) (1900). This literature is too broad to be dissected in a footnote, but one can much more easily conclude that racism unrelated to classical liberal ideology as such should bear the brunt of the blame.

CONCLUSION

1   This sparse literature includes William Cohen, *At Freedom's Edge: Black Mobility and the Southern White Quest for Racial Control, 1861–1915* (1991); Jennifer Roback, "Southern Labor Law in the Jim Crow Era: Exploitative or Competitive?" 51 *U. Chi. L. Rev.* 1161, 1169 (1984).

2   Mancur Olson Jr., *The Logic of Collective Action* (1965). As Robert Cooter explains, "discriminatory social groups suffer the same problems of instability as any other cartel. To sustain discriminatory norms, evaders must be punished by a combination of informal sanctions and formal laws." Robert Cooter, "Market Affirmative Action," 31 *San Diego L. Rev.* 133, 156 (1994).

3   See Gary S. Becker, "Pressure Groups and Political Behavior," in *Capitalism and Democracy: Schumpeter Revisited,* 120, 124 (Richard D. Coe & Charles K. Wilber eds., 1985).

4   It is true that interest groups face serious collective action problems even when they are acting in the political sphere, but these problems can be overcome through entrepreneurial strategies. See William R. Dougan & James M. Snyder, "Are Rents Fully Dissipated?" 77 *Pub. Choice* 793, 810 (1993).

    Moreover, politicians sometimes propose legislation that is only weakly desired by any particular bloc of voters. It would not be efficient for anyone to lobby spontaneously for such legislation. But because politicians are, in such cases, paying all the information costs, eliminating the costs of lobbying, and offering the legislation essentially for free (for the price of hoped-for political support), economic theory suggests that such legislation can become law. Jennifer Roback, "Racism as Rent Seeking," 27 *Econ. Inquiry* 661 (1989).

5   Richard A. Epstein, *Forbidden Grounds* (1992).

6   E.g., Norman C. Amaker, "Quittin' Time? The Antidiscrimination Principle of Title VII vs. The Free Market," 60 *U. Chi. L. Rev.* 757, 768 (1993); Gregory S. Crespi, "Market Magic: Can the Invisible Hand Strangle Bigotry?" 72 *B.U.L. Rev.* 991, 1010 (1992); John J. Donohue, "Advocacy versus Analysis in Assessing Employment Discrimination Law," 44 *Stan. L. Rev.* 1583, 1594 (1992); J. Hoult Verkerke, "Free to Search," 105 *Harv. L. Rev.* 2080, 2089–94 (1992).

7   Ian Ayres, "Price and Prejudice," *New Republic,* July 6, 1992, at 30, 31; Ian Ayres, "Alternative Grounds: Epstein's Discrimination Analysis in Other Market Settings," 31 *San Diego L. Rev.* 67, 68 (1994).

8   On violence, see 7 *African American Life in the Post-Emancipation South, 1861–1900: Black Freedom/White Violence, 1865–1900* (Donald G. Nieman

ed., 1994); Aremona G. Bennett, "Phantom Freedom: Official Acceptance of Violence to Personal Security and Subversion of Proprietary Rights and Ambitions Following Emancipation, 1865–1910," 70 *Chi.-Kent L. Rev.* 439, 461–69 (1994). On public education, see Robert A. Margo, *Race and Schooling in the South, 1880–1950* (1990).

9   Epstein acknowledges the role of social mores, at least with regard to the Jim Crow South. See Richard A. Epstein, "The Status Production Sideshow: Why the Antidiscrimination Laws Are Still a Mistake," 108 *Harv. L. Rev.* 1085, 1100 (1995). Epstein's broader thesis regarding the utility of modern employment discrimination laws is well beyond the scope of this book.

10 Price V. Fishback, "Operations of 'Unfettered' Labor Markets: Exit and Voice in American Labor Markets at the Turn of the Century," 36 *J. Econ. Lit.* 722, 741 (1998); Robert A. Margo, "Segregated Schools and the Mobility Hypothesis: A Model of Local Government Discrimination," 106 *Q.J. Econ.* 61, 62 (1991); Jennifer Roback, "Racism as Rent Seeking," 27 *Econ. Inquiry* 661, 661 (1989).

11 See, e.g., Desmond King, *Separate and Unequal: Black Americans and the US Federal Government* (1995) (focusing on the contribution of federal government policies to racial segregation).

12 Cf. Bruce A. Ackerman, "Beyond *Carolene Products*," 98 *Harv. L. Rev.* 713, 723–31 (1985); see generally Olson, supra note 2.

13 Given the inefficiency of most regulations, it is unlikely that modern Lochnerian jurisprudence would harm African Americans in absolute terms, regardless of its relative effects on them. On the inefficiency of most regulations, see, e.g., Ronald Coase, "Economists and Public Policy," in *Large Corporations in a Changing Society* 184 (J. Fred Weston ed., 1974).

14 The sources quoted, in order, are Robert McCloskey, *The American Supreme Court* 84 (1951); Gary D. Rowe, "The Legacy of *Lochner*: *Lochner* Revisionism Revisited," 24 *Law & Soc. Inquiry* 221, 222 (1999); William M. Wiecek, *Liberty under Law: The Supreme Court in American Life* 126 (1988); Bernard Schwartz, *A History of the Supreme Court* 202 (1993).

15 In addition to the sources cited in the next two footnotes, see Herbert Hovenkamp, "The Political Economy of Substantive Due Process," 40 *Stan. L. Rev.* 379, 390 (1988); Jennifer Roback, "Rules v. Discretion: *Berea College v. Kentucky*," 20 *Int'l J. Group Tensions* 47, 51 (1990); David E. Bernstein, Note, "The Supreme Court and 'Civil Rights,' 1886–1908," 100 *Yale L.J.* 725, 742 (1990).

16 See David E. Bernstein, "*Lochner*, Parity, and the Chinese Laundry Cases," 41 *Wm. & Mary L. Rev.* 211 (1999); David E. Bernstein, "The Shameful, Wasteful History of New York's Prevailing Wage Law," 7 *Geo. Mason U. Civ. Rts. L.J.* 1 (1997); David E. Bernstein, "Philip Sober Controlling Philip Drunk: *Buchanan v. Warley* in Historical Perspective," 51 *Vand. L. Rev.* 797 (1998); James W. Ely Jr., "Reflections on *Buchanan v. Warley*, Property Rights, and Race," 51 *Vand. L. Rev.* 953 (1998); Richard A. Epstein, "Lest We Forget: *Buchanan v. Warley*

Notes to Conclusion

159

and Constitutional Jurisprudence in the Progressive Era," 51 *Vand. L. Rev.* 787 (1998); William A. Fischel, "Why Judicial Reversal of Apartheid Made a Difference," 51 *Vand. L. Rev.* 975 (1998).

17 Bernard Siegan, *Economic Liberties and the Constitution* (1980); James W. Ely Jr., "Melville W. Fuller Reconsidered," 1998 *J. Sup. Ct. Hist.* 32, 46; Norman Karlin, "Back to the Future: From *Nollan* to *Lochner*," 17 *Sw. U.L. Rev.* 627, 666–70 (1988); Jonathan R. Macey, "Public Choice, Public Opinion, and the Fuller Court," 49 *Vand. L. Rev.* 373 (1996); Geoffrey P. Miller, "Public Choice at the Dawn of the Special Interest State: The Story of Butter and Margarine," 77 *Calif. L. Rev.* 83 (1989); Geoffrey P. Miller, "The True Story of Carolene Products," 1987 *Sup. Ct. Rev.* 397; Keith Poole & Howard Rosenthal, "The Enduring Nineteenth Century Battle for Economic Regulation: The Interstate Commerce Act Revisited," 36 *J.L. & Econ.* 837 (1993); Christopher T. Wonnell, "Economic Due Process and the Preservation of Competition," 11 *Hastings Const. L.Q.* 91, 95–96 (1983).

18 This problem continues to bedevil economically oriented libertarian theorists. See Daniel Polsby, "What If This Is As Good As It Gets?" 2 *Green Bag* 2d 115 (1998) (reviewing Richard A. Epstein, *Simple Rules for a Complex World* (1995)).

19 See, e.g., Ronald Coase, "Economists and Public Policy," in *Large Corporations in a Changing Society* 184 (J. Fred Weston, ed., 1974); Bernard H. Siegan, "Separation of Powers & Economic Liberties," 70 *Notre Dame L. Rev.* 415, 475 (1995). The Supreme Court opinion referenced is Planned Parenthood v. Casey, 505 U.S. 833, 861–62 (1992).

20 For a published example of this thesis, Eric Arnesen, *Waterfront Workers of New Orleans: Race, Class, and Politics, 1863–1923* (1991); see also Arthur F. McEvoy, "Freedom of Contract, Labor, and the Administrative State," in *The State and Freedom of Contract* 198, 222 (Harry Scheiber ed., 1998) (arguing that defense of free labor markets by Lochnerian courts in the face of "growing inequalities of wealth and power" "turned the free labor idealism of the *Slaughterhouse* dissents into a cruel and deadly joke").

21 This argument is made in published form by Edna Bonacich, "The Split Labor Market," 37 *Am. Soc. Rev.* 547, 553–58 (1972).

22 F. A. Harper, *Why Wages Rise* 13 (1957) (IHS ed. 1978).

23 Id. at 18.

24 Id. at 19; see also Henry Hazlitt, *Economics in One Lesson* 140 (Arlington House edition 1979) ("The belief that labor unions can substantially raise real wages over the long run . . . is one of the great delusions of the present age"); Bernard Siegan, *Economic Liberties and the Constitution* 125 (1980) (noting improvement of standard of living in the U.S. between Civil War and World War I, despite "relatively few welfare laws and unions"). For international comparisons, see E.H. Phelps Brown, *A Century of Pay* (1968); E.H. Phelps Brown, *Pay and Profit* (1968).

Notes to Conclusion

For a simple explanation of the economics involved, see Hazlitt, supra, chap. 20; see generally Morgan O. Reynolds, "The Myth of Labor's Inequality of Bargaining Power," 12 *J. Lab. Res.* 167 (1991).

25 Albert Rees, *The Economics of Trade Unions* 87–89 (3d ed. 1989); see also Hazlitt, supra note 24; Douglass C. North, *Growth and Welfare in the American Past* 179 (1966).

Bibliography

Newspaper articles are cited in the notes but not listed in the bibliography.

GOVERNMENT REPORTS AND CONGRESSIONAL HEARINGS

Advisory Committees to the United States Commission on Civil Rights, *Reports on Apprenticeships* (1964).
Comptroller General of the United States, *Report to the Congress HRD-79-18: The Davis-Bacon Act Should Be Repealed* (April 27, 1979).
Journal of the Senate of the General Assembly of the State of North Carolina (1881).
Thirteenth Annual Report of the Bureau of Statistics of Labor of the State of New York vol. 1 (1895).
"Employment of Labor on Federal Construction Work: Hearings on H.R. 7995 and H.R. 9232 before the House Comm. on Labor," 71st Cong., 2d Sess. (1930).
"Hours of Labor and Wages on Public Works: Hearings on H.R. 17069 before the House Comm. on Labor," 69th Cong., 2d Sess. (1927).
"Limiting Scope of Injunctions in Labor Disputes: Hearings on S. 1482 before a Subcomm. of the Senate Comm. on the Judiciary," 70th Cong., 1st Sess. (1928).
"Regulation of Hours Paid to Employees by Contractors Awarded Government Building Contracts: Hearings on H.R. 16619 before the Comm. on Labor," 71st Cong., 3d Sess. (1931).
"Testimony of Harry C. Allford, President & CEO, Nat'l Black Chamber of Commerce before the House Educ. Comm.," July 25, 1999.
"Testimony Taken by the Joint Select Comm. to Inquire into the Condition of Affairs in the Late Insurrectionary States," *H.R. Rep. No.* 42–22 (1872).
"To Amend the Railway Labor Act . . . Providing for Union Membership and Agreements for Deduction from Wages of Carrier Employees for Certain Purposes: Hearings before a Subcomm. of the Comm. on Labor and Public Welfare on S. 3295," 81st Cong., 2d Sess. (1950).
"Wages of Laborers and Mechanics on Public Buildings, Hearing on S. 5904 before the Comm. on Manufactures, United States Senate," 71st Cong., 3d Sess. (1931).

BOOKS

Ackerman, Bruce. *We the People: Foundations* (1993).
Anderson, Eric. *Race and Politics in North Carolina 1872–1901* (1981).
Arnesen, Eric. *Waterfront Workers of New Orleans: Race, Class, and Politics, 1863–1923* (1991).
Athearn, Robert G. *In Search of Canaan: Black Migration to Kansas, 1879–80* (1978).

Ayers, Edward L. *The Promise of the New South: Life after Reconstruction* (1992).

Baker, Ray Stannard. *Following the Color Line: An Account of Negro Citizenship in the American Democracy* 80 (Corner House 1973) (1908).

Barry, John M. *Rising Tide: The Great Mississippi Flood of 1927 and How It Changed America* (1997).

Bell, Derrick A., Jr. *Race, Racism and American Law* (2d ed. 1980).

Berger, Raoul. *Government by Judiciary: The Transformation of the Fourteenth Amendment* (1977).

Bork, Robert. *The Tempting of America* (1990).

Brock, William. *An American Crisis: Congress and Reconstruction 1865–1867* (1967).

Brotherhood of Locomotive Firemen and Enginemen: Proceedings of the Thirty-third Convention (1937).

Brotz, Howard, ed. *Negro Social and Political Thought, 1850–1920* (1966).

Buckley, F. H., ed. *The Fall and Rise of Freedom of Contract* (1999).

Bunche, Ralph J. *The Political Status of the Negro in the Age of FDR* (1973).

Burrow, J. *Organized Medicine in the Progressive Era: The Move toward Monopoly* (1977).

Burstein, Paul. *Discrimination, Jobs, and Politics* (1998).

Cantor, Milton, ed. *Black Labor in America* (1970).

Cayton, Horace R. & George S. Mitchell. *Black Workers and the New Unions* (1939).

Cobb, James C. *The Most Southern Place on Earth: The Mississippi Delta and the Roots of Regional Identity* (1992).

Coe, Richard D. & Charles K. Wilber, eds. *Capitalism and Democracy: Schumpeter Revisited* (1985).

Cohen, William. *At Freedom's Edge: Black Mobility and the Southern White Quest for Racial Control, 1861–1915* (1991).

Cooper, William J. et al., eds. *A Master's Due* (1985).

Cox, Archibald. *The Court and the Constitution* (1987).

Crow, Jeffrey J. & Flora J. Hatley, eds. *Black Americans in North Carolina and the South* (1984).

Daniel, Cletus E. *The ACLU and the Wagner Act* (1980).

Daniel, Pete. *The Shadow of Slavery: Peonage in the South, 1901–1969* (1972).

Daniels, Roger. *Asian America: Chinese and Japanese in the United States since 1850* (1988).

Darity, William, Jr. & Steven Shulman, eds. *The Question of Discrimination* (1989).

Davis, James J. *Selective Immigration* (1925).

Delancy, Francis. *The Licensing of Professions in West Virginia* (1938).

Derber, Milton & Edwin Young, eds. *Labor and the New Deal* (1957).

DeSantis, Alan D. *Selling the American Dream: The Chicago Defender and the Great Migration of 1915–1919* (1994).

Donald, Henderson H. *The Negro Migration of 1916–1918* (1921).

Drake, St. Clair. *Race Relations in a Time of Rapid Social Change* (1966).

Draper, Alan. *Conflict of Interests: Organized Labor and the Civil Rights Movement in the South, 1954–1968* (1994).

Du Bois, W. E. B. *The Negro Artisan* (1902).

Ely, James W. Jr. *The Chief Justiceship of Melville W. Fuller, 1888–1910* (1995).

Ely, John Hart. *Democracy and Distrust: A Theory of Judicial Review* (1980).

Epstein, Abraham. *The Negro Migrant in Pittsburgh* (reprint ed. 1969).

Epstein, Richard A. *Forbidden Grounds: The Case against Employment Discrimination Laws* (1992).

Flexner, Abraham. *Medical Education in the United States and Canada* (1910).

Fligstein, Neil. *Going North: Migration of Blacks and Whites from the South, 1900–1950* (1981).

Foner, Eric. *Reconstruction: America's Unfinished Revolution* (1989).

Foner, Philip. *History of the Labor Movement of the United States: The Policies and Practices of the American Federation of Labor, 1900–1909* (1964).

——. *Organized Labor and the Black Worker 1619–1973* (1974).

Forbath, William E. *Law and the Shaping of the American Labor Movement* (1991).

Fraser, Steve & Gary Gerstle, eds. *The Rise and Fall of the New Deal Order, 1930–1980* (1989).

Frederickson, George. *Black Liberation* (1995).

——. *White Supremacy* (1981).

Gellhorn, Walter. *Individual Freedom and Government Restraints* (1968).

Gerber, David H. *Black Ohio and the Color Line, 1860–1915* (1976).

Gillman, Howard. *The Constitution Besieged: The Rise and Demise of Lochner Era Police Powers Jurisprudence* (1993).

Ginzberg, Eli & Alfred S. Eichner. *The Troublesome Presence: American Democracy and the Negro* (1964).

Gottlieb, Peter. *Making Their Own Way* (1987).

Gould, John P. & George Billingmayer. *The Economics of the Davis-Bacon Act* (1980).

Gould, William B. *Black Workers in White Unions: Job Discrimination in the United States* (1977).

Greene, Lorenzo & Carter G. Woodson. *The Negro Wage Earner* (1930).

Grossman, James R. *Land of Hope: Chicago, Black Southerners, and the Great Migration* (1989).

Haines, Charles Grove. *Revival of Natural Law Concepts* (1958).

Harris, William H. *The Harder We Run: Black Workers since the Civil War* (1982).

——. *Keeping the Faith* (1977).

Harrison, Alferdteen, ed. *Black Exodus* (1991).

Henri, Florette, *Black Migration* (1975).

Higgs, Robert. *Competition and Coercion: Blacks in the American Economy, 1865–1914* (1977).

Hill, Herbert. *Black Labor and the American Legal System* (1977).

Bibliography

Hill, T. Arnold. *The Negro and Economic Reconstruction* (1937).

Hine, Darlene Clark. *Black Women in White: Racial Conflict and Cooperation in the Nursing Profession 1890–1950* (1989).

Hofstader, Richard. *Social Darwinism in American Thought* (rev. ed. 1955).

Honey, Michael K. *Southern Labor and Black Civil Rights: Organizing Memphis Workers* (1993).

Hunter, Tera W. *To 'Joy My Freedom: Southern Black Women's Lives and Labors after the Civil War* (1997).

Jacobs, Clyde E. *Law Writers and the Courts: The Influence of Thomas E. Cooley, Christopher G. Tiedeman, and John F. Dillon upon American Constitutional Law* (1954).

Jacobson, Julius, ed. *The Negro and the American Labor Movement* (1968).

Jaynes, Gerald David. *Branches without Roots: Genesis of the Black Working Class in the American South, 1862–1882* (1986).

Johnson, Daniel M. & Rex R. Campbell. *Black Migration in America* (1981).

Jones, Jacqueline. *The Dispossessed* (1992).

Kazin, Michael. *Barons of Labor: The San Francisco Building Trades and Union Power in the Progressive Era* (1987).

Kelly, Robin D. G. *Race Rebels: Culture, Politics, and the Black Working Class* (1994).

Kens, Paul. *Judicial Power and Reform Politics: The Anatomy of Lochner v. New York* (1990).

King, Desmond. *Separate and Unequal: Black Americans and the US Federal Government* (1995).

Kirby, John B. *Black Americans in the Roosevelt Era* (1980).

Klehr, Harvey et al., eds. *The Secret World of American Communism* (1995).

Klineberg, Otto. *Negro Intelligence and Selective Migration* (1935).

Kolchin, Peter. *First Freedom: The Responses of Alabama's Blacks to Emancipation and Reconstruction* (1972).

Lichtenstein, Alex. *Twice the Work of Free Labor: The Political Economy of Convict Labor in the New South* (1996).

Litwack, Leon F. *Trouble in Mind* (1998).

Logan, Frenise A. *The Negro in North Carolina 1876–1894* (1964).

Logan, Rayford. *The Betrayal of the Negro* (1965).

Maltz, Earl. *Civil Rights, the Constitution and Congress, 1863–1869* (1990).

Margo, Robert A. *Race and Schooling in the South, 1880–1950: An Economic History* (1990).

——. *Schooling and the Great Migration*. National Bureau of Economic Research Working Paper No. 2697 (1988).

Marks, Carole. *Farewell — We're Good and Gone: The Great African American Migration* (1989).

Marshall, F. Ray. *The Negro and Organized Labor* (1965).

McClain, Charles J. *In Search of Equality: The Chinese Struggle against Discrimination in Nineteenth Century America* (1996).

McCloskey, Robert. *The American Supreme Court* (1951).

McKiven, Harry M., Jr. *Iron and Steel: Class, Race, and Community in Birmingham, Alabama, 1875–1920* (1995).

McMillen, Neil R. *Dark Journey, Black Mississippians in the Age of Jim Crow* (1989).

Meier, August. *Negro Thought in America, 1880–1915: Racial Ideologies in the Age of Booker T. Washington* (1963).

Mitchell, Broadus. *Depression Decade: From New Era through New Deal* (1974).

Montgomery, David. *Beyond Equality: Labor and the Radical Republicans 1862–72* (1967).

Moore, Blaine F. *The Supreme Court and Unconstitutional Legislation* (1913).

Moore, Jesse T., Jr. *A Search for Equality: The National Urban League, 1910–1961* (1981).

Morais, Herbert M. *The History of the Afro-American in Medicine* (rev. ed. 1976).

Moreno, Paul D. *From Direct Action to Affirmative Action* (1997).

Myrdal, Gunnar. *An American Dilemma: The Negro Problem and Modern Democracy* (1944).

National Conference of Social Work. *The Negro Industrialist* (1928).

National Interracial Congress. *Toward Interracial Cooperation* (1926).

National Planning Association Committee of the South. *Studies of Negro Employment in the Upper South* (1953).

Nelson, William. *The Fourteenth Amendment: From Political Principle to Judicial Doctrine* (1988).

Nieman, Donald G., ed. *African American Life in the Post-Emancipation South, 1861–1900: Black Freedom/White Violence, 1865–1900* (1994).

———. *Promises to Keep: African-Americans and the Constitutional Order, 1776 to Present* (1991).

———, ed. *From Slavery to Sharecropping: White Land and Black Labor in the Rural South, 1865–1900* (1994).

Nordhoff, Charles. *The Cotton States in the Spring and Summer of 1875* (1876).

Northrup, Herbert R. *Organized Labor and the Negro* (rev. ed. 1971).

Northrup, Herbert R. & Richard L. Rowan, eds. *The Negro and Employment Opportunity* (1965).

Novak, Daniel. *The Wheel of Servitude: Black Forced Labor after Slavery* (1978).

Novak, William. *The People's Welfare* (1996).

O'Brien, Ruth. *Workers' Paradox: The Republican Origins of New Deal Labor Policy, 1886–1935* (1998).

Olson, Mancur, Jr. *The Logic of Collective Action* (1965).

Painter, Nell Irvin. *Exodusters: Black Migration to Kansas after Reconstruction* (1977).

Paul, Arnold M. *Conservative Crisis and the Rule of Law: Attitudes of Bar and Bench, 1887–1895* (1960).

Peterson, Florence. *American Labor Unions* (1945).

Pickens, William. *Bursting Bonds: The Heir of Slaves* (enlarged ed. 1929).

Pole, J. R. *The Pursuit of Equality in American History* (1978).

Proceedings of the Fifty-fifth Annual Convention of the American Confederation of Labor (1933).

Ransom, Roger L. & Richard Sutch. *One Kind of Freedom: The Economic Consequences of Emancipation* (1977).

Raper, Arthur F. Preface to *Peasantry: A Tale of Two Black Belt Counties* (2d ed. 1968).

——. *Tenants of the Almighty* (1943).

Reaves, Richard. *The Law of Professional Licensing and Certification* (1984).

Reed, Merl Elwyn. *Seedtime for the Modern Civil Rights Movement: The President's Committee on Fair Employment Practice, 1941–1946* (1991).

Reid, Ira D.A. *Negro Membership in American Labor Unions* (1930).

Reynolds, Morgan O. *Power and Privilege: Labor Unions in America* (1984).

Rice, Thaddeus B. & Carolyn W. Williams. *History of Greene County, Georgia* (1961).

Risher, Howard W., Jr. *The Negro in the Railroad Industry* (1971).

Roberts, Paul Craig & Larry M. Stratton. *The New Color Line* (1995).

Roediger, David. *The Wages of Whiteness* (1991).

Roos, Charles F. *NRA Economic Planning* (1937).

Ross, Malcolm. *All Manner of Men* (1948).

Ross, William G. *A Muted Fury: Populists, Progressives, and Labor Unions Confront the Courts, 1890–1937* (1994).

Rothbard, Murray. *America's Great Depression* (3d ed. 1975).

Rottenberg, Simon, ed. *Occupational Licensing and Regulation* (1980).

Ruchames, Louis. *Race, Jobs, and Politics: The Story of the FEPC* (1953).

Sandmeyer, Elmer C. *The Anti-Chinese Movement in California* (1939).

Scheiber, Harry, ed. *The State and Freedom of Contract* (1998).

Schulman, Bruce J. *From Cotton Belt to Sunbelt: Federal Policy, Economic Development, and the Transformation of the South, 1938–1980* (1991).

Schwartz, Bernard. *A History of the Supreme Court* (1993).

Scott, William. *The Journeyman Barbers' International Union of America* (1936).

Shimberg, Benjamin, Barbara F. Esser, & Daniel H. Kruger. *Occupational Licensing: Practices and Policies* (1972).

Siegan, Bernard. *Economic Liberties and the Constitution* (1980).

Simon, Bryant. *A Fabric of Defeat: The Politics of South Carolina Millhands, 1910–1948* (1998).

Sitkoff, Harvard. *A New Deal for Blacks: The Emergence of Civil Rights as a National Issue* (1971).

Slichter, Sumner H. *Union Policies and Industrial Management* (1940).

Bibliography

Spero, Sterling D. & Abram L. Harris. *The Black Worker: The Negro and the Labor Movement* (1931).

Sproat, John G. *"The Best Men": Liberal Reformers in the Gilded Age* (1968).

Stephenson, Gilbert Thomas. *Race Distinctions in American Law* (Mnemosyne Publishing Co. 1969) (1910).

Sternsler, Bernard, ed. *The Negro in Depression and War* (1969).

Stimson, Grace H. *Rise of the Labor Movement in Los Angeles* (1955).

Stokes, Melvyn, & Rick Halpern, eds. *Race and Class in the American South since 1890* (1994).

Storey, Moorefield. *Charles Sumner*. (Arthur M. Schlesinger ed., Chelsea House reprint 1983) (1900).

Sugrue, Thomas J. *The Origins of the Urban Crisis* (1996).

Sullivan, Patricia. *Days of Hope: Race and Democracy in the New Deal Era* (1997).

Summerville, James. *Educating African-American Doctors: A History of Meharry Medical College* (1983).

Thernstrom, Abigail & Stephen Thernstrom. *America in Black and White* (1998).

Thieblot, Armand J., Jr. *The Davis Bacon Act* (1975).

———. *Prevailing Wage Legislation* (1986).

Thomas, William G. *Lawyering for the Railroad* (1999).

Tindall, George Brown. *South Carolina Negroes, 1877–1900* (1952).

Tomlins, Christopher L. *The State and the Unions: Labor Relations, Law and the Organized Labor Movement in America, 1880–1960* (1985).

Twiss, Benjamin. *Lawyers and the Constitution: How Laissez Faire Came to the Supreme Court* (1942).

Van Deusen, John G. *The Black Man in White America* (rev. ed. 1944).

Vedder, Richard K. & Lowell E. Gallaway. *Out of Work: Unemployment and Government in Twentieth Century America* (1993).

Vickery, William Edward. *The Economics of the Negro Migration, 1900–1960* (1977).

Wall, Herbert. *Occupational Restrictions: A Study of the Laws of Eighteen Selected States, Covering the Requirements for Entering Occupations Therein* (1929).

Weaver, Robert C. *Negro Labor: A National Problem* (1948).

Weiss, Nancy J. *Farewell to the Party of Lincoln: African-American Politics in the Age of FDR* (1983).

———. *The National Urban League, 1910–1940* (1974).

Wesley, Charles. *Negro Labor in the United States: 1850–1925* (1927).

Weston, J. Fred, ed. *Large Corporations in a Changing Society* (1974).

Whayne, Jeannie M. *A New Plantation South* (1966).

Wiecek, William M. *Liberty under Law: The Supreme Court in American Life* (1988).

Wiener, Philip P. *Evolution and the Founders of Pragmatism* (1965).

Williams, Walter E. *The State against Blacks* (1982).

Wilson, Theodore B. *The Black Codes of the South* (1965).

Bibliography

Wolfe, Frank. *Admission to American Trade Unions* (1912).

Wolters, Raymond. *Negroes and the Great Depression* (1971).

Woodman, Harold D. *New South — New Law: The Legal Foundations of Credit and Labor Relations in the Postbellum Agricultural South* (1995).

Woodson, Carter G. *A Century of Negro Migration* (1918).

Woodward, C. Vann. *The Strange Career of Jim Crow* (3d ed. 1974).

Woofter, Thomas Jackson, Jr. *Negro Migration: Changes in Rural Organization and Population in the Cotton Belt* (Negro Univ. Press reprint ed. 1969) (1920).

Workers of the Writers' Program of the Work Projects Administration in the State of Virginia. *The Negro in Virginia* (reprint ed. 1994) (1940).

Wright, Gavin. *Old South New South: Revolutions in the Southern Economy since the Civil War* (1986).

Wright, R. *The Negro in Pennsylvania: A Study in Economic History* (1911).

Yellowitz, Irwin. *Labor and the Progressive Movement in New York State, 1897–1916* (1965).

Young, Stephen. *The Rule of Experts* (1987).

Zieger, Robert H. *The CIO 1935–1955* (1995).

——, ed. *Organized Labor in the Twentieth Century South* (1991).

——. *Republicans and Labor, 1919–1929* (1969).

ARTICLES

Abrams, Douglas Carl. "Irony of Reform: North Carolina Blacks and the New Deal." *66 N.C. Hist. Rev.* 149 (1989).

Ackerman, Bruce A. "Beyond *Carolene Products*." *98 Harv. L. Rev.* 713 (1985).

Amaker, Norman C. "Quittin' Time? The Antidiscrimination Principle of Title VII vs. The Free Market" (Book Review). *60 U. Chi. L. Rev.* 757 (1993).

Arnesen, Eric. "Following the Color Line of Labor: Black Workers and the Labor Movement before 1930." *55 Radical Hist. Rev.* 53 (1993).

——. " 'Like Banquo's Ghost, It Will Not Down': The Race Question and the American Railroad Brotherhoods, 1880–1920." *Am. Hist. Rev.* 1601 (1994).

——. "Up from Exclusion." *26 Revs. Am. Hist.* 147 (1998).

Ayres, Ian. "Alternative Grounds: Epstein's Discrimination Analysis in Other Market Settings." *31 San Diego L. Rev.* 67, 68 (1994).

——. "Price and Prejudice." *New Republic,* July 6, 1992, at 30.

Barenberg, Mark. "The Political Economy of the Wagner Act: Power, Symbol and Workplace Cooperation." *106 Harv. L. Rev.* 1379 (1993).

Bell, Derrick. "Does Discrimination Make Economic Sense?" *Hum. Rts.,* fall 1988, at 38.

Bell, Robert. "Minimum Wage and the Black Worker." *11 Opportunity* 199 (1933).

Les Benedict, Michael. "Laissez-Faire and Liberty: A Re-evaluation of the Meaning and Origins of Laissez-Faire Constitutionalism." *3 L. & Hist. Rev.* 293 (1985).

Bennett, Aremona G. "Phantom Freedom: Official Acceptance of Violence to Personal Security and Subversion of Proprietary Rights and Ambitions Following Emancipation, 1865–1910." 70 *Chi.-Kent L. Rev.* 439 (1994).

Berman, Edward. "The Pullman Porters Win." *The Nation,* Aug. 21, 1935, at 217.

Bernstein, David E. "The Law and Economics of Post–Civil War Restrictions on Interstate Migration by African-Americans." 76 *Tex. L. Rev.* 781 (1998).

——. "Licensing Laws: A Historical Example of the Use of Government Regulatory Power against African-Americans." 31 *San Diego L. Rev.* 89 (1994).

——. "*Lochner,* Parity, and the Chinese Laundry Cases." 41 *Wm. & Mary L. Rev.* 211 (1999).

——. "Philip Sober Controlling Philip Drunk: *Buchanan v. Warley* in Historical Perspective." 51 *Vand. L. Rev.* 797 (1998).

——. Note, "The Supreme Court and 'Civil Rights,' 1886–1908." 100 *Yale L.J.* 725 (1990).

——. "The Shameful, Wasteful History of New York's Prevailing Wage Law." 7 *Geo. Mason U. Civ. Rts. L.J.* 1 (1997).

Biles, Roger. "The Urban South in the Great Depression." 56 *J. So. Hist.* 71 (1990).

Bloch, Herman D. "Craft Unions and the Negro in Historical Perspective." 43 *J. Negro Hist.* 10 (1958).

Blumenthal, Henry. "Woodrow Wilson and the Race Question." 48 *J. Negro Hist.* 1 (1963).

Bogen, David S. "The Transformation of the Fourteenth Amendment: Reflections from the Admission of Maryland's First Black Lawyers." 44 *Md. L. Rev.* 939 (1985).

Bonacich, Edna. "Advanced Capitalism and Black/White Race Relations in the United States: A Split Labor Market Interpretation." 41 *Am. Soc. Rev.* 34 (1976).

——. "The Split Labor Market." 37 *Am. Soc. Rev.* 547 (1972).

Born, Kate. "Memphis Negro Workingmen and the NAACP." 28 *W. Tenn. Hist. Soc'y Papers* 90 (1974).

Boyle, Kevin. " 'There Are No Sorrows That the Union Can't Heal': The Struggle for Racial Equality in the United Automobile Workers, 1940–1960." 36 *Lab. Hist.* 5 (1995).

Brandfon, Robert L. "The End of Immigration to the Cotton Fields." 50 *Mississippi Valley Hist. Rev.* 591 (1964).

Brooks, R. P. "A Local Study of the Race Problem: Race Relations in the Eastern Piedmont Region of Georgia." 26 *Pol. Sci. Q.* 193 (1911).

Butler, Hilton. "Murder for the Job." *The Nation,* July 12, 1933, at 44.

Caldwell, Joe Louis. "Any Place but Here: Kansas Fever in Northeast Louisiana." 21 *N. La. Hist. Ass'n J.* 51 (1990).

Cogan, John. "The Decline in Black Teenage Employment: 1950–1970." 72 *Am. Econ. Rev.* 621 (1982).

Cohen, William. "Negro Involuntary Servitude in the South, 1865–1940: A Preliminary Analysis." 42 *J. S. Hist.* 31 (1976).

Cooter, Robert. "Market Affirmative Action." 31 *San Diego L. Rev.* 133 (1994).

Bibliography

Crespi, Greogry S. "Market Magic: Can the Invisible Hand Strangle Bigotry?" 72 *B.U.L. Rev.* 991 (1992).

Crowe, Charles. "Racial Violence and Social Reform: Origins of the Atlanta Riot of 1906." 53 *J. Negro Hist.* 234 (1968).

Dabney, Virginia. "Negro Barbers in the South." *The Nation,* July 16, 1930, at 64.

Davis, John P. "NRA Codifies Wage Slavery." 41 *The Crisis* 298 (1934).

———. "A Survey of the Problems of the Negro under the New Deal." 5 *J. Negro Educ.* 3 (1936).

Demsetz, Harold. "Minorities in the Marketplace." 43 *N.C.L. Rev.* 271 (1965).

Donohue, John J. "Advocacy versus Analysis in Assessing Employment Discrimination Law." 44 *Stan. L. Rev.* 1583, 1594 (1992).

Dorsey, Stuart. "Occupational Licensing and Minorities." 7 *L. & Human Behavior* 171 (1983).

———. "The Occupational Licensing Queue." 15 *J. Human Resources* 420 (1980).

Dougan, William R. & James M. Snyder. "Are Rents Fully Dissipated?" 77 *Pub. Choice* 793 (1993).

Du Bois, W. E. B. "The Denial of Economic Justice to Negroes." *New Leader,* Feb. 9, 1929, at 43.

Dudziak, Mary L. "Desegregation as a Cold War Imperative." 41 *Stan. L. Rev.* 61 (1988).

Editorial, "The A. F. of L." 40 *The Crisis* 292 (1933).

Editorial, "A Check to Union Tyranny." 80 *The Nation* 346 (1905).

"The Elimination of Negro Firemen on American Railways: A Study of the Evidence Adduced at the Hearing before the President's Committee on Fair Employment Practices." *Lawyers Guild Rev.,* March–April 1944, at 32.

Ely, James W., Jr. "Judicial Liberalism in the Gilded Age: Appraising John Marshall Harlan." 21 *Revs. Am. Hist.* 57 (1993).

———. "Melville W. Fuller Reconsidered." 1998 *J. Sup. Ct. Hist.* 32.

———. "Reflections on *Buchanan v. Warley,* Property Rights, and Race." 51 *Vand. L. Rev.* 953 (1998).

Epstein, Richard A. "The Mistakes of 1937." 11 *Geo. Mason L. Rev.* 5, 14 (1988).

———. "The Status Production Sideshow: Why the Antidiscrimination Laws Are Still a Mistake." 108 *Harv. L. Rev.* 1085 (1995).

Ernst, Daniel R. "Free Labor, the Consumer Interest, and the Law of Industrial Disputes, 1885–1900." 36 *Am. J. Legal Hist.* 19 (1992).

———. "The Yellow-Dog Contract and Liberal Reform, 1917–1932." 30 *Lab. Hist.* 251 (1989).

"The Exodus and a Bill." 1 *Opportunity* 317 (1923).

Fairlie, Robert W. & William A. Sundstrom. "The Emergence, Persistence and Recent Widening of the Racial Unemployment Gap." 20 (draft of May 1988, forthcoming) *Industrial and Labor Relations Review.*

Fellman, David. "A Case Study in Administrative Law: The Regulation of Barbers." 26 *Wash. U.L.Q.* 213 (1941).

Fischel, William A. "Why Judicial Reversal of Apartheid Made a Difference." 51 *Vand. L. Rev.* 975 (1998).

Fishback, Price V. "Can Competition among Employers Reduce Governmental Discrimination? Coal Companies and Segregated Schools in West Virginia in the Early 1900s." 32 *J.L. & Econ.* 318 (1989).

———. "Operations of Unfettered Labor Markets: Exit and Voice in American Labor Markets at the Turn of the Century." 36 *J. Econ. Lit.* 722 (1998).

Forbath, William E. "The Ambiguities of Free Labor: Labor and the Law in the Gilded Age." 1985 *Wis. L. Rev.* 767.

———. "The Shaping of the American Labor Movement." 102 *Harv. L. Rev.* 1111 (1989).

Fraenkel, Osmond K. "Recent Statutes Affecting Labor Injunctions and Yellow Dog Contracts." 30 *Ill. L. Rev.* 854 (1936).

Frey, John P. "Attempts to Organize Negro Workers." *American Federationist,* March 1929, at 296.

Friedman, Lawrence. "Freedom of Contract and Occupational Licensing 1890–1910: A Legal and Society Study." 53 *Cal. L. Rev.* 487 (1965).

Garcia, George F. "Black Disaffection from the Republican Party during the Presidency of Herbert Hoover, 1928–1932." 45 *Annals of Iowa* 462 (1980).

Goldfield, Michael. "Race and the CIO: The Possibilities for Racial Egalitarianism during the 1930s and 1940s." 44 *Int'l Lab. & Working Class Hist.* 1 (1993).

Granger, Lester B. "Negro Workers and Recovery." *Opportunity,* May 1934, at 153.

Green, Cleveland M. "Prejudices and Empty Promises: Woodrow Wilson's Betrayal of the Negro, 1910–1919." 87 *The Crisis* 380 (1980).

Grossman, James R. "Blowing the Trumpet: The *Chicago Defender* and Black Migration during World War I." 78 *Ill. Hist. J.* 82 (1985).

Guthrie, W. A. Letter to the Editors of the *American Law Review.* 38 *Am. L. Rev.* 144 (1904).

Guzda, Henry P. "Frances Perkins' Interest in a New Deal for Blacks." *Monthly Lab. Rev.,* April 1978, at 31.

Halpern, Rick. "The Iron Fist and the Velvet Glove: Welfare Capitalism in Chicago's Packinghouses, 1921–1933." 26 *J. American Stud.* 159 (1992).

Hamowy, Ronald. "The Early Development of Medical Licensing Laws in the United States, 1875–1900." 3 *J. Libertarian Studies* 73 (1979).

Heckman, James J. & J. Hoult Verkerke. "Racial Disparity and Employment Discrimination Law: An Economic Perspective." 8 *Yale L. & Pol'y Rev.* 276 (1990).

Henderson, Alexa B. "FEPC and the Southern Railway Case: An Investigation into the Discriminatory Practices of Railroads during World War II." 61 *J. Negro Hist.* 173 (1976).

Hill, Herbert. "The AFL-CIO and the Black Worker: Twenty-Five Years after the Merger." 10 *J. Intergroup Rel.* 5 (1982).

———. "Anti-Oriental Agitation and the Rise of Working-Class Racism." *Society,* Jan./Feb. 1973, at 43.

Bibliography

———. "Black Labor and Affirmative Action: An Historical Perspective." In *The Question of Discrimination* 190 (Steven Shulman & William Darity Jr. eds., 1989).

———. "The Importance of Race in American Labor History." 9 *Int'l J. Pol. Culture & Soc'y* 317 (1995).

———. "Labor Unions and the Negro." *Commentary*, Dec. 1959, at 479.

———. "Myth-Making as Labor History: Herbert Gutman and the United Mine Workers of America." 2 *Int'l J. of Pol., Culture, & Soc'y* 132 (1988).

———. "The Problem of Race in American Labor History." 24 *Revs. Am. Hist.* 189 (1996).

———. "Racial Discrimination in the Nation's Apprenticeship Training Programs." *Phylon*, fall 1962, at 215.

———. "Racism within Organized Labor: A Report of Five Years of the AFL-CIO, 1955–1960." 30 *J. Negro Educ.* 109 (1961).

Hill, T. Arnold. "The Negro in Industry." 32 *American Federationist* 915 (1925).

———. "The Plight of the Negro Industrial Worker." 5 *J. Negro Educ.* 40 (1936).

———. "Railway Employees Rally to Save Their Jobs." 12 *Opportunity* 346 (1934).

Hine, Darlene Clark. "The Anatomy of Failure: Medical Education Reform and the Leonard Medical School of Shaw University, 1882–1920." *J. Negro Educ.* 512 (1985).

Hoffman, Abraham. "Stimulus to Repatriation: The 1931 Federal Deportation Drive and the Los Angeles Mexican Community." 42 *Pac. Hist. Rev.* 205 (1973).

Holmes, Michael S. "The Blue Eagle as 'Jim Crow Bird': The NRA and Georgia's Black Workers." 57 *J. Negro Hist.* 276 (1972).

Holmes, William F. "Labor Agents and the Georgia Exodus, 1899–1900." 79 *S. Atlantic Q.* 436 (1980).

———. "Whitecapping: Agrarian Violence in Mississippi, 1902–1906." 35 *J. S. Hist.* 165 (1969).

Houston, Charles H. "Foul Employment Practice on the Rails." *Crisis*, Oct. 1949, at 269.

Hovenkamp, Hebert. "The Political Economy of Substantive Due Process." 40 *Stan. L. Rev.* 379 (1988).

Johnson, Charles S. "Negro Workers and the Unions." *The Survey*, Apr. 15, 1928, at 113.

Jones, Jacqueline. "Work Now, Get Paid Much Later: 'Free Labor' in the Postbellum South." 15 *Revs. Am. Hist.* 265 (1987).

Joo, Thomas Wuil. "New 'Conspiracy Theory' of the Fourteenth Amendment: Nineteenth Century Chinese Civil Rights Cases and the Development of Substantive Due Process Jurisprudence." 29 *U.S.F. L. Rev.* 353 (1995).

Jordan, Michael. "The NLRB Racial Discrimination Decisions, 1935–1964: The Empiric Process of Administration and the Inner Eye of Racism." 24 *Conn. L. Rev.* 55 (1991).

Karlin, Norman. "Back to the Future: From *Nollan* to *Lochner*." 17 *Sw. U. L. Rev.* 627 (1988).

Kelsey, Carl. "Some Causes of Negro Migration." *Charities*, Oct. 1905, at 15.

Kenneally, James J. "Black Republicans during the New Deal: The Role of Joseph W. Martin, Jr." 55 *Rev. Pol.* 117 (1993).

Kessel, Reuben. "The A.M.A. and the Supply of Physicians." 35 *Law & Contemp. Probs.* 267, 270 (1970).

———. "Price Discrimination in Medicine." 1 *J.L. & Econ.* 21 (1958).

Keyes, William A. "The Minimum Wage and the Davis-Bacon Act: Employment Effects on Minorities and Youth." 3 *J. Lab. Res.* 399 (1982).

Klarman, Michael J. "*Brown*, Racial Change, and the Civil Rights Movement." 80 *Va. L. Rev.* 7 (1994).

———. "Constitutional Fact/Constitutional Fiction: A Critique of Bruce Ackerman's Theory of Constitutional Moments." 44 *Stan. L. Rev.* 759 (1992).

Kovarsky, Irving. "Apprenticeship Training Programs and Racial Discrimination." 50 *Iowa L.J.* 755 (1965).

Kovatch, Kenneth A. "Should the Davis-Bacon Act Be Repealed?" *Bus. Horizons*, Sept.–Oct. 1983, at 33.

Kruman, Mark W. "Quotas for Blacks: The Public Works Administration and the Black Construction Worker." *Lab. Hist.*, winter 1975, at 38.

Lasker, Bruno. "Race and the Job." *The Survey*, Oct. 15, 1925, at 77.

Lewis, Ronald L. "From Peasant to Proletarian: The Migration of Southern Blacks to the Central Appalachian Coalfields." 55 *J. S. Hist.* 77 (1989).

Linder, Marc. "Farm Workers and the Fair Labor Standards Act: Racial Discrimination in the New Deal." 65 *Tex. L. Rev.* 1335 (1987).

Logan, Frenise A. "The Movement of Negroes from North Carolina, 1876–1894." 33 *N.C. Hist. Rev.* 45 (1956).

Macey, Jonathan R. "Public Choice, Public Opinion, and the Fuller Court." 49 *Vand. L. Rev.* 373 (1996).

Margo, Robert A. "Segregated Schools and the Mobility Hypothesis: A Model of Local Government Discrimination." 106 *Q.J. Econ.* 61, 62 (1991).

Matthews, John Michael. "The Georgia 'Race Strike' of 1909." 40 *J. S. Hist.* 613 (1974).

McCurdy, Charles W. "Justice Field and the Jurisprudence of Government-Business Relations: Some Parameters of Laissez Faire Constitutionalism, 1863–1897." 61 *J. Am. Hist.* 970 (1975).

———. "The Roots of 'Liberty of Contract' Reconsidered: Major Premises in the Law of Employment, 1867–1937." 1984 *Sup. Ct. Hist. Soc'y Y.B.* 20.

Miller, Geoffrey P. "Public Choice at the Dawn of the Special Interest State: The Story of Butter and Margarine." 77 *Cal. L. Rev.* 83 (1989).

———. "The True Story of Carolene Products." 1987 *Sup. Ct. Rev.* 397.

Miller, Kelly. "The Negro as a Workingman." 6 *Am. Mercury* 310 (1925).

Moore, Thomas G. "The Purpose of Licensing." 4 *J.L. & Econ.* 93 (1961).

Nelson, William E. "The Impact of the Antislavery Movement upon Styles of Judicial Reasoning in Nineteenth Century America." 87 *Harv. L. Rev.* 513 (1974).

Nieman, Donald G. "From Slaves to Citizens: African-Americans, Rights Consciousness, and Reconstruction." 17 *Cardozo L. Rev.* 2115 (1996).

Norrell, Robert J. "Caste in Steel: Jim Crow Careers in Birmingham, Alabama." 73 *J. Am. Hist.* 669 (1986).

Note, "Judicial Regulation of the Railway Brotherhoods' Discriminatory Practices." 1953 *Wis. L. Rev.* 516.

Note, "Restriction of Freedom of Entry into the Building Trades." 38 *Iowa L. Rev.* 556 (1953).

Osborn, George C. "The Problem of the Negro in Government, 1913." 23 *Historian* 330 (1961).

Oxley, Lawrence W. "Occupations, Negroes, and Labor Organizations." 14 *Occupations* 520 (1936).

Payton, John. "Redressing the Exclusion of and Discrimination against Black Workers in the Skilled Construction Trades: The Approach of the Washington Lawyers' Committee for Civil Rights under Law." 27 *How. L.J.* 1397 (1984).

Polsby, Daniel. "What If This Is as Good as it Gets?" 2 *Green Bag* 2d 115 (1998).

Poole, Keith & Howard Rosenthal. "The Enduring Nineteenth Century Battle for Economic Regulation: The Interstate Commerce Act Revisited." 36 *J.L. & Econ.* 837 (1993).

Pound, Roscoe. "The Scope and Purpose of Sociological Jurisprudence, Part II." 25 *Harv. L. Rev.* 489 (1912).

Powell, Thomas Reed. "Collective Bargaining before the Supreme Court." 33 *Pol. Sci. Q.* 396 (1918).

Prasch, Robert E. "American Economists and Minimum Wage Legislation during the Progressive Era: 1912–1923." 22 *J. Hist. Econ. Thought* 161 (1998).

Raper, Arthur F. "The Southern Negro and the NRA." 64 *Ga. Hist. Q.* 128 (1980).

Reid, Ira D. A. "Black Wages for Black Workers." 12 *Opportunity* 72 (1934).

———. "Negro Firemen." *The Nation*, Sept. 6, 1933, at 273.

Reynolds, Alfred W. "The Alabama Negro Colony in Mexico, 1894–1896" (pt. 1), 5 *Ala. Rev.* 243 (1952).

Roback, Jennifer. "Racism as Rent Seeking." 27 *Econ. Inquiry* 661 (1989).

———. "Rules v. Discretion: *Berea College v. Kentucky.*" 20 *Int'l J. Group Tensions* 47, 51 (1990).

———. "Southern Labor Law in the Jim Crow Era: Exploitative or Competitive?" 51 *U. Chi. L. Rev.* 1161 (1984).

Rowe, Gary D. "The Legacy of *Lochner: Lochner* Revisionism Revisited." 24 *Law & Soc. Inquiry* 221 (1999).

Savitt, Todd L. "Entering a White Profession: African-American Physicians in the New South, 1880–1920." 61 *Bull. Hist. Med.* 507 (1987).

Scheiber, Harry N. "Original Intent, History, and Doctrine: The Constitution and Economic Liberty." *Am. Econ. Rev.*, May 1988, at 140.

Seltzer, Andrew J. "The Political Economy of the Fair Labor Standards Act." 103 *J. Pol. Econ.* 1302 (1995).

Shaviro, Daniel. "The Minimum Wage, the Earned Income Tax Credit, and Optimal Subsidy Policy." 64 *U. Chi. L. Rev.* 405 (1997).

Siegan, Bernard H. "Separation of Powers & Economic Liberties." 70 *Notre Dame L. Rev.* 415 (1995).

Silver, Christopher. "The Racial Origins of Zoning: Southern Cities from 1910–1940." 6 *Planning Perspective* 189 (1991).

Soifer, Aviam. "The Paradox of Paternalism and Laissez-Faire Constitutionalism: United States Supreme Court, 1888–1921." 5 *L. & Hist. Rev.* 249 (1987).

Spahr, Margaret. "Natural Law, Due Process and Economic Pressure." 24 *Am. Pol. Sci. Rev.* 332 (1930).

"Spokesman for Negroes Condemns Anti-Injunction Bill." *Law and Labor,* Feb. 1929, at 24.

Stein, Judith. "The Ins and Outs of the CIO." 44 *Int'l J. Lab. & Working Class Hist.* 53 (1993).

Stone, Alfred Holt. "The Negro in the Yazoo-Mississippi Delta." 1902 *Am. Econ. Ass'n* 235.

———. "A Plantation Experiment." 19 *Q.J. Econ.* 270 (1905).

Strauss, George & Sidney Ingerman. "Public Policy and Discrimination in Apprenticeship." 16 *Hastings L.J.* 285 (1965).

Street, Paul. "The Logic and Limits of 'Plant Loyalty': Black Workers, White Labor, and Corporate Racial Paternalism in Chicago's Stockyards, 1916–1940." 29 *J. Social Hist.* 659 (1996).

Stroman, Carolyn A. "The *Chicago Defender* and the Mass Migration of Blacks, 1916–1918." *J. Popular Culture,* fall 1981, at 62.

Sugrue, Thomas J. "Segmented Work, Race-Conscious Workers: Structure, Agency and Division in the CIO Era." 41 *Int'l Rev. Social Hist.* 389 (1996).

Sundstrom, William A. "Down or Out: Unemployment and Occupational Shifts of Urban Black Men during the Great Depression." 16 *Research in Econ. Hist.* 127 (1996).

———. "Explaining the Racial Unemployment Gap: Race, Region, and the Employment Status of Men, 1940." 50 *Industrial & Lab. Relations Rev.* 460 (1997).

———. "Half a Career: Discrimination & Railroad Internal Labor Markets." 29 *Industrial Relations* 423 (1990).

Sunstein, Cass R. "*Lochner*'s Legacy." 87 *Colum. L. Rev.* 873 (1987).

Tarrow, Sidney G. "*Lochner Versus New York*: A Political Analysis," 5 *Labor Hist.* 275 (1964).

Taylor, Joseph H. "The Great Migration from North Carolina in 1879." 31 *N.C. Hist. Rev.* 20 (1954).

Thomas, Jesse O. "The Negro Industrialist." *Nat'l Conf. Social Work Proceedings* 455 (1928).

Tushnet, Mark. "*Plessy v. Ferguson* in Libertarian Perspective." 16 *L. & Philosophy* 245 (1997).

Tushnet, Mark V. "Progressive Era Race Relations Cases in Their 'Traditional' Context." 51 *Vand. L. Rev.* 993 (1998).

"Union Labor Again." *The Crisis*, Nov. 1934, at 300.

Valocchi, Steve. "The Racial Basis of Capitalism and the States, and the Impact of the New Deal on African Americans." 41 *Social Problems* 347 (1994).

Van Deusen, John G. "The Exodus of 1879." 21 *J. Negro Hist.* 105 (1936).

Vedder, Richard K. "The Slave Exploitation (Expropriation) Rate." 12 *Explorations in Econ. Hist.* 453 (1975).

Vedder, Richard et al. "Demonstrating Their Freedom: The Post-Emancipation Migration of Black Americans." 10 *Res. Econ. Hist.* 213 (1986).

Vedder, Richard, & Lowell Galloway. "Racial Differences in Unemployment in the United States, 1890–1990." 52 *J. Econ. Hist.* 696 (1992).

Verkerke, J. Hoult. "Free to Search." 105 *Harv. L. Rev.* 2080 (1992).

Waldinger, Roger, & Thomas Bailey. "The Continuing Significance of Race: Racial Conflict and Racial Discrimination in Construction." 19 *Pol. & Soc'y* 291 (1991).

Warren, Charles. "A Bulwark to the State Police Power: The United States Supreme Court." 13 *Colum. L. Rev.* 667 (1913).

Washington, Booker T. "The Negro and the Labor Unions." *Atlantic Monthly*, June 1913, at 753.

Weaver, Robert C. "Negro Labor since 1929." 35 *J. Negro Hist.* 20 (1950).

———. "A Wage Differential Based on Race," 41 *The Crisis* 236 (1934).

Weiss, Nancy J. "The Negro and the New Freedom: Fighting Wilsonian Segregation." 84 *Pol. Sci. Q.* 61 (1969).

Whatley, Warren C. "Getting a Foot in the Door: 'Learning,' State Dependence, and the Racial Integration of Firms." 50 *J. Econ. Hist.* 43, 44 (1990).

Wiener, Jonathan M. "Class Structure and Economic Development in the American South, 1865–1955." 84 *Am. Hist. Rev.* 970 (1979).

Williams, Walter E. "Freedom to Contract: Blacks and Labor Organizations." *Gov't-Union Rev.*, summer 1981, at 28.

Winter, Ralph K., Jr. "Improving the Economic Status of Negroes through Laws against Discrimination: A Reply to Professor Sovern." 34 *U. Chi. L. Rev.* 817 (1967).

Wolters, Raymond. "Section 7a and the Black Worker." 10 *Lab. Hist.* 459 (1969).

Wonnell, Christopher T. "Economic Due Process and the Preservation of Competition." 11 *Hastings Const. L.Q.* 91 (1983).

———. "The Influential Myth of a Generalized Conflict of Interests between Labor and Management." 81 *Geo. L.J.* 39 (1992).

Woodruff, Nan Elizabeth. "African-American Struggles for Citizenship in the Arkansas and Mississippi Deltas in the Age of Jim Crow." 55 *Radical Hist. Rev.* 33 (1993).

Woodson, Sharon L. "Exodus to Kansas." 82 *The Crisis* 239 (1975).

Wright, Richard Robert. "The Negro Skilled Mechanic in the North." 38 *Southern Workman* 155 (1909).

Zakson, Laurence Scott. "Railway Labor Legislation 1888 to 1930: A Legal History of Congressional Railway Labor Relations Policy." 20 *Rutgers L.J.* 317 (1989).

Zeichner, Oscar. "The Transition from Free Agricultural Labor in the Southern States." 12 *Agric. Hist.* 22 (1939).

Zieger, Robert H. "The Career of James J. Davis." 98 *Penn. Mag. Hist. & Biography* 67 (1973).

CASES

Adair v. United States, 208 U.S. 161 (1908)

Adkins v. Children's Hospital, 261 U.S. 525 (1923)

A. L. A. Schecter Poultry Corp. v. United States, 295 U.S. 495 (1935)

Allgeyer v. Louisiana, 165 U.S. 578 (1897)

Alliance Const. Co. v. United States, 79 Ct. Cl. 730 (1934)

Atkin v. Kansas, 191 U.S. 207 (1903)

Atlanta Oak Flooring Co., 62 N.L.R.B. 973 (1945)

Baker v. Portland, 2 F. Cas. 472 (D. Ore. 1879)

Berea College v. Kentucky, 211 U.S. 45 (1908)

Bob Jones University v. United States, 461 U.S. 574 (1983)

Brotherhood of Locomotive Firemen v. Tunstall, 163 F.2d 289 (4th Cir. 1947)

Brotherhood of R. R. Trainmen v. A.T. & Santa Fe Ry., N.R.A.B. Award No. 6640 (1st Div. 1942)

Brotherhood of Ry. & S.S. Clerks v. United Transp. Serv. Employees, 320 U.S. 715 (1943)

Brotherhood of Ry. & S.S. Clerks v. United Transp. Serv. Employees, 137 F.2d 817 (D.C. Cir. 1943)

Buchanan v. Warley, 245 U.S. 60 (1917)

Building and Constr. Trades Dept., AFL-CIO v. Donovan, 712 F.2d 611 (D.C. Cir. 1983)

Bunting v. Oregon, 243 U.S. 426 (1917)

Campbell v. City of New York, 244 N.Y. 317 (1927)

Ex Parte Case, 116 P. 1037 (Idaho 1911)

Chaires v. Atlanta, 139 S.E. 559 (Ga. 1927)

Chicago, Rock Island & Pac. Ry. v. Arkansas, 219 U.S. 453 (1911)

City of Chicago v. Hulbert, 68 N.E. 786 (Ill. 1903)

City of Cleveland v. Clements Bros. Constr. Co., 65 N.E. 885 (Ohio 1902)

Cole v. Commonwealth, 193 S.E. 517 (Va. 1937)

Connally v. General Construction Co., 269 U.S. 285 (1926)

Contractors Ass'n of E. Pa. v. Secretary of Labor, 442 F.2d 159 (3d Cir. 1971)

Coppage v. Kansas, 236 U.S. 1 (1915)

In re Craig, 20 Haw. 483 (1911)

In re Debs, 158 U.S. 564 (1895)

Dent v. West Virginia, 129 U.S. 114 (1888)

Dewell v. Quarles, 181 S.E. 159 (1935)

Dolan v. City of Tigard, 512 U.S. 374 (1994)

Douglas v. Noble, 261 U.S. 165 (1921)

Douglas v. People ex rel. Ruddy, 80 N.E. 341 (Ill. 1907)

Ellis v. United States, 206 U.S. 246 (1907)

Fiske v. People, 58 N.E. 985 (Ill. 1900)

Fulton v. Ives, 167 So. 394 (Fla. 1936)

Garbutt v. State, 77 So. 189 (Miss. 1918)

Godcharles v. Wigeman, 6 A. 354 (Pa. 1886)

Hanley v. Moody, 39 F.2d 198 (N.D. Tex. 1930)

Hawker v. New York, 170 U.S. 189 (1898)

Heim v. McCall, 239 U.S. 175 (1915)

Hitchman Coal Co. v. Mitchell, 245 U.S. 229 (1917)

Holden v. City of Alton, 53 N.E. 556 (Ill. 1899)

Independent Metal Workers Union, Local No. 1, 147 N.L.R.B. 1573 (1964)

International Ass'n Heat & Frost Insulators Local 53 v. Vogler, 407 F.2d 1047 (5th Cir. 1969)

In re Jacobs, 98 N.Y. 98 (1885)

J. I. Case Co. v. NLRB, 321 U.S. 332 (1944)

Joseph v. Randolph, 71 Ala. 499 (1882)

Kendrick v. State, 39 So. 203 (Ala. 1905)

Ex Parte Kuback, 85 Cal. 274 (1890)

Larus & Brother Co., 62 N.L.R.B. 1075 (1945)

Lauf v. E. G. Shinner & Co., 303 U.S. 323 (1938)

Lewis v. Board of Educ., 102 N.W. 756 (Mich. 1905)

Lochner v. New York, 198 U.S. 45 (1905)

McCabe v. Atchison, Topeka & Santa Fe Ry, 235 U.S. 151 (1914)

McCall v. California, 136 U.S. 104 (1890)

McMillan v. City of Knoxville, 202 S.W. 65 (Tenn. 1918)

Miranda Fuel Co., 140 N.L.R.B. 181 (1962)

Montgomery v. Pacific Elec. Ry., 293 F. 680 (9th Cir. 1923)

Morehead v. New York ex rel. Tipaldo, 298 U.S. 587 (1936)

Muller v. Oregon, 208 U.S. 412 (1908)

Nebbia v. New York, 291 U.S. 502 (1934)

NLRB v. Jones & Laughlin Steel Corp., 301 U.S. 1 (1937)

NLRB v. Miranda Fuel Co., 326 F.2d 172 (2d Cir. 1963)

People v. Brown, 95 N.E. 2d 888 (Ill. 1950)

People v. Coler, 166 N.Y. 1 (1901)

People ex rel. Nechamcus v. Warden, 144 N.Y. 529 (1895)

People v. Orange County Road Const. Co., 67 N.E. 129 (N.Y. 1903)

People v. Warren, 34 N.Y. Supp. 942 (Sup. Ct. 1895)

Phelps Dodge v. NLRB, 313 U.S. 177 (1941)

Planned Parenthood v. Casey, 505 U.S. 833 (1992)

Plessy v. Ferguson, 163 U.S. 537 (1896)

Reetz v. Michigan, 188 U.S. 505 (1903)

Replogle v. Little Rock, 267 S.W. 353 (Ark. 1924)

Ritchie v. People, 40 N.E. 454 (Ill. 1895)

Roberts v. United States Jaycees, 468 U.S. 609 (1984)

Rock v. Philadelphia, 191 A. 669 (Pa. Super. 1937)

Rolax v. Atlantic Coast Line R.R., 186 F.2d 473 (4th Cir. 1951)

St. Louis, Iron Mountain & S. Ry. v. Arkansas, 240 U.S. 518 (1916)

Shepperd v. County Comm'rs, 59 Ga. 535 (1877)

Slaughter-House Cases, 83 U.S. (16 Wall.) 36 (1873)

Smith v. Alabama, 124 U.S. 465 (1888)

Smith v. Texas, 233 U.S. 630 (1914)

State v. Bates, 101 S.E. 651 (S.C. 1919)

State v. Gardner, 51 N.E. 136 (Ohio 1898)

State v. Hunt, 40 S.E. 216 (N.C. 1901)

State v. Moore, 18 S.E. 342 (N.C. 1893)

State v. Napier, 41 S.E. 13 (S.C. 1902)

State v. Reeves, 99 S.E. 841 (S.C. 1919)

State v. Roberson, 48 S.E. 595 (N.C. 1904)

State v. Walker, 92 P. 775 (Wash. 1907)

Steele v. Louisville & Nashville R.R. Co., 323 U.S. 192 (1944)

Street v. Varney Electrical Supply, 66 N.E. 895 (Ind. 1903)

In re Taylor, 38 Md. 28 (1877)

Texas & N.O.R.R. v. Brotherhood of Ry. & S.S. Clerks, 281 U.S. 548 (1930)

United States v. Carolene Prods. Co., 304 U.S. 144 (1938)

United States v. Carpenters Local 169, 457 F.2d 210 (7th Cir. 1972)

United States v. Darby, 312 U.S. 100 (1941)

United States v. International Bhd. Elec. Workers Local 212, 472 F.2d 634 (6th Cir. 1973)

United States v. Ironworkers Local 86, 443 F.2d 544 (9th Cir. 1971)

United States v. Lathers Local 46, 471 F.2d 408 (2d Cir. 1972)

United States v. Lopez, 514 U.S. 549 (1995)

United States v. Murphy, 11 F. Supp. 572 (W.D. Mich. 1934)

United States v. W.S. Barstow & Co., 79 F.2d 496 (4th Cir. 1935)

Varner v. State, 36 S.E. 93 (Ga. 1900)

Veneer Prods., Inc., 81 N.L.R.B. 492 (1948)

Virginian Railway Co. v. System Federation No. 40, Railway Employees Dept. of the American Federation of Labor, 300 U.S. 515 (1937)

Wagner v. Milwaukee, 188 N.W. 487 (Wis. 1922)

Watson v. Maryland, 218 U.S. 173 (1910)

West Coast Hotel Co. v. Parrish, 300 U.S. 379 (1937)

Willis v. Local No. 106, Hotel and Restaurant Employees International Alliance (Court of Common Pleas Cuyahoga County, July 27, 1927)

Williams v. Fears, 35 S.E. 699 (Ga. 1900)

Williams v. Fears, 179 U.S. 270 (1900)

Winkler v. Benzenberg, 76 N.W. 345 (Wis. 1898)

Woodson v. State, 40 S.E. 1013 (Ga. 1902)

Wright v. Hoctor, 145 N.W. 704 (Neb. 1914)

Yick Wo v. Hopkins, 118 U.S. 356 (1886)

York v. State ex rel. Jones, 197 So. 766 (Fla. 1940)

Index

Cochran, John J., 77
Cohen, William, 11, 12
Communists, 96
Congress of Industrial Organizations
    (CIO): equal-wage policy, 97; merge
    with AFL (1955), 96; racial policies of,
    95–97
Connally v. General Construction Co.
    (1926), 72
Construction unions: under Davis-Bacon
    Act, 79–84; exclusionary practices,
    68–71; influence and power of, 67;
    post–Civil War goals, 66
Construction workers, African Ameri-
    can: competitiveness in construction
    trades, 68–73; conflict with construc-
    tion unions, 68–71; discrimination in
    war-related industries, 81–82; effect
    of Davis-Bacon on, 80–81; employ-
    ment in northern and southern work
    force (1930), 70–71; migration to
    cities, 68–71

Davis, Harry E., 56–57, 63, 93
Davis, James J.: racism of, 75; as Secre-
    tary of Labor, 74
Davis, John, 106–7
Davis-Bacon Act, 6; amendments to, 79,
    85; discrimination as effect of, 79–84;
    intent of, 66; local prevailing wage as
    requirement under, 100; origins of,
    71–79; revelations of legislative his-
    tory, 78–79
Davison, James, 18, 20, 23–24
Debs, Eugene V., 54
Demsetz, Harold, 105
Dent v. West Virginia (1888), 30, 34
Dewell v. Quarles (1935), 35, 134n. 30
Discrimination, racial: of AFL craft
    unions, 95; in CIO unions, 95–97; in
    construction trades, 68–71; under
    Davis-Bacon Act, 79–84; under FLSA,
    100–102; under NRA, 86–94; prac-

ticed by AFL member unions, 89; pub-
    lic support for, 106; under public
    works legislation, 66–67; under Rail-
    way Labor Act, 57–63; reasons for
    unions', 90; as unfair labor practice
    under Wagner Act, 99
Douglas v. Noble (1921), 31
Du Bois, W. E. B., 92, 93

Easley, Smith W., 20
Easterly, Charles, 76
Eisenhower, Dwight D., 82
Ellis v. United States (1907), 68
Emigrant agent laws: challenges to,
    16–22, 25; in Georgia, 12–13; U.S.
    Supreme Court upholds, 23–25; Vir-
    ginia law (1870), 12; after Williams
    decision, 25–27
Emigrant agents: effects on planters of
    recruitment by, 15–19; importance to
    African American migration, 10–11;
    interaction with African Americans,
    10–21. See also Migration, African
    American
Employers, Southern: lobbying for emi-
    grant agent laws, 11–12; response to
    large-scale migration, 11–12
Epstein, Richard, 58, 112
Equal Employment Opportunity Com-
    mission (EEOC), 83–84

Fair Employment Practices Commission
    (FEPC), 82
Fair Labor Standards Act (FLSA), 85,
    99; effect on African American farm
    workers, 103; minimum-wage provi-
    sions, 99–101; Supreme Court ruling
    on constitutionality of (1941), 99–100
Fears, Oliver, 19
Federal Railroad Administration: limit-
    ing railroad employment of African
    Americans, 52; regulations benefiting
    white trainmen, 52

Fishback, Price, 113
Flexner, Abraham, 41–44
Flexner Report, 41–43
Forbath, William, 57
Fourteenth Amendment: interpretation in *Lochner*, 2; interpretation in *Slaughter-House Cases*, 1–2; judicial review of occupational legislation under, 1–2; vagueness of, 1
"Free Labor" ideology, 2, 14, 23, 66
Friedman, Lawrence, 30–31
Fuller, Chief Justice Melville: dissent in *Atkin*, 68; opinion in *Williams*, 23–24
Fulton, Andrew, 39
Fulton v. Ives (1936), 39–40

Garvey, Marcus, 92
Government, U.S.: actions to help whites to receive employment priority, 78; establishes Fair Employment Practices Commission, 82; intervention on behalf of African Americans, 105–9; legislative intervention in labor relations, 54–55; post–World War I labor market intervention, 51–53; World War I control of railroads, 51–53
Green, William, 77

Hancock, Gordon Blaine, 88
Harlan, Justice John Marshall: dissent in *Plessy*, 24, 108; dissent in *Williams*, 24
Hart, John Collier, 20–21
Heim v. McCall (1915), 68
Hill, Herbert, 93–94, 99
Hill, T. Arnold, 58, 93, 107
Hod carriers' union, 69
Holmes, Justice Oliver Wendell, 3
Hoover, Herbert, 78, 106
Howard University Medical School, 43
Howard v. St. Louis-S.F. Ry. (1953), 64

Immigrants, 33, 66; Asian, 150n. 26; bans on employment of, 64–66; Chinese, 21, 67, 113, 131n. 86; Italian, 4, 66; Jewish, 4
Immigration Act (1924), 70
In re Debs (1895), 54
International Association of Machinists, 47
International Brotherhood of Electrical Workers, 70–72, 75

Journeymen Barbers' Union, 37

Kennedy, John F., 83
Kennedy, Justice Anthony, 115

Labor injunctions: assistance to African American workers, 55–56; to enforce yellow dog contracts, 54–55; Shipstead anti-injunction bill, 56, 63; upheld in *In re Debs*, 54
Labor legislation: Black Codes in post–Civil War South, 9–12; effect of facially neutral, 2, 111; eight-hour-day laws, 66; at federal level, 6–7; as focus in *Lochner* decision, 2–5. *See also* Davis-Bacon Act; Emigrant agent laws; Legislation, state-level; Licensing, state-level; National Labor Relations Act (Wagner Act); New Deal; Railway Labor Act
Labor market: African Americans during World War I in railroad, 51–52; effect of New Deal interference in, 94; emigrant agents in post–Civil War South, 10–21; federal intervention in railroad, 51–53; government interference in, 111–12; in post–Civil War South, 8–10; post–New Deal government intervention in, 105–9
Labor unions: banning of company unions under Wagner Act, 94; exclusionary practices under NRA, 89–94;

can workers, 86; provisions giving power to unions, 92–93; unconstitutionality of, 86, 94; wage provisions, 86–89. *See also* National Labor Relations Act (Wagner Act)

National Labor Relations Act (Wagner Act), 6, 85, 94

National Labor Relations Board (NLRB): invalidation of unions' discriminatory practices (1960s), 98–99

National Mediation Board (NMB), 59–60

National Railroad Adjustment Board (NRAB), 59

National Urban League, 52

Nechamcus. See People ex rel. Nechamcus v. Warden (1895)

New Deal: African American support for, 107; Lochnerian jurisprudence abandoned under, 98–100; long-term effects on African American labor, 103–10; Supreme Court during, 85

Nixon administration, 84

Norris-La Guardia Act (1932), 59, 63

Northrup, Herbert, 65

NRA. *See* National Industrial Recovery Act (NRA)

O'Connor, Justice Sandra Day, 115

Olson, Mancur, 111

Peckham, Justice Rufus: dissent in *Atkin,* 68; dissent in *Nechamcus,* 33, 34; opinion in *Lochner,* 30, 33

People ex rel. Nechamcus v. Warden (1895), 32–34

People v. Brown (1950), 35, 134n. 31

Physicians, African American, 41–44

Plessy v. Ferguson (1896), 24, 108

Plumbers, African American, 31–36

Plumbers' and Steamfitters' Union, 32, 70, 72

Preiss, Emil, 75

President's Committee on Equal Opportunity (PCEO), 83

President's Committee on Government Contracts (PCGC), 82–83

Progressivism, 106, 109, 114

Public choice theory: collective political action, 114, 158n. 4; government intervention to coerce, 111

Quotas, racial, 84

Racism: of employers, 91; of James Davis, 75; post–Civil War, 11; postwar shift of public opinion against, 107; race strikes, 48–50, 52; of railroad unions, 46, 64; of Robert Bacon, 73–74. *See also* Discrimination, racial

Railroad industry: employment of African Americans, 48–51, 53–58; employment practices under Railroad Labor Act, 57–64; government controls during and after World War I, 51–52, 57; laws restricting hiring practices, 50–51

Railroad unions: of African American railroad workers, 53; banning of African Americans from, 46–47; exclusionary power under Norris-La Guardia Act, 59; exclusionary practices, 46–53; monopoly power under Railway Labor Act, 49, 57–65; post–World War I, 51–53; race strikes, 52, 55; revocation of color bars (1960s), 64; role in drafting Railroad Labor Act, 57; threats related to hiring of African Americans, 52; violence against African American railroad workers (1931), 58; weakened (1920s), 53. See also *unions by name*

Railroad workers, African American: "Anti-Strikers' Railroad Union," 54; attempts to form unions (1930s), 60; effect of railroad union policies on,

Railroad workers (*cont.*)
46; entering railroad occupations
(1920s), 53–54; railroad employment
under labor injunctions, 55; railroad
porters' union, 64; under Railway
Labor Act, 57–65; strikebreaking by
(1894), 54
Railroad workers, white: attacks on
African American trainmen (1931),
58; exclusionary actions of, 46–49;
under Railway Labor Act, 57–65
Railway Labor Act, 6, 49, 57; monopoly
power of unions under, 58–59; 1934
amendments, 59–62, 85; railroad porters' union under, 64
Randolph, A. Philip, 64
Rees, Albert, 116
Replogle v. Little Rock (1924), 34
Rhodes, Robert, 69
Roos, Charles, 89
Roosevelt administration: acceptance of
discrimination against African Americans, 95; defense of NRA, 94; influence
of African Americans on, 106; refuses
to support antilynching legislation,
107
Ross, Malcolm, 62

Segregation laws: defense of (1900s–
1910s), 109; discriminatory state
action of, 111; post-*Brown*, 108
Shepperd v. County Commissioners
(1877), 13, 22, 24
Sitkoff, Harvard, 95
Slaughter-House Cases (1873), 1–2, 3
Souter, Justice David, 115
Spencer, William J., 75
Sproul, Elliott, 76–77
State v. Gardner (1898), 34
State v. Moore (1893), 15
Steele v. Louisville & Nashville Railroad
(1944), 62–64
Steelworkers' union, 96

Stewart, Ethelbert, 74–75
Strikes: African American workers as
strikebreakers, 54, 91–92; of Brotherhood of Railway Trainmen, 52; protesting hiring of African Americans,
48–50, 52
Sunstein, Cass, 3
Supreme Court: decisions related to
minimum-wage laws, 99–100; *Dent*
decision upholds physician licensing
laws, 30; *Douglas* decision upholds
dentist licensing law, 31; Harlan's dissent in *Plessy,* 24, 108; injunction
upheld in *In re Debs,* 54; New Deal
Court, 85; ruling on constitutionality
of FLSA, 99, 102; significance and use
of *Lochner,* 2–4; significance of *Adair,*
55; significance of *Allgeyer,* 30; significance of *Atkin,* 67–68; significance of
Williams, 12, 23–26; significance of
Yick Wo, 29–30; *Slaughter-House
Cases* decision, 1–2; *Steele* decision
forbids unions to discriminate, 62–63;
upholds constitutionality of Railway
Labor Act, 57, 59; upholds constitutionality of Wagner Act, 98; upholds
railroad full-crew laws, 51; upholds
state ban on employment of aliens, 68
Supreme courts, state-level: Alabama
upholds discriminatory railroad contract, 63; decisions related to barbers'
licensing laws, 37–40; decisions
related to emigrant agent laws, 12–
16, 22, 24; decisions related to
plumbers' licensing laws, 32–35

Taylor, Ben, 38
Tiedeman, Christopher, 15
Tushnet, Mark, 108

Unemployment, African American: of
construction workers during Great
Depression, 80; effect of Wagner Act

Index

188

on, 104–5; under FLSA, 100–103; under New Deal legislation, 103–10

Unemployment, white: under New Deal legislation, 103–4

Upshaw, William, 73

Virginia Commission on Interracial Cooperation, 38

Virginia Ry. Co. v. System Federation No. 40 (1937), 59

Voting Rights Act (1965), 113

Wage levels: minimum wage law under FLSA, 99–102; provisions under NRA, 87–89

Wagner, Robert, 95

Wagner Act. *See* National Labor Relations Act (Wagner Act)

Washington, Booker T., 92

Weaver, Robert, 80, 89

West Coast Hotel Co. v. Parrish (1937), 99

Wilkins, Roy, 93, 95

Williams, Robert A. ("Peg-Leg") 14–25

Williams v. Fears (1900): impact of decision, 25–27; Supreme Court decision, 12, 23–25

Wilson administration, 106

Winkler v. Benzenberg (1898), 32

Wolters, Raymond, 103

Workers, African American: barbers' licensing laws excluding, 36–41; discrimination under Davis-Bacon Act, 79–84; discrimination under plumbers' licensing laws, 31–36; discrimination under Railway Labor Act, 57–64; displacement with growth of union membership (1930s), 92–93; effect of FLSA on, 101; effects of occupational licensing laws on, 28–44; human capital of, 97; long-term effects of New Deal on, 103–10; under NRA, 85–94; post–Civil War Black Codes to control, 8–10; protection under Lochnerian jurisprudence, 7, 114–15; as strikebreakers, 54, 91–92. *See also* Construction workers, African American; Railroad workers, African American

Wright, Gavin, 104

Yellow dog contracts: constitutional protection for, 59; labor injunctions to enforce, 54; outlawed under Railway Labor Act amendments, 59; statute banning enforcement of, 54–55

Yick Wo v. Hopkins (1886), 29–30, 34

DAVID BERNSTEIN is Associate Professor at
George Mason University School of Law. He is the
editor (with Kenneth R. Foster and Peter W. Huber) of
Phantom Risk: Scientific Inference and the Law (1993).

Library of Congress Cataloging-in-Publication Data
Bernstein, David E.
Only one place of redress : African Americans,
labor regulations, and the courts from
Reconstruction to the New Deal / David E. Bernstein.
p. cm. — (Constitutional conflicts)
Includes bibliographical references and index.
ISBN 0-8223-2583-7 (cloth : alk. paper)
1. Discrimination in employment — Law and legislation —
United States — History. 2. Afro-Americans —
Employment — Law and legislation — United States —
History. I. Title. II. Series.
KF3464 .B47 2001   344.730′6396073 — dc21   00-046204